Love you
To the
WOODS
AND BACK

Kim Griffin

Kevy,
You inspire me everyday
to be better, to do better, to love better.
Love you to the woods and back.

How much do you love me?

I was asked by my Mom when I was very young, perhaps three or four years old. In my toddler mind, I knew I loved her sooo big and sooo much that, with nary a moment to think, responded with "I love you to the woods and back. Wow! Could anyone love someone as much?

Many years later, and after a rather lengthy courtship, I had found another whom I loved deeply, completely and to the woods and back. Kevin Troy Griffin.

Kevin and I have known each other since grade 7, although at that time, he thought he was "all that" and I "knew" that he wasn't! Life marched on and we went our separate ways with me moving across the country.

When people say that life is a journey, crossing paths with many, it is still a bit of a miracle when you reappear on a path you had once shared with someone years earlier. Circumstances (or God's greater plan) allowed Kevin and I to intersect our journeys five years after our first knowing each other. I quickly realized how wrong I had been about Kevin. HE WAS ALL THAT!!

An incredible courtship that ended in marriage almost eight years later presented many opportunities to have shared amazing times, and some heartache as well. The common denominator though, has always been that we are there for each other. "I promise to be true to you in good times and in bad, in sickness and in health. I will love you and honor you, all the days of my life" is the vow that we both took willingly and with complete commitment to one another.

1

During the "honeymoon" phase of the marriage, you can't wait to be together, sharing everything and anything. You are out to impress the other and have lots of PDA (public displays of affection). As the marriage goes on, you begin to grow as your own person, although never wavering from the partnership. It begins to take some work to keep things fresh and new.

We began to build a family adding Troy Michael Griffin to our mix in 1994. Troy, our "preemie," was born at 33 weeks and spent his first 23 days in the hospital. From the first time we saw him (Kev saw him first, as I was under general anesthesia for his emergency entrance) we were in love.

As a toddler, we would tuck him in at night and after story time would say prayers together. As we would kiss him goodnight, and get up to leave the room, he always stopped us in our tracks by saying "Father, father" and putting his hand to his forehead to make the sign of the cross. He figured if we kept saying prayers, he wouldn't have to go to sleep.

Liam Alexander was also born early, but this time I was awake and very involved in his arrival. The first thing I noticed about him was how quiet he was, and how his huge dark eyes were taking in everything that was happening around him.

Liam has always been into art. As a youngster, he watched a show that had an artist making pieces of art using different mediums. He was fascinated and one day decided to do his own "art attack". He took all the towels and sheets that he could reach out of the linen closet and went about placing them on the floor to make a picture. He was so proud, and had to have Kev and I see it. To this day, I cannot tell you what he was trying to make, but to us it was a masterpiece.

The two most perfect children in the world. I continue to thank God everyday for these babes who are loved to the woods and back. What an extraordinary addition to our happy marriage.

During the building of our family, Kevin continued growing his very successful career in international sales while our sons began their journey into high school and I fulfilled a lifelong desire to work in elementary schools. A full and overflowing heart was housed within my soul. A wife, a mother of two extraordinary sons, and a fulfilling career in education.

I blinked. Why did I blink? In that moment, a new set of sashes were made for me to wear across my heart. Caregiver. Advocate. Grief stricken partner. My husband, at 44 years old, was diagnosed with colon cancer. CANCER. Everything fell away to the depths beyond hell.

The man whom I had told so many times that I loved to the woods and back, was now encased in the mist at the edge of the woods and would begin a strenuous, complicated, debilitating, exasperating and ultimately grace filled journey back. One thing that neither he nor I knew was that the journey would not be alone.

Stumbling around trying to figure out how to do this thing called "cancer" I decided that I would begin a journal dedicated to our family and friends who lived far and wide across the country and in Canada, letting them know how Kevin was doing, and what steps were taking place to care for my favorite husband. This was the beginning of not being alone on this sucky journey.

August 23, 2010 12:50 pm

After experiencing what now appear as obvious symptoms, Kev was finally convinced to go for a colonoscopy. While hoping for the best, we received the worst. Kev has colorectal cancer. We are still in the finding and gathering information stages, but are anticipating surgery, hopefully within the next week.

We have a strong faith and are moving forward optimistically. We believe in the power of prayer and ask all of you to take a moment and firstly thank God for all the goodness in your life; and secondly to watch over Kevin as he goes through this journey.

As you know, Kevy is a phenomenal man who has made an impact on many people's lives. If you have been lucky enough to receive his warmth and love over the years, please take a moment to drop a note and let him know. If I can quote Kevin, he doesn't like "people caring about me". However, deep down I know it will help to sustain him and our family if you are willing to share those thoughts.

As we learn more, I will post the info here so you can all be kept in the loop.

Take a moment today to tell your loved ones that you love them, and take the time to do something nice for others. What goes around comes around, and if that is true, Kevin will come though this with flying colors (colours for our Canadian family and friends).

Let love, prayers and laughter abound!

Love Kim

I found that writing a journal and inviting all of those whom we knew to come along and be part of this experience would harness a couple different responses. Firstly, it was a way of not having to repeat the health updates, therefore making sure everyone had the same information. It was also, as I look at it five years removed, a veiled attempt or unspoken desire for many to come with us and be the support that we didn't realize would be needed almost immediately.

Augst 27, 2010 4:51 pm

Thanks to all who have visited the site and who have offered prayers and good thoughts for Kevin. Please keep those comments coming - Kev looks forward to reading it at the end of the day.

Today we have found out that his surgery is scheduled for Friday, September 3 at Edward Hospital in Naperville. We have also been told that his cancer is a stage III - it has been found outside of the colon, although at this point has not entered any major organs.

We continue to think optimistically, although if you had talked to Kev today, he is annoyed that the surgery wasn't scheduled for Monday or Tuesday.)

I think I would rate today on a scale of 1-10 with 1 being horrific and 10 being euphoric, a 7. Fear and sadness have definitely taken hold (at least on me). Boys are telling us that they are okay and want the surgery over with as soon as possible.

Love the loves of your life as much as you can, and show them as much as you can.

Anymore info, I will let you know.

Have a great weekend!

Love, Kim

The result of the journal had an immediate response. It truly lifted us all up and reminded us of how wealthy we were - friends and family rallying around us and offering prayers, good thoughts and their help with any and all things. While we may not have known exactly what kind of help we needed as we moved forward, knowing we had a multitude of warriors to lean on was greatly appreciated.

The first of September Kevin began to prepare for surgery that would remove the cancerous part of his colon. The warriors began in earnest with Kevin's brother Brian and his family - Anne his wife and Brenna and Steven, their kiddos, coming down from Canada to be with us. My great friend Stacy who was an RN, flew in from Phoenix and as a bonus, was going to be our interpreter of the "doctor talk" after the surgery.

September 4, 2010 7:02 am

Good morning everyone.

I am Anne Griffin (married to Kev's brother, Brian). Kim asked that I send along info about Kev on her behalf.

Kim has been overwhelmed by your kindness and outpouring of prayers & good wishes for Kev.

Kev has made it through surgery and the doctor is very optimistic that he removed the entire tumor. He also removed some lymph nodes from the site and the results from tests on these will be back by the end of next week. The treatment plan will be determined after the results are back.

Kev got to his room about 9:00 pm last night and he looks good. Still groggy from the pain meds but he looked really good and trying to crack jokes (so we know he is getting back to his old self). Right now, it looks like he'll be in the hospital for about 5 days or so.

Kev is not ready for visitors yet but we will let you know when he is.

Thank you so much for all of your good thoughts & prayers. They have really helped him get over this first significant hurdle so please keep them up as he continues with his fight.

Since I have the keyboard, I would like to say something about Kim. Kim is an amazing woman who has held up incredibly well over the past 2 weeks (which have seemed like a lifetime). She is being such a rock for Kev and I know with her devotion & love, Kev will be better than ever. I am in awe of Kim's absolute faith & strength in a time of extreme uncertainty. I love her so much and I am so proud to be her sister-in-law.

Please keep up your good wishes & prayers for Kev. Thanks.

Kevin's first night after surgery was tough. He didn't get much sleep as there were too many monitors and wires hooked up to him. As Anne said, they were confident they got the whole tumor out, and weren't sure if the lymph nodes located nearby were cancerous or just extremely irritated from the tumor. I had stayed with Kevin from the beginning but got a reprieve from Brian. Brian stayed with him so that I could go home to grab a nap and a shower and head back later on. Later, during a quiet moment, I posted, thanking everyone for their generosity and kindness. It was a moment when I realized that we were surrounded by so many, many people who cared for us, loved us and were in for the long haul.

September 6, 2010 8:13 am

Kev has passed gas! Trust me when I say that this is probably one of the only times in the 27 years of being with Kev that I am thrilled and excited about this event. Of course, the doctors were happy too. He has moved to a soft food diet and is up walking, although somewhat gingerly. He has taken himself off of the IV hard pain meds, and will be taking them orally. Looks like he will be home tomorrow. We will have to continue to wait until Wednesday (ish) for the results of the lymph nodes. Thank you for everything, but most especially the love and caring you have been sending our way. Today is a blue day for Kev and me, sort of like having the baby blues. Love to all.

September 7, 2010 12:48 pm

KEV IS HOME!!!!!!

We got home around 11:00 am this morning and he is currently sleeping on the couch with a big smile on his face.

We are expecting to hear about the lymph nodes hopefully tomorrow or Thursday.

While this part of our journey is over, the long road has just begun. Thank you to all who have prayed for Kevin, who have cooked for our family and for all of you who have offered your help in any and all ways. We may be reaching the point where I may need to call on some of you when I go back to work next week. It would be to maybe sit with Kev over lunch time etc.

We are truly blessed and Kevin and I agree that God must have some greater good at work here. Please continue to let your family and friends know how important they are. You never know when things can change. Will update when we hear back on the pathology report.

Love (and a huge sigh of relief), Kim

September 10, 2010 5:07 pm

CANCER SUCKS!!!!

Got the results back about an hour ago. Eleven of the 18 lymph nodes taken out and tested came back positive.

Kev will be receiving chemo and quite possibly radiation. We have an appointment with the head of the oncology department at Edward on Friday September 17.

To say that this has taken the wind out of our sails is an understatement. While we thought there was a chance they would come back positive, until you hear that it's a definite, there is that little ray of hope that there would be none found.

We are saddened by this news, and could really use some guestbook visits.

Please continue to hold Troy and Liam close in your prayers and thoughts - they are trying so hard to be strong.

Will update soon.

Love Kim

If there is one thing that comes from being blindsided by something like cancer, it's that you begin to notice the little things that have surrounded you day in and day out. As part of the healing Kevy and I would take walks. September is an incredible time to be outside to see the world showing us its beauty and plethora of colors.

On our walks, Kev and I noticed how many cute babies were out in strollers, smiling and pointing to things as their parents walked by. It sort of encapsulated what we were now doing. While I always thought that Kevy was handsome, I don't think I ever truly realized just how blue his eyes were. Or how incredibly deep the dimples are on his face.

Holding hands has become a priority, as has telling each other "I love you" sporadically throughout the day, not out of habit, but because we truly mean it. Decorations for the house or the newest gadgets seem so frivolous now, when before they could become all consuming.

During this difficult time, we have also come to realize how many true friendships we have. Some have been over many years, while others have only recently begun. ALL are precious to us and help us to face each new day as it comes. I would share my observations and ideas in the journal. Stop and smell the roses is not a bad idea. Even as fall approaches, notice how beautiful the leaves are in their new coat of orange, red, purple. Look at your kids and breathe in their innocence and joy and make it last you throughout the day.

Kev was healing really well. He had incredible energy for someone who had just gone through such a difficult surgery. We knew that harder days were ahead. But it was so important for me to encourage everyone who was reading the journal to enjoy their day, say hello to someone they hadn't before, and to know that both Kevin and I were extremely grateful for their continued love and support.

September 15, 2010 5:52pm

Turn your face to the sun and the shadows fall behind you.
~Maori Proverb

Kevin returned to the surgeon today to see how he was healing. The doctor was very happy with his progress and has given Kevin the OK to eat whatever he wants. Let this be a warning to all fruit and vegetable sections of our surrounding grocery stores - I'm coming and I'm armed with a list of wants thiiiissssssss long! We have scheduled surgery for Kevin to have a port put into his upper chest which will be used for the chemotherapy. The date is October 1, although that could change depending on what the oncologist says to us at our consultation this Friday. It's possible they may move it up. We will let you know. Kev was ready to go in right now for the procedure. No surprise right?

How I love Kevy's attitude about this whole situation. While we have the odd "down" night , Kev picks himself up and hits the ground running, straight into optimism. I have to admit that it is quite contagious. We both believe that he will conquer this and become even better than before. I suppose it is already a fact that he is better than before. As I have said in the past journals, when you get hit with cancer, you stop and realize all the good and beautiful things that are around you. Kev has always been affectionate and a fabulous hugger. It just seems now that he holds the hug a little longer, smiles a little wider, and gives thanks constantly.

When Kevin was being rolled away to the operating room for his surgery, he told me he didn't want to get upset. So I told him this joke: Two guys walk into a bar; and you have to ask yourself, why the second guy didn't duck! This is now our running theme. Thanks for your continued support and notes of encouragement. We both read them over and over again. Slow down and really enjoy your dinners this week and remember to watch out for "bars" - you don't want to walk into one!:)

Love, Kim

Overwhelming was an understatement. Meeting with doctors and finding out the regiment that was planned for the attack on the cancer was intense, incredible and inevitable.

We had met with Dr. Alexander Hantel, an oncologist whom Kev and I really liked. He has become an honorary member of our family. He came highly recommended and from what we gathered during our meeting, it was going to be a good partnership.

Kev had a port placed in his chest to receive his intravenous chemo treatments. He started chemotherapy on Friday, October 1. Kev was facing six months of chemo with five weeks of radiation sandwiched in between treatments.

He would be going every two weeks, for approximately 3 hrs each time. He would also come home with a pump attached to continue meds for 46 hours. The good thing is that the treatments were scheduled for Fridays, in the hopes that Kev would be able to recover over the weekend and tackle work on Mondays.

Because the cancer was labeled stage III, Kevy was going to have a hard battle ahead of him. This was when we both needed the strength of all who were reading our journals.

My entries always included suggestions for ways to pay it forward or show random acts of kindness. Cherishing every moment was also a theme that was peppered throughout the journal. Ideas such as letting a car merge into your lane, holding a door open for someone, or bringing a grocery cart back to the store after a fellow shopper has finished loading their car with food and sundries, are small gestures that go a long way. Ultimately, the goal is to rise above the little things and act in kindness.

I used to worry about having a brand name purse, or having someone like me. Now I worried about Kevin struggling with the physical and emotional strain being forced on him. I was agonizing about my sons trying too hard to be strong for their dad and me. I was concerned that I wouldn't have enough strength to hold Kevin up when he became weak. Kevin was feeling like he was letting us down.

September 20, 2010 4:44 pm

Okay, I have realized that there is no down time when it comes to dealing with cancer.

Just when we thought we got the right play to the field, the doctors have called an audible.

Kev will be getting his port put in tomorrow during an outpatient procedure at Edward Hospital. Not sure of the time yet, but it will be tomorrow.

Chemo treatments now start this Friday, not a week from this Friday as we were originally told.

I like to think that the doctors are being so aggressive because Kev is healing nicely from surgery, and that he will be able to withstand the treatments sooner. I guess when you are fighting an enemy that you can't see and therefore not sure how big they are, you want to get in there and do as much damage as possible before they get a chance to make their next move.

Prayers and more prayers are requested. Please stop and tell your family that you love them - even those lacrosse players who think they may be too "macho" for such a thing. I love Kevin and Troy and Liam so much and I won't stop telling them that.

Hopefully things go smoothly - I'll update tomorrow.

Thanks for your support. Now let's get out there and win!!!

Love, Kim

September 21, 2010 6:15 pm

Hope you all have your seat belts on and please remember to keep your arms and legs inside the ride at all times...

Kev got his port today - quite the trooper. His arm and shoulder are a little sore, but not too bad. Dr. Park, who assisted Dr. Joo with Kev's colon surgery was the surgeon today.

Here is where you need your seat belts:

Kev and I ran (not literally) into Dr. Hantel in the hospital this morning, on our way to his outpatient procedure. Seems like Kev's case was the talk of the "tumor board" at Edward where many doctors come together to discuss "unique" cases.

After the meeting of the minds, they have decided on a change to his treatment. This time, Kevy will be receiving chemotherapy for six months first. Once he has completed the chemo, they will start him on radiation.

Kind of relieved, as they are mostly concerned with the systemic spread of the disease. The CEA marker in Kev's blood prior to his surgery was 29. Normal range is 0-5. The number indicated that there was cancer in the body. Had blood work done this past Friday after our first visit with Dr. Hantel and Kev's CEA is now 9.2. Certainly better, but they anticipate it will go down more after he starts his treatments.

My Mom and Dad are coming down here this weekend and while I know that Kev will probably be spending the weekend sleeping, I will certainly appreciate their support. If I slow down long enough, it's amazing how tired I get. That's when having my Mom around will help.

Kev is resting on Troy's bed right now, admiring the beautiful aquarium that is in his room. The heavens have opened up and we are in the midst of a downpour. The boys are playing Xbox and I am writing this, once again overcome with such joy when I read the messages, and see how many people have visited Kev's website. We stand now at 1350! Please keep visiting.

Kevin is so grateful for all of your support and prayers. I am in awe of his strength and positive mind set. He definitely is kicking cancer's butt because he is already fighting - two surgeries, numerous blood tests and soon enough the first of 12 chemo treatments.

As this ride comes to an end, please wait until we have come to a complete stop before you exit. Have a fantastic day and remember random acts of kindness!

Love and an "air" high five, Kim

September 23, 2010 4:13 pm

Just going through our list for tomorrow:

Kevin - CHECK
Port implanted - CHECK
Nausea medicines picked up - CHECK
Comfy clothes -CHECK
A movie or two - CHECK
Our faith - CHECK
All of your prayers and thoughts - CHECK

That does it, we are READY!

Love, Kim, Troy, Liam and of course Kevin

September 24, 2010 3:32 pm

1 down... 11 to go...

You know how your anticipation always ends up being worse than reality? It happened here as well. Now granted, we are only a few hours removed from Kev's first treatment, but surprisingly, there were no monsters underneath his chair, and no blob thingy ready to pounce from the corner of his treatment room.

Nope.

It was just Kev and a port and a couple of bags of meds. We had lunch in there (he had soup and veggies) and watched the best of Will Ferrell from SNL. We also had a surprise visitor: Troy. Seems he felt he should be there with us for this first step into a rather long and yucky journey. We were glad to have him and I think that it helped him to lose some of his fear and at the same time made Kev feel good.

Kevy has come home with 2 anti nausea meds which are on top of the really strong one he had before the treatment started. He has his pump attached to his port which is pushing the 5FU meds (yep, that's the name) through his body.

I am so proud of how Kevin is handling this so far. We know we have some very hard days ahead, but seeing Kevy, Troy and me laughing in our little room makes us truly believe that we will get through it.

I'll update on Sunday when he gets his pump taken off.

Love and less anticipation,

Kim

September 26, 2010 3:06 pm

Kevin is officially pump free. Aside from getting wrapped up by the IV tubing the first night in bed, he handled it pretty well. No major side effects as of yet, although the nurse did say that the next few days will be telling.

Kevin is proud of how well he is doing and I have to give him credit. His attitude about this whole treatment is incredible. We know we have the tough hills to climb coming up, but for now we are going to stop and rejoice in strapping on our climbing boots and having our picks ready.

Oh right, we need our helmets...

Thank you for your prayers - they are keeping Kev warm and ready to go.

It was great having my parents here - they handled all four of us with the kind of care you can only get from parents/grandparents.

Have a great week and don't forget random acts of kindness.

Love Kim

I had a lot of time during all of this to think. And not surprisingly I did most of my thinking at night, when the world was at its darkest, and I could not sleep. I was finding that the journal gave me an opportunity to talk and thank all who had passed through the pages, who had left messages of hope and prayer and unending love. I could let all know that I was thinking about them and what that meant.

As you can see from the time of this entry, sleep is a pretty hard commodity to come by. Lying in bed, and unable to sleep, I thought about YOU. All of YOU.

What a whirlwind journey we have been on since August 20. It has gone by so fast, and at the same time feels like this has been our life forever.

From the moment of discovery, we have chosen to reach out to our family and friends to help us through these dark times. There is such comfort in knowing that there are so many people who love and care for Kevy and our family that at times it's overwhelming.

I began to think about YOU and what it must be like for you to have found out that your son, brother, uncle, in-law, friend, co-worker, coach was facing such a huge battle.

The constant thread through all of YOU is your immense ability to truly love someone with such depth and honesty that it changes the world into a much warmer, inviting and loving place.

Can you even begin to imagine how many people YOU have come in contact with since finding out this news? People you see every day, once a week, a few times a year, and those who YOU will never see again?

The goodness that has transpired from this sadness is immeasurable. YOU have unknowingly made other people's lives a little better because of your renewed awareness of things around you.

But selfishly, YOU have made Kevin feel like he can do anything. YOU have made Troy and Liam feel like they are not alone. YOU have made me thank God for each and every one of YOU. Every day. YOU are amazing.

With incredible love and gratitude, Kim

Life was moving on. Being in a household that was in overload of testosterone, where there is a lot of chest thumping, wrestling, and the occasional wedgie, Kevin's struggle with colon cancer had come in like a strong wind and knocked the hell out of the walls that are naturally put up by men. Walls to keep emotions in and ways to evoke those emotions, out.

Troy has always been more willing to climb over that wall and tell us if something is bothering him. Since Kev's diagnosis, he has loaded up at least 2 trucks to take away any remaining walls he may have had. He is constantly finding an excuse to hug Kev and tell him how much he loves his dad.

Liam, who's wall is taller than he is, has finally requested a truck to come and take away some of the wall that has started to crumble. Kevin always tells the boys he loves them, and Liam would normally respond with "me too". At some point during a school day, Liam text Kev and told him that he loved him more than Kev loved him. Kevin was so moved by the text - and couldn't wait to tell me about it. Liam has taken it on as a challenge to find ways to keep Kev laughing through this process. We find him hanging out in our room at bedtime, sitting on the bed telling us about funny things he has seen or heard.

In reading the book "The Five Love Languages" about different love languages and how each of us has a unique one, I found out that Kevin's love language is "quality time". He loves to spend time with our family. Sitting down to have dinner together is a big deal for him and we are able to accomplish that 99% of the time. He also loves us watching movies together. To look over and see Kevin laughing so hard at a movie, and the boys laughing right along with him, makes all the difficulties we are going through worth it.

I would like to think that those bricks being hauled away from our home are meeting up with other trucks having just left our friends and family's homes and are making their way to find a new use for all the bricks. Maybe they are helping to build bridges, where past ones have been ruined by hurtful words and gestures. Or maybe they are being used to build roads that lead to the front doors of people who need to have their own walls taken down. No matter the use, Kevin's journey was allowing so many to let down their guard and feel. Sometimes for the first time.

Things happen for a reason is something I truly believe. We may not always know why at the time, but soon enough it shows itself, at the right time, and in the right place. You need to know that Kevin being a rather talkative guy with an Irish background, has probably kissed the blarney stone a few times. Okay, many times. But the reality is, never having been to Ireland, he just comes by it honestly. One thing, however, that Kevin rarely talks about, are the things he has done in his life to make it a better place for one and all.

Being rather neurotic first time parents, just after Troy was born, I enrolled in a CPR class that included a session on how to revive infants and children. I was eager to share the information with Kevin, just in case.

Literally the next day, Kevin was out for lunch with a coworker at a restaurant, when a mother with a child not much older than 1, began panicking and screaming for help. Her child was choking and she was frozen with fear. The restaurant was fairly busy, and while others seated at tables nearby just watched, no one got up to help the child... no one that is, except Kevin.

Remembering what he had learned the night before, he scooped the child up and immediately began the maneuvers to help the child lose the food that it was choking on. After some rather tense moments, the child started to regain a pink glow in her cheeks and lips, and let out a huge scream. Those sitting nearby started clapping for Kevin, and as the mother took her child back in her arms, she informed Kevy that she was a nurse and could not believe she had become immobilized with fear.

When Kevin's coworker went back to the office and shared what had happened, Kevin was less than happy. He didn't want a big deal to be made of it. As far as he was concerned, he was in the right place at the right time. While he may have the gift of gab, he also has the gift of humility, and an unwillingness to have the spotlight pointed at him.

So, as Kev has said, things happen for a reason. We may never know the reason for this illness, but we have to believe that Kevin is in the right place at the right time. Maybe it will encourage some of you to have a colonoscopy; or others to reach out and talk to someone you love and tell them to go and have the procedure. Maybe, just maybe in partnership with you, another life may be saved.

October 21, 2010 9:22 pm

Tomorrow brings round number 3 which leaves only 9 more to go!

Isn't it funny that an exclamation mark can make the above sentence sound exciting? Actually Kev will be a quarter of the way through his chemo and that is exciting.

We went to see the oncologist yesterday a few days ahead of his treatment as the doctor was not going to be in tomorrow. He ran the labs and did his once over and was very happy with what Kev is presenting. First off, he has healed very nicely from the surgery, his weight, bp, pulse etc. were all great.

The best part however, was that his CEA number was 2.7, which is down from 4.8.

Now granted, the doctor did say that once this number is below 5, there isn't much distinction between a 2.7 and a 4.8. I would like to disagree with the good doctor. While he may be medically correct, it is amazing to see the response from Kevin and yes, his wife, when told the new number.

I think what it does is reaffirms that the tough days are worth all the aches, pains, nausea, fatigue and rough going. We are gaining the upper hand in this fight, and for those of you who know Kev, when he is fighting for anything worthwhile, he doesn't cry uncle. He will see this through until the end and will be able to turn to all of us and say it was all worth it.

Will update tomorrow after he has his treatment and let you know how it went. Until then, God bless all of you who have taken time out of your own very busy lives and given us your love, support, prayers, laughs and tears. For those who have been part of the cooking crew, there isn't enough money in the world to tip you all what you are worth.

Love, Kim

October 22, 2010 8:28 pm

It's far more important to know what person the disease has than what disease the person has. ~ Hippocrates

Hippocrates is known as the father of medicine and for him to be credited with the above statement goes to show you that Kevin would have been invited to join Hippocrates at his home for dinner and conversations many times over. Days before Kev had his latest blood work, we made a bet on what the new CEA number would be. I guessed that the number would be 4.3, down from the prior 4.8. Kevin just smiled and said that it would be 2.7. So when he got the call from the lab with his results, you wouldn't believe it. Through the miracle of Alexander Graham Bell's invention, Kevin was told that his CEA number was 2.7. He couldn't wait to tell me the news... I gave him the accolades he deserved for being right on with his "guesstimation." I was never so happy to lose a bet. I still won though, because we bet a kiss!!

From the first fearful steps into the world of cancer, both Kevin and I, although truth be told, more Kevin, decided that we were going to approach this from a position of the cancer being a "phase", and not life ending or life debilitating. We have each faltered ever so slightly from this vantage point. However, it always seems that when that is happening, our partner is telling us to continue to believe and pray. Every time, we have survived and renewed our faith in how much our mind plays in healing our bodies. So Kevin's positive outlook and belief that he in fact is a vital part of his recovery, seemed to simply live on in him knowing on some level what his number would be.

Cancer doesn't know who it is up against and perhaps that's okay. Having the sneak attack of belief in God, prayers, love, support, and laughter from soooo many people has helped to level out the playing field.

Hippocrates would most definitely have been on Kev's team. After all, his quote above seems to say that Kevin is in fact a winner. Treatment number 3 was today, and so far the only side effects that he has noticed, are the increased sensitivity to cold and the tingling in his hands and feet. No nausea to speak of, thank God.

We are having a quiet weekend, with lots of opportunities to rest and rejuvenate. Random acts of kindness would be a great thing to do this weekend. Maybe all reading this will join us in this and quietly do something nice for someone else. It certainly makes your heart feel full. Love and big time high "2.7"s to all,

Often times, my journal entries would be without medical jargon, appointment reminders or CEA numbers. There were times that I just wanted to share something about Kevin so that the people who were checking in on the journal, might get to know the man I knew, just a little bit more and on a deeper level.

October 27, 2010 2:51 pm

Man Card Please?!

After sharing this story, I'm sure that many of you "dudes" will probably ask Kev for his man card - but before you do, take a moment to read this and share it with your significant other. You just may change your mind.

A few years ago, it was just before Valentine's Day and Kevin had not done his usual "so if someone were to get you something for a certain holiday that is coming up, what would you want?"

I chalked it up to maybe he forgot, or had decided to do something else. However, what did transpire that Valentine's Day has forever marked Kevin as very much a romantic.

We usually only exchanged small things for Valentine's Day - something to show that we were in fact thinking of the other. This time, Kevin handed me a gift bag that was topped off with colorful tissue paper and a beautiful card.

When I removed the tissue paper, the bag was full of what looked like shredded bits of paper, almost like packing material. I looked at Kevin with what I'm sure was a rather odd expression, but honestly, I thought he may have forgotten to put the gift inside.

He encouraged me to take a little piece of paper out of the bag, which I did and almost immediately started crying. On the piece of paper

31

was a message—"Barbados". I instantly started thinking about Barbados (which is where we had our honeymoon) and starting throwing out "I remember when we did this trip; it was a beautiful beach; remember the drinks with cute umbrellas?"

Kevin stopped me after a while of reminiscing and went on to tell me what the gift was. He had typed out 365 different things on little pieces of paper that I was to put in a ceramic container on my nightstand. Every morning I was to take one of the pieces of paper out, and read it. It was a memory of our life together, or simply a gesture of kindness:

> *Senior football championship game*
> *Buy yourself a magazine*
> *Woodland Beach and the cottage*
> *Snowball fights*
> *Let me brush your hair*

These were the things he knew would mean the most to me. Memories of being together, and things for me to do for myself that would make me feel good.

Now, for all of the women reading this entry, sorry but he is taken. The good news is that maybe the men in your life will read this and think it a good idea for the women who are special in their lives.

I kept some of the wishes and look at them often. My favorite one simply said: I Love You. Show your special someone how much you love them today. It would mean the world to them. Do not leave things unsaid.

So, I love you Kevin Troy Griffin more than you will ever know. Thank you for being the father of my sons and for loving me like no one else would. Elephant Shoes.

Love Kim

November 6, 2010 10:41 pm

"If you're going through hell keep going." ~ Winston Churchill

Kevin is now officially a third of the way through his chemo treatments and Friday was the toughest day yet. Now toughest takes on many different meanings here, so let me explain.

Kevin was truly happy with his appointment with the doctor and the lab numbers were fantastic. The infamous CEA number went from 2.7 to 1.6!!!!! Now for those of you who have been following consistently, you know that the normal range is 0-5, and that while our doctor told us that there really isn't much difference in the importance of the numbers once they are under 5, he was very happy to see the number. I think he actually said "great".

So, how could Friday have been a terrible day? Kevin received a 1.6, had his good friend Randy join him for his treatment, and got to watch more humorous videos that made his sides hurt. What Kevin wasn't expecting or anticipating, was running into a dear friend in the cancer center, who was there receiving her own treatment for a recurrence of breast cancer.

To say Kevy was shocked and stunned would be an understatement. It was she who noticed Kevin first and called out to him. After doing a double take, he realized that it was in fact his friend. As a teacher assistant, I relate it to running into some of my students at Border's or McDonald's. When they see you, they appear like deer in headlights, wondering how you actually got out of the school.

Once Kevin realized, he was quick to embrace her with one of his great hugs. He sat and talked with her for a while and reminisced

about the past and shared war stories about their respective fights against cancer. After a while, Kev made his way back to his own chair and continued his treatment. He told me that he couldn't shake the sadness that he felt in seeing her there. As he said, it's not the place to run into a friend.

After coming home from the cancer center, Kev was hit really hard by side effects. The neuropathy came on full force and his hands, feet, lips and forearms were tingly and very sensitive to the cold. His stomach was cramping up and he was incredibly exhausted. He was looking forward to going to bed for the night.

As is our custom, we began our bedtime prayers with thanks to God for giving us so many wonderful friends and family and thanking him for all the goodness in our lives. We also ask for strength for our family to be able to continue the good fight against this horrific disease. The difference last night was that we had one more person to add to our list for God to watch over and help to heal.

When I told Kevin that I was going to be updating the journal, he asked me to pass along to all who are reading this to please say an extra prayer for his friend. Until Kevin clears it with her, he does not want to use her name, so please ask God to watch over "D".

I love this man so much, and this is just another example. While having one of the worst physically challenging days of his own treatment, his biggest concern and illness was the heaviness he was carrying in his heart for his dear friend. Once again, he is putting others ahead of himself.

Please remember to show your love to those closest to you, and to take a few moments to think of "D" and her struggle. We know that the strength of your prayers has been doing wonders for Kev, Troy, Liam and me and that they can do the same for her.

May God continue to bless you with his overabundance of love and allow me to remind each and every one of you that the circle of love that you are surrounding us with is truly life changing.

Love, Kim

Opening up our home to visitors is something that Kevin and I enjoy doing. It allows us to entertain, share conversation, reminisce... which sometimes may include re-writing history, and ultimately reconnecting with those in our lives who are important. These are the visitors that we welcome with the front door held open, arms wide with an embrace, and usher in to the heart of our home. We quickly reconnect and pick up conversations that were started the last time we were together, share a refreshment, have something to eat, and if you are in our home, probably play a game. We kick back, relax, with a smile on our face and a warmth in our heart.

There are, however, those visitors that ring the doorbell unexpectedly, in the middle of the night, who come bearing doom and fear. They have not been invited, and this is when you wish you could pretend not to be at home. They peak in windows, through the curtains until they know we have seen them, and are forced to make the long walk to the front door. They have different names, but in this instance, it's name is Cancer.

The dread that comes when you open the door, even a fraction, to get a better look at the unwanted visitor, is pushed in by a huge gust of wind. The door flies open, you stumble over the mat, and any papers that were lying on the hall table are instantly airborne, preparing to land near and far in a huge jumble. The dog starts to bark, the cold of the wind is bone chilling, and you instinctively try to close the door to no avail. The visitor is inside, making a comfortable spot for itself on the couch, and waiting for you to come back into the room.

When you ask it to leave, you are met with silence, and find yourself in the middle of a staring contest that you ultimately lose. Looking around to find your family so you can stand united against this visitor, you find that everyone is standing alone, afraid, unable to take a step toward the others. Immobilized with fear, you find yourself trying to yell to your loved ones to look away from the visitor, and to remain strong.

Suddenly, the uninvited visitor pulls itself up from its comfortable spot on the couch, and taking its glare off of you, looks back toward the front door. The door is wide open and an enormous light and warmth is filling our home. Cancer begins to look to its left and to its right, searching for a way to get out of the focus of the warmth and bright light. It moves toward the back door that is instantly unlocked and opened for it to slither through.

Instantly we are once again able to move, and quickly find each other with a warm hug and comforting words. As we come back into the reality of what just happened, we begin to wonder what sent the unwanted visitor away.

Glancing back to the front door, we see what was able to do what we alone were not. Our friends and family, all standing together, key to our front door in hand. It was all of you, who through your unwavering support and love, showed the unwanted visitor, that we are not alone, and that you, Cancer, are not welcome here. Thank you for all standing with us as we continue this very aggressive fight against Cancer. Our home is always open to you, our family and friends. God is good... He has given you all the map to our doorstep and hearts.

November 8, 2010 10:04 pm

When we were little, the boogeyman lived under the bed or in the closet and we were sure that we saw him peering at us through the darkness. Now most of us came to realize that there was no such thing. However, since August 20, I have begun to be afraid of the dark and fearful of the silence that night brings and am certain that the boogeyman is back.

Kevin has had the worst day yet of his treatment, sleeping fitfully for a stretch of 16 hours, only to get up for a drink and nap for 3 more hours. When he is awake he is nauseous and feeling numb.

Today the boogeyman was cornering me in broad daylight. I am so overwhelmed, sad, and feel completely vulnerable. I also feel ashamed that I am using this avenue and sharing my gut wrenching heartache at seeing the man I love most in this world suffering so.

I started this journal as a way to keep family and friends informed of Kevy's journey through and over cancer. Little did I know that it would end up being a therapy for me. I am scared of being the keeper of all answers for Troy and Liam and Kev. I don't have all the right answers and am afraid of making a misstep. I am overwhelmed with anguish when I see my 6' husband barely able to pick his head up off his pillow. When he moves during the night, I am immediately awake, asking if he needs any help.

I know that we will make it through, but I have to tell you, I couldn't do this alone. Thank you to those who are keeping me in their prayers as well. I could use a few more helpers in warding off the scary monster. Goodnight to one and all...

Angel of God My guardian dear
To whom God's love commits me here.
Forever this day be at my side
To light, to guide
To rule and guard
Amen

Love Kim

Everyone needs a little inspiration once and a while and for Kevin fighting a tough fight, nothing brings him that feeling of contentment and drive to continue than when he is talking about one of the loves of his life... lacrosse!

In November 2010 at Marmion Academy, Kevin took center stage, under the bright light, to present the plans for the 2011 Marmion Lacrosse season to a roomful of young men and their parents. For an hour, Kevin was in his glory, talking about one of the greatest loves of his life. He didn't miss a beat, and from what I have heard, he was able to convince many new players to become part of a team that is made up of incredible boys who are fantastic athletes, but more importantly, wonderful, caring young men.

This team has among its members, players who visited Kevin in the hospital and brought with them laughter and smiles that helped jumpstart Kev's healing. They were front and center this night for the presentation, fully supporting Coach, and sharing his famous saying from the sidelines "on the hop". He couldn't love these guys any more if they were his own.

Kev came home completely drained from the night, but as we settled in our bed to sleep, Kevy could not wipe the grin from his face as he revisited the joy from the night at Marmion. The twinkle in his blue eyes was reminiscent of a child hiding on the stairway, peering through the spindles to get a glimpse of Santa on Christmas Eve. The only thing that could come close to this incredible feeling is when Kev gets a chance to watch our boys play lacrosse.

November 14, 2010 7:16 pm

If you have been out doing any kind of shopping, it is clearly evident that we have hit the holiday season. The marketing departments of the stores don't leave anything to chance, and have placed their twinkling lights, ornaments, scented candles and tinsel in all the right places.

When I was out and about (not aboot), a common thread of small talk this weekend seemed to be about the cool/cold weather that has moved in. Of course, among colleagues and friends, the jokes are always there that being from Canada, this must feel like springtime etc. Nothing better than cuddling with your hubby and having a warm cup of tea and apple pumpkin loaf (thank you Margie) when it's 40 degrees outside. Most I'm sure would admit that their favorite season is summer, or maybe spring. I have been looking forward to the winter time, especially this year with Kevin being housebound so much of the time.

I have always loved the feel of being secure, inside a warm house, with pjs and slippers on while the wind whistles outside the windows. We tend to all be together more often, Kevy, me and the boys. We spend time watching movies together, with the lights off and the fireplace on.

I have always felt safe and loved during this time of the year. We pull out the old movies like "Going My Way" and "The Bells of St. Mary" with Bing Crosby. While the boys may not admit it, we all recite the same old lines, and hum along to the old songs.

I think this year, more than ever, I am looking forward to the cold dark nights that will find all of us home and together. We will share our days with each other over a bowl of chili; find another blanket to climb under; and laugh through "White Christmas" until the time comes to cry through it.

This time of year is so magical, and this year is no different. The magic is happening right in front of us. Kevy is beating the cancer back and down and we are right there beside him helping. We are all so grateful for the love and support that has been bestowed and entrusted to us, that we will not waste a drop. Paying it forward is the name of the game and we plan on paying it big time.

Snuggles and huggles and healing, OH MY! Bring it on.

Love Kim

While there are some moments of levity during a difficult journey through cancer, it is never far from our everyday. The following entry gives a glimpse into that every day.

November 24, 2010 12.08 am

While many in our adopted homeland began their travels to meet up with family and friends, we started putting up Christmas decorations.

Kevin had treatment 5 on Friday, and we have begun to have a rough idea of how long the good days will be around before Kev does a sudden 180 and ends up flat on his back. We got the tree up and after coming back from having the pump removed on Sunday, were going to start decorating while listening to Christmas music. Up to this point, Kevy was responding fairly well. Somewhere between a penguin ornament and "Our First Home -1988" ornament, Kev was suddenly sitting down, watching us decorate.

He was trying to stay in the moment for the boy's sake, but he lost all his energy in mere moments. He slept fitfully the rest of the day on the couch, sneaking a peak at the tv to see who was winning the various football games, and to see how badly he was letting Rich down in his football fantasy league. By the way, pretty badly.

Sunday night and into Monday morning, Kev was up frequently with incredible stomach cramps. It is difficult to describe how heart wrenching it is to hear your loved one wincing and moaning in pain. You want to reach out and help, all the while knowing you cannot. The best I can do is hold his hand, and help him to the bathroom.

Monday found him tackling both the cramps and the sweats that tire him out, not to mention making him feel gross. The good that will come of this is when I go through the "change". I believe I will have the most compassionate and caring husband this side of the American border.

As I rubbed Kevy's face and ears tonight to help him get to sleep, I found myself wiping away his tears, so quiet they were, marking their path down his beautiful face. He whispers to me that he doesn't think he can do this, and I respond, with a catch in my throat, that he is doing it. I tell him, let's just get through the next half hour. He finally succumbs to a restless sleep, here beside me in our warm, safe, comfortable bed. I find myself watching his chest rise and fall, just making sure.

While I know the road to recovery is littered with pain and tears and cloaks of worry, I want to run the other way. I want to scream out that we are lost and can't make it. But then I turn around and find Kevin picking himself up, and allowing Troy and Liam to carry him. How can I possibly put down the walking stick, or not move the obstacles out of the way?

And so we carry on, knowing that tomorrow is another day, and perhaps realizing for the first time that we don't know what to expect after the treatments, and maybe that is somehow better. This way, we, our small immediate family, must stay on our toes, and watch out for falling branches, and potholes in our path. As soon as you put down your guard and begin to take things for granted is when you stumble and fall.

At this time of thanksgiving, I am thankful for all of you. I am thankful for our extended family and friends. I am grateful for Troy Michael, and Liam Alexander. But most of all, I am thankful that Kevin went for his colonoscopy. I am so blessed to have Kevin sleeping beside me as I write this, and even his snoring is tolerable.

Thank you God for the love of my husband and sons. Thank you for the strength to carry on, day after day, especially on days when my tears outlast Kevin's. He is so worth this. He will overcome this adversity and be better for it. Thank you God for carrying us when we cannot carry ourselves. Thanks be to God. Amen!

December 3, 2010 7:29 pm

Eight is Enough!

Christmas came early for Kev and our family today. The CEA number came back at 1.5, the lowest it has ever been! Our doctor was quite happy with the results, and how well Kevin is tolerating the side effects (which he himself admits are brutal). We were originally told that Kev would have to face 12 chemotherapy treatments, because his cancer was so aggressive. However, based on those and other factors, Dr. Hantel has decided that...

8 CHEMO TREATMENTS ARE ENOUGH!!!!!!!!!!!!!

This does not mean that the fight against the ugly monster cancer is over, rather it will be moving to the final round. A bell has been rung, and Kev is in his corner feeling overly blessed and happy that he only has 2 more chemo treatments left. We haven't seen cancer, and according to the numbers, he has left the ring at least. I'm not prepared to say it has left the building just yet.

December 31st will be Kev's last chemo treatment. What a way to bring in the new year. He will have a reprieve of two weeks, then begin his radiation treatments, which total 25 over five weeks.

We will be meeting the radiation oncologist on Tuesday, and at the same time, also meet a genetic counselor to discuss if Kevin has a genetic predisposition to this kind of cancer. It's important for him to find out, so Troy and Liam know if they will have to be tested in their twenties. It is also information that his siblings will want, in addition to their scheduled colonoscopies.

Please please please get yourself checked. This applies to both men and women. If you have had a close relative with this kind of cancer, you may feel better getting checked.

Women, get your mammograms too!

Prayers are continuing to be answered so please keep them coming. We are cautiously optimistic that 2011 will be a better year for us.

May God continue to bless all of us with health and happiness, with perhaps an extra serving of health dished to Kev! If it tastes anything like turkey, he will "gobble" it up.

December 8, 2010 2:53 pm

Radiation A Go Go!

After a rather euphoric weekend, what with being told Kevy only has to have 2 more chemo treatments, we had our appointment with the radiation oncologist on Tuesday. He seems to know his stuff when it comes to radiation, although not really sure of how to take our humor. That MUST mean he is not funny! :)) Once Kev is done with him, he will be spinning jokes like nobody's business. He was, however, very informed about Kevin's case, and rather definite in the next steps.

We will meet with him on January 10 at which time they will make a mold of Kevin's body once they find the perfect position for him to lie on the table for his treatment. They do this so that when he comes in for the radiation, he will always be lined up correctly for the beams to do their work. By the way, I told the doctor that I want to make sure that they break the mold when we are finished with the treatments, because there is no one else in this world who could fit into the mold of Kevin Troy Griffin!

Kevy will receive 28 treatments, probably starting around January 17th and will go M-F for five and a half weeks. He will be receiving 5000-5400 rads of radiation. The doctor told him that in comparison, a man coming in for radiation for prostate cancer would receive 8,000 rads.

What we weren't completely clear on, but are now, is that Kev will be taking chemo pills throughout the radiation treatment. He will not have the 3 hour sessions at the hospital anymore, rather take a pill a day. Kevin was a little disappointed in that news, but when you are tackling something that is so serious, you have to bring all your guns.

We also met with a genetic counselor, to determine if Kevin has Lynch Syndrome. This is important for his siblings to know, as well as himself but of course, the most important thing to him is that Troy and Liam know if they are facing increased risks for cancers later on. We are sending a sample of the tumor off to the Mayo Clinic for them to check for the syndrome. Will keep you posted in the weeks to come. Enjoy the rest of the week, and crank those Christmas songs!

Love and Blessings,

Kim

December 11, 2010 9:16 pm

Bah Humbug!

Troy and Liam will not be seeing mommy kissing Santa Claus underneath the mistletoe... this year. While it may be the season for "making merry" and joyfully greeting one another, because of Kevin's precarious health situation, we are going to have to be sensible. Air high fives, pound it, and blowing kisses into the air will be the plan of "love" attacks.

Kevin has had a rough week, even more so because he contracted a cold. I know it's the season of giving, but please, whoever gave the cold away, take it back!! It's not the right size, color or style for Kevin.

Colds are bad enough, (especially, it seems, for men), but putting it on top of chemo treatment - I'm surprised Kev is able to blink, not to mention anything else. While I am usually the first to see his yuckiness, I was somewhat taken back when Kevin actually decided that he was going to miss Rich and Maria's annual Christmas party.

As you all know, Kev is an extrovert who needs to have his battery charged by being around others. He requires this jump start to sustain himself. He loves joining in with others to celebrate this most holy and wonderful time of the year, whether sharing stories, singing songs, and even dancing in the middle of the group. For him to miss this celebration, speaks volumes for how he was feeling.

Today was slightly better. I am pretty sure I heard him singing while he was sitting in the family room. I am hoping that this week, we will see the twinkle back in his eyes, and maybe some pep in his step.

One thing, however, that will not be seen is a kiss... a simple loving gaze is going to have to suffice until he is better. But with the right flutter of eyes, and tilt to the head, Kevin will know he is loved and that he is the best present any of us could ask for this, or any other year.

Love and an air embrace,

Kim

December 12, 2010 6:48 pm

Ladies, ladies, ladies,

Kev here. Based on Kim's last entry I was compelled to steal the computer away from her and put in my own entry. I love Kim, and know she is looking out for my best interest. She usually reads the journal to me before she posts it, but I must have been resting at the time.

Please disregard Kim's comments about bypassing any hugs and kisses. Sure I may catch a cold, but believe me ladies, it will be worth it. During this tough time, the one thing I have enjoyed is the women fussing over me. Keep your smiles, hugs and kisses coming!

Best regards, Kevin

P.S. Don't make me strap a piece of mistletoe to my head!!!!

December 17, 2010 10:14 pm

Kev had his seventh chemo treatment today but we weren't sure it was going to happen. It seems that Kev's platelets were off somewhere with a sandy beach, fancy drinks and dazzling seas, instead of being in his blood stream where they belong!!

After waiting for almost one hour, we were finally given the go ahead. Kev reacted pretty well to the treatment, although the neuropathy is at its worst. He can't drink beverages that are at room temperature - they are too cold for him. Lots of tea is coming his way.

The CEA was 1.8, slightly up from last times 1.5. However, it was pointed out again, that this is just a marker and as long as the number stays below 5.0, it's all good. His final IV chemo treatment is slated for Dec 30, with the pump being removed on New Year's Day. Hope the platelets plan to show up this time in greater numbers!

Rich and Maria Licata invited us to join them for a Candlelight Christmas Dinner at the Butterfield Golf and Country Club. It was a magical evening, with incredible ambiance, delicious food, and spectacular music from over 40 violinists. The best part of the evening though, was being with family and friends.

Since being down here in Illinois, Rich and his family have been there for us from day one. They have welcomed us into their home with open arms, and always include us in holiday celebrations as well as weekly Sunday dinners. They are more than friends, they are truly our family and we couldn't feel more loved if we shared the same last name.

It can't be said enough, Rich and Maria, we treasure your friendship and love and total acceptance of us from the first day, some eleven years ago. Thank you from the bottom of our hearts.

Please continue the prayers and enjoy the last "weekend" of shopping. Remembering the true meaning of Christmas is the ultimate gift and best way to celebrate the holidays.

Love and Blessings, Kim

December 22, 2010 6:50am

Be kind, for everyone you meet is fighting a hard battle. ~ Plato

Kevin is struggling through number seven, and it has definitely been the hardest. He has pretty much slept since the weekend. He gets up for very brief moments to have a drink, eat a small meal, or shower. Last night he had a bath - he never takes baths - and just like a little baby, after he got his back scrubbed, and his hair washed, he got out, ready for bed and has been asleep ever since.

We are hoping that today is a better day, one filled with a little more energy.

I thought the quote above spoke volumes. While we are often our most kind for those we know are sick, or in pain, we should be blanketing everyone we meet today with our kind words, gestures and smiles. Especially at this time of year, when everyone is in such a rush to get their last few gifts bought, or hurrying to an office luncheon, it's easy to push our kindness way down, and dish out some frustration, or even worse, dismissiveness.

Spread your kindness that you shower so lovingly on Kevin and our family and share it with someone else who may be in need. Kindness is one resource that replenishes itself in greater amounts than we can possibly share.

Kev is stirring - time to make some tea! Have a great day.

Love, Kim

December 29, 2010 10:09 am

As Christmas approached, Kevin was hoping that he would feel good, so he could enjoy the blessed holiday with all of us. It is a blessed time, and magical things happen. For the first time in almost six months, Kevy felt fantastic. His side effects have been minimal, almost able to be ignored. He was so excited and overjoyed!

It was just the four of us on Christmas day, but the love that filled out home was immeasurable. We took our time opening gifts and sharing stories of past Christmas'. We watched more movies together and all of us napped at some point during the day.

The highlight of the day for me was when Kevin got up and started dancing with me to "Dominic the Donkey" that was playing. Nothing better than when the urge to dance hits you, and a kitchen floor and funny Christmas carol complete the scene. A turkey dinner followed and Kev was thrilled that he could taste it. and. more importantly, go back for turkey sandwiches later on.

A wonderful gift that we received this Christmas, was having Kevin's Mom and Dad and his sister Joanne, and Maureen (with her hubby Mike, and kiddos Michaela and Mikey) come down on Boxing Day (Dec 26 for our U.S. friends). It was the first time that Joanne has seen Kevy since his diagnosis and so tears flowed rather freely. The embrace that Joanne had for Kevin went on for some time, but no one complained. It was great to see Kevin being loved.

Our last night together was to include an early dinner of salmon and salad. Apparently Commonwealth Edison had other ideas. Our power went out around 4:00 pm. We weren't sure how we were going to fix dinner, but a call to ComEd told us that they were on the problem and would have power restored by 6:00 pm.

So what do you do with a house full of 2 toddlers, 2 teenagers, 5 adults and 2 seniors when the lights go out? You have an incredibly magical time. We lit candles and had them around the family room, where the fire was crackling in the fireplace and extra comforters were brought down to help keep everyone warm. We used a flashlight so Kevy could make animal shapes with his hands and shine it on the ceiling so the kiddos would laugh. Uncle Kevy also made up silly stories that made us all chuckle and then we sang songs. We sang Too Ra Loo Ra Loo Ra all together and it caused the hair to stand up on my arms. It was truly magical and something none of us will soon forget.

Today, Kev has his foot reflexology appointment and then we are off to see Dr. Hantel this afternoon, a day ahead of Kevin's final chemo treatment. Hopefully he will see that Kev is doing great and sign off on #8. We are scheduled in tomorrow at 9:00 am for his treatment. If you are in the neighborhood, feel free to swing by the Edward Cancer Center tomorrow!

I hope you all had a wonderful Christmas, and received all the love and prayers that we are sending your way. We couldn't make it through this journey without each and every one of you who have taken the time to send a note, make a meal, say a prayer or phone us. There is power in numbers and we will hold on to this power and use it to propel us through radiation and then at the end of February, begin to plan a celebration to which you will all be invited.

God is great and He has blessed us with all of you! Thank you for checking in on the Caring Bridge to find out how Kevin is doing. It's an honor to be among your company.

Will update on Kevy's final chemo tomorrow afternoon, unless something else comes up before then.

Love and Hugs,

Kim

Seeing 2010 come to an end was something that couldn't happen soon enough. Perhaps the further we got from the diagnosis of cancer, the closer we would get to healing and ultimate cure. Here is my last entry for the year.

December 31, 2010 7:09 pm

One Last Note from 2010

While I hoped to use this venue as a way of sharing how Kevin is doing on his long road to recovery, I have at times, shared with you how I am doing. Today is a tough day, and maybe more for me than Kevin.

His chemo treatment on Thursday was delayed a while because his platelet count was low (73). The doctor did give the go ahead and we proceeded with the final IV chemo! As Troy joined us for our first treatment, it seemed only fitting that Liam join us for the last one. It was great to have him there with us as he once again, didn't leave us without laughter and smiles. We are very lucky to have Troy and Liam. They have been wonderful.

When the treatment was over, our nurse Julie presented Kevin with a "Certificate for Meritorious Accomplishment" on behalf of the staff at the Edward Cancer Center. He received it for "exhibiting courage, bravery, and perseverance during chemotherapy". His feet didn't hit the ground, as he floated around the nurses' station, giving hugs to all the nurses, some who have never had Kevin as their patient. As he said, he didn't care, everyone was getting a hug no matter what.

On the way home, Kevin got the neuropathy feeling back, but less stomach cramps this go-round. When we arrived home, he developed debilitating muscle pulls in his legs. He was in real pain. Every time he tried to sleep, they would pull again.

Sweats showed up again, and it became a kind of game of whether or not to have the fan on for the sweats, or a blanket over his lower legs to keep them and his feet warm. We somehow found the right balance to address both issues.

So why do I feel down? I am chalking it up to seeing the holiday come and go, and allowing a little darkness to enter my mind, allowing me to think... this can't be the last Christmas... ..

Many of you have told me that cancer doesn't just touch the life of the patient. It goes for the family supporting the patient, as a way of perhaps getting us to back down and let it have its way with our husband, wife, sibling, parent or friend. I am upset with myself for letting it get in between Kevin and I. I am angry that Kev is a cancer patient. I am sad that Troy and Liam's dad is sick. I am sorry for Kevy's parents and siblings, that their loved one is suffering. I am devastated, beat down, overwhelmed, and so sad that my life partner, best friend, head of our household, incredibly great guy and phenomenal person is wondering if the chemo has done all it can do.

Sorry for the sadness on New Year's Eve, but I know you will understand. I want to rid myself of this heartache before the stroke of midnight so I can be open to receiving all the glorious best wishes and prayers that we continue to have bestowed upon us. I want to welcome the new year with such brightness and openness that all the darkness I may have developed over these past few months will move into the light and be gone.

Good bye 2010... Hello bright future!

Kevin has had a multitude of tests during this "cancer" thing. One such test is a PET scan. He was scheduled for one prior to the beginning of his radiation. He had to fast and psych himself up for the 3 hours that he would be at the hospital. Now, by description alone, the test is hardly fearful. He is given an IV and through the IV a radioactive compound which goes through his body. Once the substance has had a chance to move around and know the ins and outs of Kevin's body, he is put through the scan machine, with his arms above his head and his feet held together by bands. He then has to lie there quietly while they take the scan. He is unable to move, and wait out the 36 minutes it took for the procedure to be done.

So, as described above, the PET scan should not have the power to cause a melt down on my part. First of all, it was Kevin going through it, and aside from him possibly feeling a little fearful of the quiet and still part (haha), he was fine. Not until he was done and we were on our way home, did I realize that I had been holding my breath, gripping tightly to myself the whole time. Once I realized that he was done, and that we will find out if our unwanted visitor is lurking around, perhaps hiding in plain sight, I broke down and cried.

Stress is an incredible thing and plays tricks with you even if you aren't aware. Of course I am confident most of the time that the chemo has done the trick, and that nothing will be found. But, it makes you feel vulnerable knowing that this test is searching near and far and may find something.

When I was crying on our way home, I started talking to Kev about the day he had his colonoscopy, August 20, 2010 at 12:00 pm. They had medicated him pretty heavily because they had found the tumor early in the exam, so after it was done, he was unaware of everything. The doctor wanted to do a CT scan right away, seeing as we were already in the hospital. Kev was awake and was told of the findings and that he was going to have a scan. He had to drink a cocktail, and then he was rolled into the room, and I was left alone, for the first time since finding out he had cancer, sitting in a chair in the hallway on the other side of the door. I openly sobbed as people walked past. Someone did stop and ask if I was okay. How do you answer that question? My voice said I would be fine, but my mind and heart were screaming NO NO NO. HE CAN'T HAVE CANCER! WHAT IF IT IS SOMEWHERE ELSE?

The fear is there, and this scan sent me back to that horrible time. I know we have come such a far way and I know that the surgery and chemo have laid the path for radiation to come in and beam any last remnants of cancer. I know, yet I still cried.

My tears were met by Kev with open arms, and his shoulders that I have loved to sink into. There is less of him there, but he is still here and we are fighting and winning. Nevertheless, I feel somehow guilty because of my meltdown. On one hand, I am saying I am confident and full of faith that it's fine, and on the other, I am crumbling.

I am feeling better now, and Kev has been OK. He is gaining back his strength every day, and everyday he tells me he loves me. Every day I say a prayer to ask for strength, and everyday God delivers. And every day, when I tell Kevin that I love him, I say a silent I love you to one and all who have read the journal. It has allowed me to regain my strength, after sharing the bumps in the road to recovery. The messages left by visitors gives me the boost I need to keep moving. It allows me to be the best partner for Kevin as we move on.

FOOTPRINTS

One night a man had a dream. He dreamed that he was walking along the beach with the Lord. Across the sky flashed scenes from his life. For each scene, he noticed two sets of footprints in the sand: one belonged to him, and the other belonged to the Lord. When the last scene of his life flashed before him, he looked back at the footprints in the sand. He noticed that many times along the path of his life there was only one set of footprints. He also noticed that it happened at the very lowest and saddest times of his life. This really bothered him and he questioned the Lord about it.

"Lord, you said that once I decided to follow you, you'd walk with me all the way. But I have noticed that during the most troublesome times in my life, there was only one set of footprints. I don't understand why when I needed you the most you would leave me."

The Lord replied, "My son, my precious child I love you and I would never leave you. During your times of trial and suffering, when you see only one set of footprints, it was then that I carried you."

January 10, 2011 1:22 pm

Blessed is the servant who loves his brother as much when he is sick and useless as when he is well and can be of service to him. And blessed is he who loves his brother as well when he is far off as when he is by his side, and who would say nothing behind his back he might not, in love, say before his face.

~St Francis of Assisi

This may very well be one of the hardest journals to write.

We have known since November, but out of respect for Kevin's brother Brian and his family, have not posted this until they were ready. Today they are ready. Brian has stage II colon cancer.

Kevin and Brian have been this close since childhood. They are 17 months apart in age, with Brian leading the way. They shared a bedroom where you would find them together on the bunk beds, Kevy on the top and Brian on the bottom bunk.

They played together constantly and were each other's best friend. They played hockey together with Kevin on right wing, always looking for a chance to feed Brian the puck to score. The two of them would play golf together, often being dropped off at Northridge Golf Club to play 36 holes. No surprise here, but they also played lacrosse together, with Brian being the scorer, often with passes from Kevy.

Brian always included Kevy when he would go out. They went to university together, stood in each other's wedding, married their respective spouses in the same year, and as grown men, travel and vacation with their families together. We have been to Mexico and Hawaii together, not to mention the numerous days at Woodland Beach, at the family cottage. Quite simply, they are each other's "other" half.

Those who have been reading from the beginning of Kevin's journey know that Brian has been here for Kevy since day 1. He flew down from Toronto to attend the Dr. appointment when we got confirmation of Kev's cancer and subsequently returned with Anne and their two kids to be here while Kevy had surgery and then, made yet another trip to go with Kev to one of his first chemo treatments.

Unlike Kevin, Brian did not have symptoms and simply went and had a colonoscopy after Kev's diagnosis to be proactive and show his support. It came as a complete shock to Brian and Anne, and us when Brian was told of the findings.

Brian told us on Kevy's birthday. Brian said that Kevin saved his life. Kev told Brian that hearing that he went and they found something at an earlier stage, was the best birthday gift ever.

I know from seeing with my own eyes, that Brian's diagnosis was crushing to Kev. Kevin reacted with more raw emotion at that news than he did to learning of his own cancer. I also know from speaking to Anne, that Brian's response to Kevin's illness affected Brian the same way.

Brian will start radiation and chemo on January 20 for five weeks. He will have surgery in April. God Bless you Brian. We love you.

Please get checked... especially if you have a family member who has been diagnosed with colon cancer. It may just save a life...

What greater thing is there for human souls than to feel that they are joined for life - to be with each other in silent unspeakable memories.

~ George Eliot

In 2000 Kevin and I moved our sons down here for a job opportunity that held great promise and challenges for Kevin. We made the journey to Aurora, leaving our family behind. We forged ahead to make a life for ourselves here, in the U.S.

Since we have been here, we have made wonderful friends and found new "family". The support for us at this time is so appreciated, especially since our family is not here. You have picked up the slack and ran with it, and continue to do so. While we have known for a long time that we are "not alone here", all of you have folded us into your families, and you have all earned your own spot in ours.

Thought I would introduce you to Kevin's family, for those of you who have not had the privilege. Kevin's parents, Jack and Theresa, moved to Canada from Belfast, Ireland over 50 years ago. They went on to have six children and today have added 13 grandchildren to the mix.

Kevin has two brothers, Jack and Brian and three sisters, Joanne, Sue and Maureen. Kevin's brother Jack and his wife Carolynn have two children, Courtney and Jack Jr. Growing up, Jack had the role of disciplinarian. He made sure that his siblings towed the line and followed his example. He has been a mentor to all his brothers and sisters.

Joanne has two children Tiffany and Josh. Joanne is a high school teacher, and was known as the sensitive and artistic one. Joanne made our wedding flowers, and they were amazing. She is a free spirit who loves her family very much. We were grateful to have her join us over the Christmas holidays.

Sue comes next and is married to Ron. They have three sons, David, Griffin and John. Sue was a collector. As she got older, she was a collector of harlequin romance novels, and the homeless. It was not uncommon to find new faces around Susie's table at Thanksgiving. Her heart is as big as any I've come across.

Brian, the brother just ahead of Kevy, was and still is Kevin's right hand. They grew up doing things together all the time. They will even finish their radiation treatments on the same date... Feb. 23. Brian has always been there for Kevin, and included him in all aspects of his life. His wife is Anne, my roommate from university, who is an awesome woman. She is an executive at a large corporation, and is raising, along with Brian, their children, Brenna and Steve.

The baby of the family is Maureen, who is the "go to" one. She is aware of all things family, in a good way, and has taken on the role of caring for their parents in their golden years. Maureen makes sure they get to doctor appointments, to church, trips to the cottage etc. She is an elementary teacher and is married to Mike. They have two kiddos, Michaela and Michael. Maureen also joined us during Christmas and New Years.

An extra special shout out to Kevy's Aunt Maureen and his Aunt Sue. Sue has had a 30+ year career as an oncologist. She has been instrumental in helping us understand the ins and outs of the cancer treatments, and willing to take our calls at any time. Boy, we are blessed.

While they are not here locally, the love for their son, brother, uncle, in-law and nephew is immeasurable and they continually show it with phone calls and visits. His family has shared with Kevin, funny, scary, silent, remarkable, run of the mill and unspeakable memories. And lots and lots of love.

January 30, 2011 11:43 am

Nothing is more desirable than to be released from an affliction, but nothing is more frightening than to be divested of a crutch.

~ James Baldwin

As you may have noticed, I love to include quotations in an entry that perhaps encapsulates exactly where we are in Kevin's journey. He has officially completed 10 of his 28 radiation and oral chemo treatments, leaving 18! He has three and a half weeks to go. While we are extremely relieved to know the end is in sight, a different kind of fear or uneasiness has crept in.

When Kevin was diagnosed way back on August 25, fear was all encompassing of every wakeful moment, and also crept into our dreams, turning them into nightmares. However, in quick succession, he had surgery to remove the tumor and do a res-section of his colon and three weeks to the day of his surgery, started chemotherapy. A funny note to add here - not until we were well into the chemo treatments, did Kevin share with me that it was he who pushed everything ahead by a week. Both the surgeon and oncologist wanted Kevin to heal from the major surgery for at least four weeks. Their preference would have been six weeks. However, Kevin took it into his own hands and told them he wanted to start at three weeks. No surprise that they went ahead - he is quite an incredible salesman, and has quite the persuasive nature.

From September 24 to January 1, Kevin tackled the grueling treatment, rarely wavering. Waves of fear and unknown pushed us around constantly in the beginning, but began to only ripple in the end.

Now we find ourselves in the home stretch. I hate to say it, but those ripples are gaining momentum, and are slowing growing larger and stronger every day. You see, once February 23 comes, Kevin and I will be waving and smiling and possibly hugging staff at the Edward Cancer Center goodbye, knowing that this incredible dark period of our lives is over. As we exit through the revolving door, and have Ivan the valet parking attendant retrieve our car, the ripples will be full blown waves again... waiting to push us home.

From the first hint of cancer, Kevin has had a life preserver around him. First surgery, then chemo and finally radiation coupled with chemotherapy. During this whole time, there was something working toward ridding Kevy's body of the cancer.

February 24 we will awake to the first day in six months of Kevin swimming alone, without the life preserver of treatments to support him. How do you go from feeling like you are fighting the disease somewhat proactively, to nothing?

There is no question that we are both a little uncomfortable about that first day. Do the cancer cells, if there are any left, know that we are not sending in the poison, or radiation anymore?

So this is when our faith and the support from all of you come in to play as the lead role. All of you who have been following this journal, and know Kevin and our family, will now be the front line for us. Fear isn't so scary when you are with others. Knowing how supportive you have been to us during this difficult time, has always been essential in moving us forward and looking ahead to tomorrow.

Two different kind of support: medicine and love. They have been working in harmony this past half year. As we say goodbye to the medicine, we now have the spotlight on the love. So, as I write this, I am beginning to feel my fear subside - it always helps me if I talk things out - the crutch of medicine may be removed, but we still have all of you at our backs, holding us upright! Thank you will never be enough....

One thing left to say... Anchors Away!!!!!!

Love Kim

February 3, 2011 11:58 am

Well the blizzard of 2011 left behind 20 inches of snow for us, 2 snow days, and one day without radiation. Kevin's radiation and chemo scheduled for Wednesday was cancelled. While we were told that it is okay to miss a day, it does mean that we will add the day on at the end and therefore our new last day is February 24.

I'm pretty sure that Kevin's body was thankful for the delay. It allowed him to rest his body and battle the fatigue and diarrhea at home. He is an incredible trooper and I am so proud of him.

March is Colon Cancer Awareness month and I am planning on making sure that my place of employment has posters up reminding people to get checked. If you are over the age of 50 or have a family history of colon cancer, you owe it to yourself and your family to get checked. Kevin can assure you that the procedure itself is nothing. If he can do it, you can too.

Kevy meets with Dr. Hantel tomorrow for the first time since starting radiation. They will do blood work at which time, we can find out his CEA number, which should still be under 5. We also meet again with Dr. Das Gupta, the radiology oncologist to review the process and answer any questions.

From my perspective, the radiation aspect of the treatment makes it very difficult to be an active supporter. When Kevy was receiving the IV chemo, the treatment was evident. You could see the drugs in their bags, hanging from the pole. The line delivering the drugs to Kevin via his port is obvious, as is the nurses coming in frequently to check on Kevin and see that he was comfortable.

67

The radiation treatment leaves you having to believe that treatment is happening. Kev is alone in the room receiving the radiation, and is still and quiet for 8 minutes. He is then told that it's all done, and makes his way to the change room to give back the pretty hospital gown, and dress to go home. That's it. No warm and fuzzies here. Our only way of having a clear picture of the treatment was when Dr. Das Gupta showed us the computerized pictures of Kevin's body and exactly where the beams are aimed. That helped to make it seem more real.

So tomorrow should have some new info to share and will bring us one day closer to being done. If you are in the area where the storms hit, stay warm and safe, and if you are lucky enough to be beyond its path... enjoy!

Love Kim

February 4, 2011 4:08 pm

Today the lyrics of Bon Jovi's *Living on a Prayer* were on a loop in my head, causing me to sing and hum it over and over. Around the seventeenth time, (give or take a few), I made the connection and realized that we ARE living on a prayer... perhaps quite a few.

Kevin received his 14th radiation treatment today. He has 14 more to go!!! Happiness is knowing that we are on the downward side of the mountain.

Prior to the radiation, we met again with Dr. Hantel - I can't say enough nice things about this man. He is a great guy, and very much involved in Kevin's recovery. He is caring, compassionate, and quite funny. Kevy continues to hug him whenever he sees him, which brings a smile to both their faces.

Because Imodium is not working for Kevin, the Dr. has given him a prescription to help with the diarrhea. The doctor is concerned that Kev could become dehydrated, and has therefore booked him in for blood work for the next three weeks. He wants to keep an eye on his electrolytes.

The blood work done today gives us our first CEA number since back in December... 1.5! Oh yeah. We want it to stay below 5 and so far, it's cooperating.

We are pushing forward, and have our eye on February 24th. It comes just before the start of Colon Cancer Awareness Month

(March). I have heard rumors about a "Cut for Cancer" by the lacrosse team, to help raise money for colon cancer research. It is coming at a good time as Kevin is losing more of his hair over these past few weeks than throughout the whole time of treatment.

Thank you for your continued support of Kevin, the boys and me. Without doubt, you are why we are half way there and have the staying power to finish this journey.

Time to listen to some Bon Jovi! Enjoy the weekend, and keep thinking of ways to show random acts of kindness.

Sleep would escape me and my mind drifted. I found myself reading the journal entries, going back to the beginning. It seems that when the house is still and all are asleep, I am most vulnerable to sadness and fear.

While sitting on our bed, complete darkness envelopes me, and only the light from the screen gives away my loneliness and aloneness. Reflecting on the past six months brings a mixed bag of goods. Disbelief, fear, grief, sadness, faith, inexplicable joy, love, laughter and tears.

The questions, the rants, the tears and guttural cries are not new to my bedroom walls. The pillows are active participants in holding the tears and muffled cries. The man I love most in this world is dealing with pain, nausea, embarrassment and life, everyday. Only now, while the silence in the house is deafening, is Kevy able to fall into a restless slumber and escape the heaviness of his cancer.

Most of the time I was able to see the glass as half full. However, reflecting on this long and difficult journey, the darkness kept me from seeing the glass at all. The only cure for this was to turn off the computer, pull the covers up, and let the pillows do their thing.

God Bless. I know this will pass... come on sunshine!

Love, Kim

February 7, 2011 9:02 pm

There is one friend in the life of each of us who seems not a separate person, however dear and beloved, but an expansion, an interpretation, of one's self, the very meaning of one's soul.

~ Edith Wharton

Kevin Troy Griffin is my beloved friend who is, in fact, an extension of myself. He is the extrovert to my introvert, the strong to my weak, the childlike to my serious side, the protector to my fear. He quite simply is my everything.

Many years ago, I remember reading an article that discussed marriage. There is one thing that has stuck with me since that time. It is that everyone wants someone to walk with, and be a witness to, their life.

What good is it if you can't share the good and the bad with someone who is right there, every step of the way? While they may have seen what you see, you are still able to describe the vibrant colors that you found in the vision. Your partner is standing on the same path as you, and can add more details, to things we may have not noticed.

The saying that two heads are better than one is true... such can also be said about two sets of eyes. Going through life, the obvious things are seen by both, but one pulls out all the obvious shades of color, while the other is able to paint the picture with subtle nuances and shades which in turn make the view beautifully perfect for each.

Kim Griffin

Kevin's cancer diagnosis is a great example of us having each other to walk the path and be on the lookout for any and all things. We have both experienced the fear and pain, although somewhat differently, yet we are able to enhance the others vision and help to calm and comfort the other. We have always been good partners - when one of us is down, the other is able to stop and pick them up. If one is hurt, the other helps to dress the wound with love, words, or chicken soup.

I have been having an incredibly difficult time these past 2 or 3 days, and Kevin has been there for me. I feel selfish, but not because of anything he has said. In fact, today while I was at work in my first grade classroom, there was a knock on the door, and who was standing there but Kevin... with a bouquet of flowers in his hands. It took everything in my power to hold it together. He knew. He knew.

And I know. I got the right one. I know.

February 13, 2011 8:34 pm

To weep is to make less the depth of grief. ~William Shakespeare

Tears are never far from my eyes. I've been told forever that my bladder is too close to my eyes. I think that's a whole other problem... haha.

Laughing and crying are great ways to release your feelings. Over this journey, I have done both, and although I prefer to laugh, the tears come on, wind down my cheeks and land softly on my shirt. I have always let myself go there when I feel like crying because to me, if I deny it, the sadness will only sit there, gain strength and present itself again.

Tears deserve to flow, and lessen your grief. Life is too short to carry around grief. It takes away room for joy, love, happiness, goofiness. I want to get it out of the way, and then focus on the good feelings.

I know that with continued prayer, and the love we both feel from our friends and family, we will stop those tears from running down my cheeks by breaking out a huge smile, causing them to detour and land on my shoulders. Lord knows that all your support makes me feel like I can shoulder anything... including salty tears.

February 15, 2011 8:42 pm

Be the change you want to see in the world. ~ Ghandi

Kevin is hanging in there, knowing that there is only 7 more treatments left. He still suffers from neuropathy side effects in his hands and occasionally his feet. Some days his hands are completely numb, and other days there is only a slight numbness in the tips of his fingers.

He has no mouth sores, and has been able to go back to drinking cold drinks. He actually had a slurpee the other day! Fatigue is still milling around, but is less pervasive. Diarrhea is a constant and cramps as well. We have to keep an eye on him, making sure he does not get dehydrated.

Perhaps the most noticeable thing now is his hair. It has really thinned out. He has always had a head full of thick wavy/curly hair. It's not so right now. I think because it is such an obvious sign that things are not the same as they were, that we both have reacted to the absence with sadness and a few tears.

From that first moment of being pulled into a small waiting room at the hospital immediately after Kevin's colonoscopy, I began to wonder what good could possibly come from this.

I will tell you the good.

I am more in love with my husband than at any other time during our almost 20 year marriage.

Kevin's heart is full of love after seeing all of the friends and family and acquaintances who have taken the time to let him know that he is thought of and important. Sometimes it takes something this earth shattering to realize how much you mean to so many people.

It's a shame that we don't take the time more often to celebrate each other, and to come together to put words to our feelings for another person. Too often it takes the end of one's life before we reflect on how they impacted us.

I have tried to take the time to realize that like a pebble thrown into a pond, our lives ripple and affect so many others, to the point of never truly knowing if it ever stops.

Many who have reached out are those who know Kevin as a coach, co-worker, parent or neighbor. Beyond that, we have heard from elementary school friends, high school friends, university friends, Kevin's client's (past and present), past employers, old girlfriends (I can handle it :)), parents of friends and co-workers of mine.

We have had prayers said for us and Kevin from as far away as the Congo, France, Switzerland, England, Hong Kong, Canada, and, of course, all corners of the U.S.A. We have never realized how small the world really is.

Thank you are only words - but the actions that we are and will continue to put behind them will begin in a small way, to pay it forward.

Love, Kim

February 19, 2011 12:10 am

While I don't yet know how March is going to come in - like a lamb or lion, I know how Kevin's cancer journey came in - like a lion. So for some reason I thought it would go out like a lamb. Nope. Can you say "One really pissed off Lion?"

Kevin has recently been suffering from acute diarrhea, which in turn has caused extremely painful rectal spasms. He is in so much pain when they hit that he becomes faint, breaks out in a sweat, gets an incredible headache and then, mercifully, makes his way to the couch or bed and is soothed by the fatigue, falling into a fitful sleep.

Really? While we are grateful that only four treatments remain, Kevy could have done without all this last minute hoopla.

Man, this colon cancer has truly been a pain in the a$$! Four more... Get ready, Lion... you have met your match!!

Love, Kim

February 21, 2011 12:57 am

One Tear.

How can something so small cause a flood of epic proportions?

Kevin has been in incredible pain for most of the weekend. Today it came on after we left Marmion where we were joining forces with Diane, Teri and Randy (incredible lacrosse parents and amazing people) to organize lacrosse uniforms. Spasms are gripping Kevin and not letting him go.

If the purpose was to bring a grown man to his knees, then success was achieved. Bedtime couldn't come soon enough. Kevin pulled the blankets up close around him and prayed for a way out of the agony he has been feeling.

He struggled with shivers and pain and finally let a tear flow.

Kevin is a strong man, but during this last push to the finish line, cancer is overtaking him and bringing out all it has.

One tear... a flood of pain and agony and finally sleep.

Please God help Kevin get through these next few days of treatment and let him awaken on Friday ready to face the rest of his life... with one tear... of joy.

Amen.

Love Kim

February 22, 2011 8:55 pm

After two days in the hospital, I took a turn for the nurse.

~W.C. Fields

Edward Hospital was where Kevin and I spent a good part of our day today. We met with Dr. Hantel and went over Kev's next steps on his road to remission. Have I mentioned before how much we love Dr. Hantel? He is laudable, incredibly competent, intelligent, a leader, not to mention a man with a good sense of humor. He gave Kevy a prescription for the spasms that have been holding him hostage these last few days. He listened to our questions and once again made us feel like we were in the best possible hands.

Kevin has only 2 treatments left... can't believe it! Once he is done, Dr. Hantel is going to have him do a CT scan March 25. We will do some blood work before then, but the scan will be what will hold at least the first true signs of remission (we hope).

Kevin then received his radiation treatment. These last three therapies are being called boosts, because they narrow the scope of the radiation beams to a more specific location in the pelvic area. Like a mother who does final preparations on her young son for the family picture - you know, pats his hair down, fixes his shirt, and uses her own spit to clean a spot off his face - the radiation therapy wants to send Kevin back out into the big world as prepared as possible for the rest of his life.

After Kevin's appointments, I had my mammogram. Ladies who have been reluctant to go because you are afraid of the pain, or the experience itself, let me reassure you that it's worth it. The pain and experience are inconsequential, but the outcome is a sense of relief and reassurance.

After I finished the mammogram, and before I went back to the waiting room to get Kevin, I made my way upstairs to the endoscopy department (where Kevin had his colonoscopy) to see if one of the nurses who was there on that frightful August 20th was in today.

Sure enough Michelle, the nurse that I remembered the most from that day was in fact working. I was led back by another nurse to say hello. She somewhat remembered me, but there was no question that I remembered her. She was there for me when the doctor told me that he found cancer in Kevin. While Kevin slept off the medication, and was oblivious to the results, she stood with me while I made those difficult phone calls. Michelle made sure that I was offered something to drink and eat - I didn't want anything - and she sat with me, holding my hand and offering soothing words.

She was so appreciative of me stopping by, and got the okay to come down to the waiting room to say hello to Kevin. As we approached Kev, I could tell he had no recollection of Michelle. She quickly remembered Kevin (surprise surprise) and after a brief retelling of the story, Kev gave her a big hug. She was interested in hearing about Kevin's journey and we shared a great few minutes together. At the end, I wanted to remind her that she in fact made a difference in someone's life. She was there for me when even I wasn't there for me.

Michelle, thank you again for the encouragement and incredible care you gave to both Kevin and I. You have a permanent place in our hearts.

If you have had a great experience with a nurse, please let them know. They are the heart and soul in healthcare.

On that note, Stacy thank you once again for flying up to Chicago to be with us during Kevin's surgery. I know you did it from your role as my friend, but it sure helped that you are a nurse. Your ability to decipher the pig Latin that was spoken after surgery by the doctor was appreciated.

While I may not have the authority, I am going to declare tomorrow February 23, 2011 as Hug a Nurse or Doctor Day.

Love, Kim

February 24, 2011 6:57 am

THIS IS IT.

2:15 pm

Last radiation and chemo treatment.

February 24, 2011 8:05 pm

Now for continued healing and health.

I will keep writing as we continue with follow up care. Please continue to stop by and leave a note for Kev. It's bad enough going through withdrawal of not going to the cancer center every day, Kevy couldn't handle having to withdrawal from all your love and support and notes!

We couldn't have done it without all of you!!!

Love Kim

March 2, 2011 8:22 pm

If things go wrong, don't go with them. ~ Roger Babson

Just got word that Kev's CT scan originally scheduled for March 25 has been rescheduled for March 22.

This will allow Dr. Hantel enough time to get the results and talk to us before the weekend - we are grateful for this change because going into a weekend not knowing, would be enough to send us over the edge!

We are expecting good news but I would be lying to say that we aren't a little anxious. Please keep Kevy in your prayers.

Love to all, and may God continue to bless you for your strength and friendship to us.

God is good! Kim

March 6, 2011 7:33 pm

I had the blues because I had no shoes until upon the street, I met a man who had no feet.

~ Denis Waitely

Thankfully most of the side effects have left, but for some reason Kevin is making neuropathy feel really comfortable and at home. The loss of sensation in his fingers, feet and lower legs is at an all time annoying level.

Dr. Hantel has told him that this may last for up to a year, but I know that it is frustrating Kev. He is dropping things all the time, and while I love him scratching my back, he doesn't feel his fingers so has no idea how much pressure, or lack thereof that he is applying.

Of course, the opening quote just goes to show you that while Kevin has occasionally complained of the lack of feeling, he knows and appreciates the fact that the chemo was necessary for him to be cleared of cancer. I know it will be even easier to accept once the CT scan comes back clean.

Have a great evening, and enjoy the upcoming week. We love and are thankful for all of you.

Love, Kim

I am an avid reader and many years ago I came across a book that dealt with relationships and how to find happiness within one. The main thing that has stuck with me some 15 years later is this: all relationships, be they a marriage, courtship, sibling to sibling, friend to friend, boss to employee, coworker to coworker; require the three "A"s.

Acceptance
Acknowledgement
Appreciation

Traveling life's path, has thus far been pretty smooth. Of course, there have been bumps along the road. Let me share a few.

I was estranged from my father for quite a few years after my parents divorced. In my early 20s, I felt a need to reach out to my dad and try one more time to reconnect. I sent him a letter acknowledging that both of us had stopped trying to repair our relationship. I told him that I was willing to take half the blame (acceptance) and went on to tell him that I thought that I had grown into a nice young woman and that he was partly responsible for it. I was therefore letting him know how much I appreciated him. This letter opened the door, and we were able to come together and rebuild our father daughter relationship. We remained connected and loving toward each other until his passing 3 years later.

With Kevin, not unlike most other couples, we had our ups and downs along the way, but those bumps were never strong enough to send us off our path as husband and wife. Perfection is not a word I would ever use in describing our relationship, but I would say that we have both in the past and present, practiced the three "A"s. It's not always easy; frankly it can be quite difficult. But hear me now. Since Kevin's diagnosis, we have upped our efforts 100 fold to make sure that we accept, acknowledge and appreciate each other.

Kevin's cancer has given me a new perspective on many things. When I am a witness to a petty argument among co-workers over trivial things, I am able to give it the weight of my time and thoughts that it deserves - none. I will not be drawn into such messes. I would rather put my energy toward making sure that the relationships I have with my husband, sons, family and friends are acknowledged and appreciated. I also accept them for what they each individually hold.

When you find yourself ready to blow your top, or rehash something that happened a fortnight ago, stop. Remember to give the other person what they and you need. Someone in the relationship has to go first. The payoff is incredible. Like with my dad, I was the first to reach out and offer the three "A"s. The payoff? Having my dad feel that he could reach out to me and not be turned away. He got to know me as an adult, and I got to feel like daddy's little girl again. Holding his hand those last three years made me realize how big and strong his hands were, and how perfectly my hand fit inside of his.

I never want to waste another moment with any and all of you: I so greatly appreciate all that you have brought to my life, both from those who have known me before I was born through to and including my newest friends. I want to acknowledge that you have helped to make me the woman I am today. A woman of strong faith and full of life's riches, and that my heart is accepting of all your love, effort and prayers. I stand before all of you knowing that it is because of you that Kevin's healing has begun.

March 14, 2011 11:38 pm

Kevin is almost back to his old self, with only neuropathy and fatigue hanging around. He keeps hoping to be rid of the last side effects soon.

The neuropathy is the most significant symptom. There is very little feeling in his fingertips, but what's worse is that he is numb from the knees down. Walking at times resembles a person on stilts. He is bumping into things, and not feeling it.

Kevy's hair is quite thin, but he won't have to worry about that for long. The Marmion lacrosse team is raising funds for Colon Cancer Alliance by holding a hair cutting fundraiser. The players are collecting money from sponsors and in turn will be having their heads shaved in a show of solidarity for Kev and the many thousands of people who have been struck by cancer. We are blessed to be part of such a great "family".

Have a wonderful day, and remember you make a difference each and every day!

March 20, 2011 11:31 am

On Friday the lacrosse team was volunteering at Feed My Starving Children packaging food for those around the world who go to bed every night hungry. In the two hours we were there, we packaged enough food to feed 74 children for one year. What a success!

Well lacrosse season is now underway, with Marmion having their first games of the year. The Fresh/Soph team put up a good fight, but lost by this much... the JV team won their game 13-1, and Kev's varsity team won 3-0. Kev was there to coach his team to their first of what we hope are many victories.

I look for meaning behind things and am hoping that this victory is a sign that Kevin's scan on Tuesday will be the messenger telling us that Kevin is in remission. Of course, we know that this is always going to be part of our lives from this point on, but we are hopeful that all the pain and suffering that has happened has not been in vain.

This upcoming week will probably be the worst we have faced since August. How can we sleep, or move forward knowing that the scan could show cancer that was hiding somewhere. Please say an extra prayer that the treatments have driven the cancer out and that the DO NOT ENTER sign we put up after Kev's surgery and treatments, will be obeyed.

Thank you for your continued support by following along on Caring Bridge. We have been so blessed to have a place to share the good and the not so good news with all of you.

Love Kim

March 22, 2011 5:06 pm

"All human wisdom is summed up in two words - wait and hope"
~ Alexandre Dumas Père

Our first stop today was at the cancer center, where Kevin had blood drawn to get a count and to find out his CEA number. It was eerie being back in the center, but surprisingly not too much anxiety. That didn't come until a little later. We were told the results wouldn't be available until tomorrow.

We then moved on to the main hospital where Kev had his CT scan surrounded by a little bit of drama. He had changed into a cute hospital outfit, and was waiting for his turn to be called. As they came around the corner to get him, the hospital fire alarm system went off and the loud speaker proceeded to announce over and over "Code Red".

We had to be placed in a room off the hallway until the code was cleared. Some fifteen minutes later, Kev was able to proceed into the scanning room. Low and behold, as he was being positioned on the table, the alarm went off again with the loud speaker blaring "Code Red" over and over again. In the waiting area, I didn't know whether or not to evacuate the building, leaving Kevin and his clothes behind :).

From Kevin's perspective, lying down on the table, he could hear the nurses place a call to see if they were to continue with the CT scans or have the patients leave. They did get the OK to go ahead, and after much anxiety Kevy had his scan.

Kevin says he doesn't remember having the scan immediately following his colonoscopy back in August. It wasn't as bad as he thought. We will not have the results until Friday, possibly Thursday. We will receive a call from Dr. Hantel.

Please give an extra squeeze to your loved ones tonight, and hold them close. The pit of my stomach is heavy with the unknown. I guess the only thing I know for sure is that I could sure use a bigger dose of patience.

Will let everyone know any and all results as they become available to us.

Love, Kim

March 24, 2011 7:23 am

CANCER FREE!

March 27, 2011 7:35 pm

God has not called us to see through each other, but to see each other through.

~Author Unknown

Since Thursday, it seems as if we have been riding a huge wave of relief, joy and thankfulness.

Dr. Hantel called us at 7:00 am on Thursday and asked Kevin how he was feeling. When Kev responded by saying he felt great, Dr. Hantel said that he should because the CT scan came back clean.

Kev repeated the result for Troy, Liam and myself as we were all standing still, waiting for the news. We were embracing each other and tearing up, and Kevy told Dr. Hantel that if he were here (meaning our house) that he would kiss him. Dr. Hantel quickly said that he was glad he was not!

Kevy will go for blood tests every two months for the next year and then eventually that will stretch out to longer increments. He will also receive scans every four months for the first two years and again will fade out over time. The blood work that accompanied this past CT scan came back with a CEA number of 0.9. As a refresher, 0-5 is the normal range. Upon finding the cancer, Kev's number was 29. After surgery and prior to chemo, it was 9.2 and since then went as low as 1.5. Therefore the reading of 0.9 is the lowest it has ever been.

As was mentioned in previous journals, the lacrosse players from Marmion Academy wanted to shave their heads in a unity of baldness as they all anticipated Kevin losing his hair from chemotherapy. When that didn't happen, a fundraising idea was born. The boys would get sponsors and they would shave their heads and the funds raised would go to Colon Cancer Alliance.

We are very proud to say that the players raised over $6,000.00 for a very worthy cause. Kev gladly shaved his head using a number 1 clipper, and paved the way for some 50+ players to some level of baldness.

We continue to be thankful for all that was done for us during these past seven months and what a wonderful way to end - paying it forward. God saw us through this difficult journey, but only after all of our family and friends parted a path for him. We have been carried by so much love, faith and hope.

Thank you all for caring so much for a man who gives so much of himself to all who know him. A man willing to do for all his fellow men; who never says no; who loves deeply and completely; who has impacted so many lives and who continues to make a difference each and every day. Thank you for lighting our way through this dark journey, and never letting us fall.

God has blessed us all by putting Kevin Troy Griffin in our lives.

Love and many blessings,

Kim

April 12, 2011 9:54 pm

Thanks for all who are following along on this second Griffin colon cancer journey. Brian did have surgery today and came through it pretty well. Apparently his scar starts above the bellybutton and Kev was ticked. He says that Brian always has to one up him.)

Kev has had a rough couple of days leading up to Brian's surgery and feeling as if he is letting him down by not being there. Let me assure you that there have been joyous tears and smiles today from all.

Please continue to overlook the small things in life and hug your loved ones a little tighter. Random acts of kindness never go unappreciated.

Now let's hope Kev gets through the neuropathy side effects. He is still pretty numb from his knees down and in his fingers.

Will update over the next little while as we get more back from Kev's visit to the doctor coming up and from Brian's recovery.

Love, Kim

May 17, 2011 5:25 pm

Hello to one and all. Just wanted to provide an update on Kevin, as he had his first blood work and appointment with the oncologist since being given the "Cancer Free" banner to carry.

Kevin met with Dr. Hantel, to go over Kevin's side effects of neuropathy that have been with him since last fall. We were reassured that it could still take many months for the feeling of numbness and tingling to go away. I'm guessing that I may want to purchase a few more lanyards for his keys for work, home and lacrosse. Note to everyone, if you have found keys as of late, they are probably Kevy's... even if found in Mississauga, Missouri or Marmion. If, however, you found them in Winnipeg, they are not his!!! (hahaha)

Kevin's blood work took a long time to get back today, but when it did come back it showed his CEA number to be 2.1. Very well within the normal range. All of his other blood work numbers were great, and he has only gained 2 pounds.

Kev will have to continue carrying the Cancer Free banner which I know he does not mind in the least. He has another CT scan at the end of July at which time the CEA blood work will be done again. He will have a colonoscopy in August (August 20 will be one year since diagnosis).

Walking back into the cancer center is not recommended for those of us who have their bladder close to their eyes. I felt like the calendar

95

had turned back to September. It was nice to see some of the nurses that were there for us during the long haul and they were thrilled to see how good Kevin looked and how well he is doing.

We are in the final push for lacrosse, and are have a winning season. It's been great for Kevin to be back doing what he loves, with those he loves, his teams.

Thanks for continuing your prayers, and acts of kindness. It never gets old thanking you for being there for us, and I hope you all know that you have continued in our prayers as well.

Continued health to one and all and don't forget to pay it forward.

Love, Kim

October 18, 2011 10:27 pm

It feels like only yesterday that I last posted here, but I see that it has been quite a while. This week is crunch time for Kevin's CT scan and results.

To recap, we found out in July that Kevin's cancer had returned, although in only one lymph node and another suspicious spot just up the lymph node chain from where it was originally discovered.

You would think by now that Kevin and I would be old pros at this game called "Life", but you would be wrong. Kevin has been incredibly stressed the past week or so, and I am following along like a good soldier. Kevin has mentioned that he doesn't think he can go through this again, and of course I answer that yes he can. But then I begin to wonder…

The wear and tear that this journey has put on Kevin and our family is indescribable. We are up, then we are down, we are praying, we are crying, we are laughing, we are holding our breath. Right now, I would say that we are holding our breath, while praying and jumping up and down.

The impact that this disease has had on all aspects of our life has lead us into a corner. Emotionally, financially, spiritually, even our ability to make it through this week has been labeled with the cancer stamp.

Kevin has his scan on Thursday at 8:45 am. We were originally scheduled to meet with Dr. Hantel on Friday for the results, but the doctor will not be in the office that day and had us reschedule the appointment for Monday. So not only do we have the stress leading up to the scan, but we now have the added burden of having to wait over the weekend before we find out.

To top off this week, we are also waiting on results for a very dear friend who has pancreatic cancer. Another dear friend of mine lost her father last night after a long battle. Oh, and did I mention that it's application time for Troy and colleges/universities?

The biggest thing though is that this week Troy is at a religious retreat with 30+ seniors. It just brings home how close we are to seeing him off to school and ultimately off into the big wide world. This time for him is going to hold lots of opportunity for self reflection, faith reflection, and an opportunity to build on his personal relationships with his dear friends. We feel his absence incredibly so at this time. Liam is really beginning to miss him, and I think he is getting the idea that it won't be the same when he is gone.

Anyway, felt like I could share some of this burden of mixed feelings knowing that I always feel better. I have to get into a good place so I can be strong for Kevin and the boys when we find out the results.

Love your kiddos and give them extra hugs this week. Please keep us in your prayers, and know that we appreciate all of you who leave messages.

I'll keep you posted about the scan and the blood work and I will let you know the results as soon as we get them.

Thank you for your continued friendships and support.

Love, Kim

October 20, 2011 10:29 pm

And so we wait... until Monday. That is unless we can track the good doctor down before then!

Lots of prayers are appreciated. And bloodhounds!

Luv, Kim

October 22, 2011 10:30 am

Perseverance is not a long race; it is many short races one after another.

~Walter Elliott, The Spiritual Life

Okay.

Take a deep breath and give someone you love a hug.

Fortunately, or unfortunately, depending how you want to look at it, we were able to get some feedback yesterday about Kevin's scan. The great news is that the scan did not detect any new spots, which is fantastic. It also had in its viewfinder the 2 spots we were concerned about located in the "retro peritoneal" lymph nodes. This is why Kev started a second round of treatments during the summer, finishing up Sept. 9.

One of the cancerous nodes measured 1.5 cm by 1.5 cm. Since the second round of treatments, all other spots have vanished, therefore no cancer there. This one node, however, is still there having shrunk by a 1/3. So, if I am wearing my pink colored glasses, this is all encouraging news. I am, however, not wearing those glasses.

The initial comments from the doctors (thanks to Sue Aitken) are that they are not concerned with the CT scan. However, the concern, and there is some, is that the infamous CEA number is rising.

If you can go back to the beginning, you will recall that the CEA number was a marker that indicates there is cancer somewhere. Prior to Kevin's surgery and treatments, he was at 29. From the time he started chemo it dropped to under 5 (which is the area you want). It also doesn't matter if the number under five is 4.9 or 1.1, they are all considered the same. However, when the number is above 5, there is considerable concern given the higher the number rises. Right now, the blood work shows Kevin's CEA to be at 17.

We meet with Dr. Hantel Monday at 9:00 am. It's possible that the CEA number is higher because the one spot is still alive, and that the radiation is still completing its work. Unfortunately, that is not a for sure. We are anticipating the good doctor to schedule a PET scan which is more intense, and able to pick up any cancer anywhere. That way, if they find no other areas to be cancerous throughout Kevin's body, then they know the source of the increased CEA number.

Kevin was truly nervous and depressed leading up to this CT scan. I can honestly say that this time around has been the hardest. He is still incredibly fatigued from the radiation, and going to bed very early to help ward it off, but also, I think, to escape the thoughts of further treatments. He has said that he just wants a break from treatments to allow his body to completely recover from the past year. I am finding out more about the fatigue caused by the treatments, and that it usually takes 6-8 weeks after completion for the patient to begin (begin) to have some feeling of less fatigue. Because Kevy has had two rounds, it is not surprising that he is still incredibly fatigued.

We could really use your prayers right now. We are cautiously optimistic that nothing will be found elsewhere, but dismayed that the node has not died off.

Thank you for your prayers, your humor, but most importantly, thank you for your friendships that have sustained us over the years. We are in real need of that right now.

"Let Go, Let God". I'm borrowing this and making it my new mantra.

Love, Kim

October 24, 2011 11:52 am

Our appointment with Dr. Hantel was very different this time around. As he showed us the CT scan from this time in comparison to the July scan, it shows that the spots have shrunk, even the bigger one is about the tenth of its size from before.

Dr. Hantel was visibly concerned with the CEA number. In July the marker was reading 10. Last week it was 17.9. Because the scan shows that all areas of concern have disappeared as a result of the chemo and radiation, he is leaning toward it being somewhere else.

We are awaiting a PET scan appointment, sometime this week. Dr. Hantel will have the results the day after the scan, and inform us.

We are truly heavy hearted.

October 25, 2011 12:13 pm

Kevy's PET scan is set for Monday at 8:00 am. We should have results on Tuesday. Yesterday was a horrible day, and for Kev so was last night. This is the lowest I have seen him, and it breaks my heart.

Keep him in your thoughts and prayers. Liam and Troy too - who tried really hard to handle the information yesterday in a noble way. They too are scared, sad and overwhelmed.

God Bless,

Kim

October 26, 2011 6:57 am

Dear friends,

Kevin is weary and finding it near impossible to go on... let's rally around him and help him to keep going. He is hurting so much. So many tears have fallen. Keep praying.

Love, Kim

October 30, 2011 9:30 am

Kevin's Dad and brother Brian flew down here to be with Kevy during this difficult time. I know it has been a great source of comfort for him, and for the rest of us. It's a great example to our sons of what a brother relationship looks like as adults. Kevin and Brian are extremely close, and it shows.

They took Liam to the driving range yesterday, and enjoyed the nice fall weather. Liam also cornered Grandpa with questions about life, religion, and history. It was a nice moment for me to watch.

I tried explaining to my father in law that even going through this horrific situation, both Kevy and I find ourselves counting our blessings. We have so many people, all of you, who support us with your words, thoughts, prayers and the memories we have made with you along the way.

Kevin is trying really hard to stay positive, and has been helped along this past week with support from all of you, with a special nod going out to the Clarks for dinner on Wednesday and for Rich, Maria, Chris and Margie and their kids for dinner and games Thursday night.

As I am writing this, we are preparing to go to mass at the Abbey. My hands are sweating, my stomach in knots, and I have to remind myself to take along some Kleenex. The anxiety about tomorrows scan is catching up with me. I was up from 4:00 am until 5:30 am just thinking. I've heard "them" talk about fight or flight response of the body *when in a dangerous situation. I can so understand that. My stomach is in knots, my hands sweaty, my head pounding, which makes it hard to hear. I can't focus on anything for long, and man I just want to run.*

I know your mind can play tricks on you and that sometimes your fears are much more than the truth will ever reveal. I can only hope that is the case here, because this is not the way to go through day after day after day.

I've never been more afraid in my life. Or sure of how lucky we are.

November 3, 2011 3:24 pm

Kevin had his PET scan today, after much hard work on his part, and some prayers answered on all of your part.

They are going to try and have the results by tomorrow - please hope this happens because the idea of waiting over the weekend, while of course is doable, is certainly a heavy load.

Kevin was blessed to have his friend Mike join him through today's process. Mike and his wife Christine are incredible people who have a very strong faith, and a very deep love. After the procedure, Kevin and Mike went for lunch at a Vietnamese restaurant. That certainly brought a smile to Kev's face. They were able to enjoy a good meal and great conversation. Kevin was very happy that Mike was there.

So now we wait and hope that the scan can give us the map of our next plan of attack.

Random acts of kindness are a great way of thanking God anytime, but especially with answering our prayer to get Kevin through the test so we can breathe again.

As usual, your comments in the guestbook are greatly appreciated and we look forward to reading them at bedtime. It has become, in a way, the best bedtime story of all. It is full of love, joy, hope, friendship and grace.

Love, Kim

November 4, 2011 2:37 pm

During the darkest indigo midnight, yet will countless stars blossom.
~ Dr. Sun Wolf

The boogeyman has been revealed. Dr. Hantel got in touch with Kevin around 1:00 pm today and told him the findings of the PET scan. It is evident that Kevin has a fight on his hands, but the good news is that we have four different treatment options available.
A spot has been found in the liver, in a somewhat awkward position. Dr. Hantel is pretty sure that this is the source of the spike in the CEA number, although he is not saying absolutely. He is in the process of scheduling an MRI to better pinpoint the disease in the liver.

Dr. Hantel has said that there are four options available for treatment: the first is chemotherapy, which he says would be very difficult; radiation because it is outside of the previously radiated areas; going in laparoscopically to burn the spot, and finally surgery. He will be conferring with a team of other doctors, to determine which path we will be taking.

Waiting for the boogeyman to come out from behind the curtains has been emotionally and physically draining. Now that we know what we are up against, it seems slightly less scary. Don't get me wrong, it's not the cancer free diagnosis of earlier this year, but considering some of the other possibilities, this is at least attainable. Like Kevy said, we are going to chase this thing until it's caught.

Thanks to all of you who have been turning up the prayers to heaven - it appears that they have worked.

Grab a few extra hugs and kisses from your loved ones. We can't thank you enough for your support. You are what sustains us when we feel we can't go on. We are so lucky to have you in our lives.

He who has a why to live can bear almost any how.
~ Friedrich Nietzsche

I kept asking myself, how is it that, at this sorrowful and most dark time in our lives, I can be so full of joy, love, and happiness?

Tears and laughter are divided by the thinnest line. The journey that we are on has presented numerous examples of stepping over the line from one abyss to the other. We seem to move seamlessly from sadness to happiness in the blink of an eye.

Many of you are aware that Kevin is known for crossing the "line". We are forever calling him back to the line time and again. It usually happens as he is sharing a story or tale and can't help himself when he realizes how many people have stopped to listen to him. You can almost see the wheels turning in his head "I'm just going to push this a little further..." which is usually met with groans, chuckles and belly laughs.

When I saw Kevin for the first time since elementary school, he was 17, and I was 18. It was a gorgeous July night in 1983 with "Little Red Corvette" by Prince blaring on the car stereo. He was wearing a blue golf shirt, jeans and Adidas running shoes. A group of us met up behind the elementary school that Kevy attended years before. I remember thinking that he was gorgeous and very different from our elementary encounters. Looking at him, I had forgotten how blue his eyes were and how his hair was curlier and more lush than I recalled. I remember the smell of the poplar trees, and the heaviness of the air.

I remember the butterflies I was feeling as I talked to him. I remember doing all those stupid girlie things to get his attention, and being met with a bit of "hard to get" attitude. Many years later, I remember that I was falling hard.

Kevin was the first guy to give me a dozen long stemmed red roses. They were treasured then, as they are today, being pressed into my bible after they had dried and begun to shrivel. Over the years, he has surprised me with flowers time and again, and they are always received by me with a smile and sometimes tears.

During this grasp that cancer has, we have both shed tears, but we have also laughed so hard that it hurts. We have hung our heads low, and made ourselves dizzy looking up at the sky full of stars. We can't go on; we get up and dance to Phil Collins "Don't Let Her Steal Your Heart". We stare blankly into the fire; we look at each other and smile. I can see his blue eyes twinkling. I get lost in his dimples and I cherished his curly lush hair. I felt like I was hanging by a thread and realize that yes, I am.

November 8, 2011 7:28 pm

I have heard there are troubles of more than one kind. Some come from ahead and some come from behind. But I've bought a big bat. I'm all ready you see. Now my troubles are going to have troubles with me!

~ Dr. Seuss

Things certainly happen quickly when it comes to Kevin Troy Griffin.

I don't have many specifics from the MRI other than the cancer presents itself as a solitary mass in the liver. I will know more after our meeting tomorrow. We do, however, have our plan in place.

The determination has been made that Kevin will go through a third round of chemotherapy....starting tomorrow (Wednesday). We meet with Dr. Hantel at 11:00 am and immediately following the appointment, we will scoot across the way to start Kevin's new cocktail infusion.

He's a big fan of coconut, so here's hoping they can dress this one up with a little flavor, tiny umbrella, you name it.

Prayers are greatly appreciated, and from what we have been told, this chemo will most likely be more difficult to go through. While Kevin is a little scared, he is happy to get going. I have to agree. I don't like the idea, but the sooner we get started, the sooner it will be over.

I'll post tomorrow after the treatment.

Love, Kim

November 9, 2011 7:37 pm

We met with Dr. Hantel today to discuss the plan for this recurrence. By the way, if you can love your oncologist, we do. He showed us the CT scan, PET scan and MRI so we could see where the disease has made its new home.

The tumor is 1/2" to 3/4" in size and is located very close to the vena cava, towards the back of the liver. Our first course of attack is to use a new mixture of chemo drugs - irinotecan and avastin. The side effects include incredible stomach cramping, diarrhea, nausea, fatigue, and hair loss. Last time Kev chose to shave his head because his hair thinned. This time, he will most likely lose it all.

We also have to be careful of blood clots. Kev has agreed to take part in a clinical study where he will be watched to see if the drugs cause any blood clots.

Now, if the chemo does its job, the tumor should shrink. Dr. Hantel described it as saying if the tumor were a weed, the chemo will take the head of it off, but we have to go in a dig up the root. After round 4, we will discuss the possibility of surgery to remove the remnants.

Right now, Dr. Hantel is having Kevin's case reviewed by doctors who specialize in liver surgery to see if they think surgery is possible. When we meet with Hantel in two weeks, we will see what kind of feedback the doctors have given.

Kevin had immediate side effects from the chemo, with incredible nausea. He is still not feeling very good, but we hope it will subside soon. He has his pump which will continue to deliver the drugs for the next 46 hours. He will have it removed on Friday afternoon.

So, for the next 8-16 weeks, Kev will be receiving chemo every other week. Looks like he will receive it the day before Thanksgiving, and return the pump on Friday of that holiday weekend. It may be déjà vu, but I'm pretty sure we were in the same place last year.

Kevin's CEA number on October 20 was 17.9. Today it was 21.0. Please pray that the number is lower in two weeks. That's all for now, please keep Kevin in your prayers, and say one or two for the boys as well. They are being so strong. I am the luckiest Mom in the world, and the luckiest wife.

November 11, 2011 11:02 am

Kevin has had some nausea and cramping and an incredible headache that has lasted since Wednesday. He is frustrated that he is feeling so poorly so soon after the start of treatment, but I keep reminding him that it's new meds, and this stuff is the real deal.

He will have the pump removed today, and will not be sad about that. A note to the lacrosse boys: he will also be losing his hair this time - showing off his nice and shiny head!

I'm hanging in there too, although I am pretty sure that my stomach is tied up in knots. Also a little on the tired side, but one thing that is strong is my faith. We have so much love coming our way that it is helping to carry us over the rather ragged bumps on this road.

This time of year it is so important to help your fellow man in any way that you can. If you have an opportunity to volunteer, donate food to a food bank, take gently used items to Good Will or say hello to someone new, do it with purpose and love.

God is great and all of you are incredible! We couldn't keep going without you.

Thank you for caring. Love, Kim

November 13, 2011 11:19 pm

Not being able to sleep, again, I started looking back through the journal entries, specifically those from last year at this time. It is so surreal to me that we are still dealing with this all this time later. For the second time, Kevin will be celebrating his birthday (Nov. 15) while going through chemo. I know I should be thankful that we are going to celebrate, but I'm beginning to see and feel the toll that this illness is taking on Kev.

Of course the meds this time are different than the last chemo, so therefore there are different side effects. He has had a constant headache, stomach cramps (like Charlie horses), nausea and fatigue. I know the fatigue is still part of the past year, and he had truly not been able to completely recover from the last round of radiation and chemo.

When he is not at work, or the cancer center, you can usually find Kevy lying down on the couch, or in bed. He has incredible sweats, and fitful sleep. He has admitted that he is really having a hard time emotionally dealing with this third round.

As I look at him, and see the change in his color, and notice little differences in his eyes, I stop and remember that toxic poisons are running through his body, all in the hopes of stopping a spot in his liver from sending cells to other destinations.

I have felt like I am walking through a movie, having an out of body experience. I know that I am going to work, cleaning, laundry, spending time giving Kevin his foot rubs, and talking and being with the boys. I know it because I can see it as if I'm hovering above the scenes, and not because I feel them. I am becoming numb, and so very tired.

If Kevin is having such a strong response to the treatment after the first one, and I am feeling so tired, and down, can we really make it through? It is so draining to watch him struggle, and it is of course even more difficult for him.

My cheery facade is cracking, and I'm afraid if I let go, I won't be able to pull it back together. I feel our whole family shuddering and I need to be there for them, but at this very moment in time, as tears are streaming down my face, it's too much to bear.

I know you have been praying for all of us, and for that I am eternally grateful. I find when I write about my feelings, I usually begin to see the light at the end of the tunnel. I know this moment will pass. It is too easy to be consumed by grief and pain when the house is still, the darkness is everywhere, and the silence is deafening.

I also know that when I finish, and go to sleep, that tomorrow I will awaken and feel somewhat embarrassed by this entry. However, I have been honest with all of you from the beginning about how this journey is affecting Kevin and me, and our sons. If I only show the sunny side of things, and not the grey gritty side, I'm not being truthful.

Heavenly Father, please bring Kevin some relief from his pains, and help both of us to reignite the fire of optimism. I know you are with us always, as are our family and friends. Sometimes, despite being surrounded, you can't help but feel alone.

My tears are drying, and I have stopped my shuddering. I will leave my sadness and fears here, and climb into bed to the sounds of Kevin tossing, and turning. Tomorrow is another day, and gives me another chance to thank all of you for your love. Not to worry, we will rise and face the morning with a renewed sense of hope and purpose.

Thank you for letting me share my grief.

Love, Kim

November 15, 2011 10:31 pm

Kevy was feeling great today and enjoyed his birthday, thanks to all of your birthday wishes.

He is so strong... not to mention handsome as well.

Looking forward to a good night sleep for everyone.

Love, Kim

November 18, 2011 9:01 am

Too often we underestimate the power of a touch, a smile, a kind word, a listening ear, an honest compliment, or the smallest act of caring, all of which have the potential to turn a life around.

~Leo Buscaglia

Kev and I are going to Northwestern today to meet with another doctor to get his take on our treatment plans. It never hurts to have another opinion. The bigger the army, the more chance we have of coming out on top.

I want to thank everyone from Marmion who came out for lacrosse registration and after they had filled out all the paperwork, signed the checks, and ordered apparel, they still had enough ink in their pens to sign up as providers of meals for our family. We are more than lucky, we are blessed beyond belief. Thank you and I can promise you that we will all pay this love forward.

I also want to thank my friends who took me out for dinner last night. Teri, Laura, Renee, Sheri, and Cathy - you ladies rock, and I love you all.

Kevy is feeling good today and I'm so happy to see him laughing and smiling. We should have a good weekend, as we look forward to having Brian and Anne and Brenna and Steve come down for Thanksgiving. We love you guys.

Here is praying for a good meeting today, and that all of you can feel the love and appreciation Kevin and I have for everyone reading this, and supporting us in ways big and small.

I'll let you know how the appointment goes.

Love Kim

November 20, 2011 8:58 pm

Sometimes the questions are complicated and the answers are simple."

~ Dr. Seuss

I have always been a fan of Dr. Seuss, and this quote sums it all up for me. As an author of children's books, he writes for the innocence that is the child's mind. A clean slate. As we grow older, our slate has been written on by all the life experiences we have undertaken or endured. It marks our minds, and seems to make us unwilling to accept that answers to our questions can be simple and straightforward. We are looking for an angle, wondering what message is behind the words that we hear. Can you picture yourself as you are waiting for an answer to a complicated question? Forehead scrunched, eyebrows framing our narrow eyes, and most likely having our arms crossed?

Jump to Friday afternoon when we were downtown to meet with Dr. Vergo, a doctor from Northwestern who was recommended to us to give a second or third look at Kevin's case. We were meeting with him to get his opinion about Kevin's most recent scans and tests.

We are rarely downtown, although Kevin has certainly been there more than me. We found our way to the hospital in good time, which allowed for us to have lunch before our appointment. We ate at the Corner Bakery across the street, enjoying our paninis and salad.

Being downtown with the crazy drivers, and crazier pedestrians, honking horns and cell phone talkers, not to mention that whirring in and out of the restaurant by doctors in white coats with beepers; my senses were at an all time high. And just as we were finishing our talk and listing our questions for the doctor, an eerie calm came over me.

I took the page with our questions listed, and put it away in my purse. I thought to myself, let's just go in there and ask "Okay, are we on the right path?" Walking back to the hospital, I took a deep breath, grabbed Kevin's hand, and marched in through the glass door.

The waiting area was quite large, and we were given a pager when we got there, just like we were going to a restaurant. Finally our pager flashed and vibrated, and we were taken to our room. By the way, not only was the waiting room purple, so were the uniforms on the nurses. Every last one of them. (Purple is my favorite color). We waited a little longer (okay 1 1/2 hrs) before we met Dr. Vergo.

He is a young guy, originally from the Boston area (yeah Rich Ford!) Very knowledgeable, and well informed about Kevin and his case. While the importance of this meeting was not lost on either of us, we listened as he told us the simple answer. Yes, we are on the right track, it's the treatment that he would have ordered, and he actually said the word "cure". He is going to present Kevy's case to the GI Board that meets weekly at Northwestern, with physicians from various specialties, who will review the scans, pathology reports, blood work etc., and chime in on whether or not they have other suggestions.

Dr. Vergo, like Dr. Hantel, figures after 4 treatments, Kevin will have surgery (which is how you cure cancer found in the liver - and yes, it's still colon cancer, not liver cancer). This will be followed up with four more treatments of chemo. We meet with Dr. Hantel this Wednesday, and he will let us know if a surgeon has been found who is willing to sign on for the task of ridding Kevin's body of the diseased section of liver.

So, after all is said and done and the difficult or complicated questions are asked, the simple answer is YES - there is still options, and still hope.

I realized that sometimes all you have to do is slow down, and stop to hear the answer, not only from the doctors, but from God, and ourselves. YES, there are options. YES, we are on the right track. YES, you are loved, and YES, you are blessed with incredible friends and family.

YES!

November 23, 2011 11:35 pm

I know we have said it many times, but we love Dr. Hantel. He is straightforward, incredibly tolerant of our list of questions, and perhaps just as important, laughs along with us while at the same time throwing his own zingers in there now and again.

Kevy went for his second treatment today, leaving only six more. Dr. Hantel has sent Kevin's case to two top surgeons to see what their take is on the positioning of the tumor, and if we can resection or ablate. You'll excuse my medical terminology - it kind of makes me feel somewhat in control of a very uncontrollable situation. It boils down to removing the diseased part of the liver, or burning the tumor. We expect to get some feedback next week.

So the plan continues to be 4 treatments, surgery, 4 treatments. The earliest we could look to have the surgery is six weeks from today making that the early part of January. The Avastin chemo which blocks blood vessels from feeding the tumor has to be out of his system at least that amount of time. Today was his last dose of Avastin, at least for this round.

The CEA number did NOT go down, in fact it went up from 21.0 to 21.7. However, we have been told not to worry about it, as it shows the tumor was viable and growing when it was found and that this first round has stabilized the tumor which is good news too. Kev was very upset that it didn't go down.

Our dear friend Randy went with Kevy today for the chemo treatment allowing me to leave after the meeting with Dr. Hantel and get some running around done. Brian, Anne, Brenna and Steve arrive from Canada to spend a few days with us on Thursday. They have to have frequent driver miles by now! We are so lucky. By the way, Randy, Kev was in tears talking about how you helped him through the tough part of the treatment by keeping his mind off of how he was feeling. He and I love you very much.

Happy Thanksgiving to all of you who are celebrating! May you find comfort in the company of your family, fullness from the plethora of food, and joy in knowing that we truly feel all of your love and prayers, every minute of every day.

And every day that Kevin is here fighting this fight is a day of thanksgiving for the Griffin family.

Love Kim

November 28, 2011 11:56 am

Well, Thanksgiving weekend has come and gone and so has our wonderful family... Brian, Anne, Brenna and Steve. It was so great to have them here to be with us and just enjoy each other's company.

Rich and Maria invited us along for a night of fun and laughs at Zany's a comedy club on Friday night. The six of us had a great time with lots of laughs and tears from laughing so hard.

Kevin has been on a roller coaster ride this past five days since his last treatment. He has suffered incredible fatigue, headaches, nausea and stomach cramps. There were moments over the weekend, where Kev was able to join in on the fun. However, there were more moments where sleep was the only thing that was doable.

I have to take a moment and remind Kevin and those around him of managing expectations. Kevy wants to be there for everyone and everything, and musters as much energy as he can find so he does not let anyone down. Including me. We decorated the Christmas tree, and for such a traditionalist and loyalist and all around emotional person like myself, it was difficult to watch Kev try his hardest to participate. He was doing it for me, and all he really wanted to do was go and rest on the couch. He stuck it out for me for as long as he could, and then retreated to the couch. It touched me, and saddened me at the same time. I know there are others who he is trying to impress with his efforts and energy, but we all have to remind him and ourselves to take it slow and easy.

We prayed for all of you and your families over this holiday weekend. We wished for you to have a fun and healthy holiday, with lots of food, conversation, and laughs. We felt your prayers too, and thank you again for your immeasurable care and concern.

Happy Leftover week!

Love, Kim

November 30, 2011 11:56 am

Sorrow is like a precious treasure, shown only to friends.

While I'm not looking in the mirror, I am pretty sure I have my miner's hard hat on, with its light brightly shining. I probably have some black stuff on my face, though, although, for them it's coal, for me, it's mascara that has run. I am carrying around a pick, and pretty sure that these weights on my feet are work boots.

This mine I find myself in is so deep down and feels so heavy. My shoulders are aching, my mouth is dry, and there is no visible light. Every step is harder than the one before, and I am cringing at the thought that there are at least a million more like the last. I hear the creaking around me, and sometimes feel the trickle of water on my face. It must be from a weak spot in the wall right?

I keep waiting for the whistle to blow ending my time down here. This is now my third straight shift here, and I am more than ready to hand it off to the next crew. I want to see the sunlight, feel the brightness on my cheeks, take a deep breath of fresh air and feel the weight on my shoulders disappear. I want to put on some dancing shoes, get all dressed up, and go dancing with my partner, my best friend my love... my Kevy.

What a down time this week has been for me. Again I feel guilty complaining because Kevin is the one who is battling the hardest. But let me tell you, I am pretty sure this is the lowest I have been. I am crying at the drop of a hat (probably because it's a miner's hard had) and feel surrounded by doom. Now this isn't because of any news, I think it's just a compilation of feelings that I have kept in check for a while, but are making me very aware that they want out. What a glorious day it will be when I can take my hat off, hang up the pick and walk into the sun. Until that time, I will continue to show my sorrow on occasion. After all, it is our friends and family that turn here.

Much love, Kim

December 5, 2011 12.48 pm

The season has officially begun with Kevin and I attending the Marmion Parents Christmas Dinner and Dance this past weekend. Thankfully the timing was good for Kevin. He was feeling really good and was the first one on the dance floor, encouraging everyone else to get up and boogie. And boy did he boogie. Even when I couldn't keep up with him, he was out there with a bevy of beauties. It's wonderful to see him so happy and enjoying himself.

Kevy goes for his third treatment on Wednesday. We are both beginning to feel the anticipation and anxiety. We now know what to expect, and how long Kev will feel like crap. It's a vicious cycle, but the good news is that in about 9 - 10 days from now, he will be feeling good again.

Thanks to all who made Saturday night so much fun. We have a great group of friends at Marmion, and enjoy spending time with all.

Will update after Wednesday's treatment.

Love, Kim

December 8, 2011 6:31 pm

Kevin came through treatment three, this time without the chest pains that he had been experiencing during the first two. Dr. Hantel listened to Kevin's description, and was confident in surmising that it was all brought about because of anxiety. He told Kev that subconsciously he was hyperventilating, causing a buildup of CO_2 in his body which was causing cramps and pain. Kevin was not completely convinced that it was anxiety, but was a believer after the doctor gave him some anti-anxiety meds prior to the treatment. Kevin was free of chest pain throughout the infusion.

He did experience the other side effects such as headache, nausea, sweats, cramping in his stomach and fatigue, but let me assure you, he was relieved to only suffer from these.

The CEA number did come down, but not very much. It went from 21.7 to 20.3. We asked Dr. Hantel for his thoughts on this, and his was response was that as long as it is going down, whether by a little or a lot, he is happy. I think we will say that we are slightly disappointed that it didn't move anymore than that.

We have two appointments with the two different surgeons next week. We will meet with them to discuss what they think is the best way to approach this newest home for the cancer i.e.) the liver, and if it is operable or if we may have to look at ablation of the tumor. Our want of course is to have it cut out, which in our understanding, is the only way to truly "cure" the cancer at this site. As mentioned before, it's location in the liver is what is causing the problems. The doctors have to make sure that whatever procedure they do, they are not taking unnecessary risks and putting Kevin's life in danger. Our first appointment is Tuesday, followed on Thursday with the second surgeon. I'll update after Tuesday's appointment.

The anxiety in our home during this time was at an all time high, just waiting and hoping for some good news from the surgeons. The boys were reacting in their own way to the situation: Troy was finding many reasons to be out of the house, and Liam was in lock down with his emotions. I knew they looked to us for a read as to how they should be reacting, and I have to say that I was probably not the greatest when it came to that. Prior to Kevin's afternoon appointment, I ended up being sick to my stomach. I couldn't stop shaking, and had an incredible headache. Worst case of sympathy pains ever! I wish I knew if the boys were truly okay—so I asked for any whose path crossed with theirs to check in on them and let us know if we were missing any signs.

For those of you old enough to remember *The Flintstones*, it felt like our life, at that moment, was like an Upside Down Flint Rubble Double Cake. We go through the motions of living, but don't know which end is up. Just when we think we see the light at the end of the tunnel, we realize that it's just Wilma opening the oven to check on us.

December 13, 2011 2:56 pm

Location

We travelled to nearly hell and gone to get to North Shore Hospital in Evanston, IL to meet with Dr. Talamonti. We planned two hours to get there as there is no straight path. I'm pretty sure that the crow doesn't fly there either!! As the head of surgical oncology, we were very impressed with the good doctor. The best part was that he said he could do the surgery, removing the right lobe of the liver. He commented that he would do an ultrasound while they are in there, making sure they aren't missing anything. We were also told that in the event they see something different once they get in there, they are prepared to ablate any other spots.

Location

When you talk about location, the doctor said the placement of the tumor was pretty good. It's far enough away from the vena cava, the portal vein and the hepatic vein, which allows us to proceed with the removal. Any closer to any of these three and removal would not be an option.

Location

So we are in the land of Hope, and the view is quite promising. Surgery could happen at the end of January, with a stay of 5-6 days. We have a meeting this week with another surgeon to see what she has to say. But for now, at least today, we love our location. What a view!

Love Kim

December 22, 2011 4:27 am

Kev had his fourth chemo treatment yesterday, and for the first time, slept through it. His blood counts are down so he will be receiving neulasta by injection on Friday when he returns the pump.

The CEA went from 20.7 to 16.9, which put us all at ease (at least a little).

Dr. Hantel told Kevin he wants him to have a pet scan the same week he will do his CT scan and other prep work for the surgery. He wants to make sure that there is nothing hiding anywhere else. At this point, surgery will take place the third week of January at Loyola. Dr. Shoup will be the surgeon, and we are both happy with the choice.

Kev is experiencing the same side effects... cold sweats, cramping, headache, nausea, fatigue. I would have to say however, that right now the biggest thing for him is the emotional roller coaster that he finds himself on. He is quite down, and tearful. He broke down with the boys, and has become quite in need of extra hugs and cuddles. I don't mind of course. Here beside me in bed, he just stated that he can't wait to see his mom when they come down on the 30th. He is also is going crazy for Canada Dry Gingerale. He says it makes him feel good.

This time of year is so hard having a loved one ill. It's the one time of year when in my romantic vision of things, joy, smiles, warmth and celebration abound. I know Christmas day will be hard for Kevy, who will most likely spend it sleeping both in bed and on the couch. I know he wishes things were different, as do we all, but I hope he embraces the idea that having him with us, in jammies on the couch, is the best Christmas present for all of us.

My wish for all of you is peace, joy, love and hope. Please know that on behalf of Kevy and Troy and Liam, we are so thankful to have the love and support of so many. We continue to pay it forward, and have visual confirmation that your giving, prayers and love have gone on to help so many others as well. The world is a better place for having all of you in it.

Merry Christmas and wishes for a healthy and Happy New Year.

Much love, Kim

December 25, 2011 1:11 am

Wishing you all a very blessed and Merry Christmas. May the holidays be full of love and peace.

Love, Kevin, Kim, Troy, and Liam

December 26, 2011 12:29 am

We were saddened to hear about the sudden and unexpected passing of a friend on Christmas Eve. Rich Green was a witty, charming, smart, approachable man who was deeply committed to his children and to life. He was very involved in the lacrosse club at Troy and Liam's high school and assisted Kev with the core conditioning program that they put on for the boys. We last saw him 3 weeks ago at the Marmion Parents Christmas Dinner/Dance with his bow tie lit up like a tree! He was enjoying himself so much on the dance floor, and had a constant smile.

Please say prayers for his children, girlfriend, and the many friends he had. He will be missed.

God Bless you Rich.

December 28, 2011 11:34 pm

Santa Claus was good to us this year, as we were all together, just the four of us. While we were blessed with gifts, the one thing we didn't get was Kevy time.

Christmas Eve has traditions for our family that include mass, watching White Christmas and enjoying Spaghetti Pie. This year we had to improvise and take dinner to Kevin... up in bed. We decided that we would all eat in our bed, keeping us together, as our tradition dictates. It was magical to have an impromptu picnic in bed. We laid out a sheet on the bed, and ate as we watched the movie.

Since his fourth treatment, the cumulative effect of the chemotherapy has had Kevin MIA from the start. He has slept for the past week up to 20 hours a day, and on Christmas Day itself, was able to join us for a short time in the morning, followed by a day of napping, and a quick visit to the dinner table before bed time.

At this time of year, it becomes so much more evident just how ill Kevy is. Anyone who knows Kev, knows how much he likes to be with people, especially the boys. Not having him with us is tough. The thing too is that no amount of sleep can ever help him catch up. Unlike the flu, or mere tiredness, sleeping does not take away the feeling. Rest does not build your energy and stamina. Fatigue is here all the time, and couples itself with nausea, stomach cramps, and sweats so intense that Kev has to change pjs 2 or 3 times a day. He has incredible headaches, and the loudness of everyday life strips him of any strength he has.

137

Kevin is the biggest kid I know, and for him not to be able to shine is heartbreaking. As mentioned in the prior journal entry, we lost a friend on Christmas Eve, which is weighing on Kevin quite heavily. It seemed to highlight his own mortality even more.

Being Kevin, he is going in to work tomorrow, hoping to get caught up on some paperwork. Thankfully his company moved a couch into his office for him to nap on. I'm pretty sure that the drive alone is going to take a lot from him. I know he will rest if needed, and based on his record, I hope he saves enough energy to get home.

Thanks to all for their best wishes and cards. The meals have been a welcome support for us from our Lacrosse families these past months, as was the surprising gift delivery a few days before Christmas from the Marmion Football families. Coach Dan Thorpe, who works as a guidance counselor at Marmion, was aware of our situation and felt that some support from the football families would be a great way to show Gods grace and love. After collecting donations, we had a plethora of gifts delivered for the boys, and for us as well. Humbled and blessed does not even begin to explain how we felt. To all of our supporters, we promise to pay it forward, as there is no way we could ever repay you. God is good and has blessed us with an incredible support system.

Please hug your loved ones a little longer today, and remember how great God is.

We hope Kevy will get stronger over the next week or so, as he heads toward another surgery and the final (hopefully) four chemo treatments.

Love and blessings,

Kim

January 2, 2012 10:34 am

While typically someone with cancer may not label their life as the title states, Kevin and I agree, that It Is A Wonderful Life.

Family around us at Christmas time is great, and a welcome respite from the ordinary. Laughs, some tears, and more laughs have been the items on the agenda. My sister Karen and her two kiddos joined us on Boxing Day (Dec. 26) and stayed for 3 days. I love her so much, and she brings such pain to my stomach from laughing! Kev spent most of this time still trying to sleep away the nausea, and was happy that Karen was here for me.

The 30th saw Kevin's parents come in as well as his three sisters, 2 brothers in law, 3 nephews and one niece. Kevy was very happy to have most of his family together. We kind of rang in the new year together, albeit all in our separate beds. The stroke of midnight was not heard by this crew, but that's fine with us.

On New Year's Day, perhaps the best part of the whole season happened. Kevin contacted Father Nathanael from Marmion to ask him if he would be willing to bestow the anointing of the sick on him. This is in anticipation of Kevin's surgery which has been set for January 16 at Loyola. Fr. Nathanael suggested that he could do it after New Year's Day mass, in the chapel off of the main abbey.

All of us went to mass and proceeded to the chapel immediately following. While Abbott John was preparing to give the Anointing of the Sick to Kevin, Fr. Nathanael ushered us into the chapel to take a seat. Little did we know that an email had been sent out the night before letting all lacrosse families know that this blessing was going to be happening after mass.

What we initially thought would be an intimate gathering of our family (all 13) and the Abbott and Fr. Nathanael, in fact turned into an intimate gathering of approximately 55-60 of our extended Marmion/Lacrosse families. ABSOLUTELY INCREDIBLE. The anointing included beautiful prayers, Kevin being blessed with holy oil, the Miter of Columba Marmion being held against Kevin's chest, and Fr. Nathanael sprinkling holy water over everyone who was there. When it was over, Kevin was inundated with hugs, tears and more hugs. We were all overwhelmed.

The movie by the same name as the title, is to me a great comparison. When George Bailey is at his lowest, it is those around him that rise up and end up carrying him away on a wave of support, giving and love. Kevin could not feel any more loved than he did at that moment in time. No question that Kevin has impacted the lives of so many people, both far and wide, and those who are here are helping to show him that they have been blessed by him.

God is amazing and we are so grateful that He has brought us to this place. He has shown us that no matter how difficult things have been for Kevin and our family, and how much more of the mountain Kevy has to climb, we are surrounded by an incredible embrace of love and faith.

It's a Wonderful Life!

January 8, 2012 6:49 pm

Kevin is scheduled for a PET scan tomorrow to see if cancer is found anywhere else prior to the surgery. My understanding is if they find it somewhere else, they may have to rethink their plan. We are not expecting to find it anywhere else, in fact Dr. Hantel said that Kevin looked great. We will have the results on Tuesday sometime.

Provided that goes the way it is expected, Kevin goes to Loyola for his pre-surgery prep, CT scan, blood work, etc. Then we wait and wait and bite our nails some more until Monday, January 16, 2012 when he will have his approximate 6 hr. surgery. The surgery is scheduled to start around 11:00 am.

He is expected to be in the hospital approximately a week, give or take a few days.

Thank you to all who continue to pray, and are doing random acts of kindness. Spreading the pure love and joy that you all have shown us has undoubtedly made this world a better and more peaceful place.

I'll let you know how the PET scan goes. Love to all.

January 10, 2012 6:11 pm

After nearly twenty-four sleepless hours, and probably as many phone calls, Kevin's PET scan results came back... and the news is GREAT! There is no sign of cancer anywhere else in his body, and the one tumor that was known has stabilized and shrunk.

This means that Kevin will be allowed to go ahead with the surgery on Monday, January 16 at Loyola Hospital. The plan will be to remove the right lobe, and while he is open, the Dr. will use a specialized ultrasound machine to check other areas.

We are getting good news all around, and we are so grateful. If you are near someone (preferably that you know) grab them and give them a big hug!

Next plan is his pre-op workup on Thursday.

Thanks for your constant checking of this site. We both appreciate the support as the anxiety level is ever increasing here as we count down our way to a table for one, with a side of liver (too much? ;)))

Kim

January 13, 2012 10:26 am

As the angst of wondering how the PET scan would turn out has passed, and thankfully left in its wake great news, the daunting reality of what lies ahead is firmly in place.

Kev had his pre-op appointments at Loyola yesterday including a CT scan, vitals and meeting with doctors. On a day where we were fully involved in a snow fiesta, Kevin was finding out the good and not so good about the surgery.

The CT scan did not show the cancer at all - although the more thorough PET scan did show the hot spot. This is a double edged sword. It tells us that all the treatments that Kevy has been going through have been doing their job, but it also is making it slightly more difficult for the doctor, as she no longer has a visual of the tumor itself. She will be able to use the last CT scan from a few months ago, along with the PET scan as a map of the liver.

The most troubling thing to come from the meeting, however, was Dr. Shoup's comments of how extremely close the tumor is to the venae cavae. While we were aware of this before, she reemphasized the seriousness of the surgery. I suppose she has to do this, but it is really unnerving to hear. Any nick to the venae cavae could have an outcome that none of us wants. She said her objective is to go in and remove the right lobe, but her goal is to have Kevin come through the surgery, and if necessary, she will use ablation (burning) on the tumor.

Kevin has been so strong and positive about this whole ordeal, and though he has suffered dearly with side effects and the emotional roller coaster of having cancer, I have to believe that he is going to *make it through the surgery, with the diseased liver portion removed, and a great outlook for complete recovery. Right?*

This is where my printed words and private thoughts begin their battle over which one is forefront in my mind at any given moment of the day. Right now, my private thoughts are winning out, and it has me on my knees praying harder than I have ever prayed before. The world needs someone like Kevin, and without question I need and the boys need the one man who loves us unconditionally, who always puts us first, who leads us down life's path and has fulfilled us in ways we will find out over time.

Your support for our family has been a source of strength and such a feeling of love that we have cloaked ourselves in from day one. While I know you are, it's the mother in me that has to ask you anyway to please keep praying for Kevin and that he is able to withstand the seriousness of the surgery. Ask God to watch over the doctor and her team as they prepare to undertake this task. Finally ask God to hold Troy and Liam in his warm embrace, while I sit at His feet.

I have included a prayer we received from the Keilty Family. It's beautiful.

A PRAYER FOR COURAGE

God, make me brave -
Let me strengthen after pain
As a tree strengthens after rain,
Shining and lovely again.

As the blown grass lifts, let me rise -,
From sorrow with quiet eyes,
Knowing Thy way is wise.

God, make me braver - life brings
Such blinding things!

Help me to keep my sight,
Help me to see aright -
That out of dark - comes light.

January 16, 2012 8:42 am

Surgery started at 8:40 am. Say it will be about 4 1/2 hrs and then 2 hrs in recovery. Will update soon.

Luv Kim

January 16, 2012 10:33 am

Two hour update from OR... everything is going fine!

January 16, 2012 11:20 am

Surgery is continuing and they have cut out the tumor!!!!!!!!!! More updates as they become available.

January 16, 2012 1:39 pm

Kev is out of surgery, with more than half his liver removed, a huge scar but most importantly... CANCER FREE... from the mouth of the surgeon. He responded well to the surgery, and may go home by the weekend.!!!

God and all of you are amazing!

Love and thanks,

Kim, Troy, and Liam

January 17, 2012 12:09 pm

I'm sitting here in Kev's ICU room watching him try to sleep. Beeps and machines don't know how loud they are for someone who wants nothing but the tranquility and peace of sleep. The lights are off and the room is cool... just like he likes it.

He had a pretty good night, but early this morning after sitting up for a few minutes, he passed out. I'm being told that his heart rate is up, urine output is down, and he is requiring oxygen today, unlike yesterday. While these setbacks are somewhat expected, they are expressing some concern.

I'll post later, but know that I am keeping Kevy up to date about all the entries, prayers, tears and cheers.

Please keep them coming.

Luv Kim

The old saying "you don't know what you've got 'til it's gone" is so true.

With Kevin in the hospital, our king size bed is huge and I don't remember it ever being so big. I found myself sleeping diagonally across the bed, with my head on Kevy's pillow. When Kev was home, we would usually hold hands or touch feet as we drifted off to sleep. My feet kept dancing around the sheets, searching for their partner. My hands ended up holding Kev's pillow, and eventually I found the strength to give in to the tiredness and sleep.

January 19, 2012 10:35 pm

Well Kev has finally been given a room, and it's a beauty. He is settled in, and very exhausted. Tonight while I was there, I had the good fortune to run into Dr. Shoup. She continues to be very happy about Kev's recovery.

There is talk about my hubby coming home on Saturday. I can't see it but what do I know. Kev walked about 40 ft tonight and had to sit down half way through. His fatigue is all consuming. He has been put on a solid diet, although he is only drinking the boost.

The 55 stitches that are in his chest will apparently be going home with him. They need to stay in for about two weeks.

I'm not sure what kind of medical home care we may receive, but it's gonna have to be a doozy. Kevin is in such a fragile condition that I am afraid I may break him. Anyway, off to sleep and dream about the impending storm and how on earth I'm going to get Kevin upstairs. I couldn't be happier!!!

Good Night, Kim

January 20, 2012 4:48 pm

Kev is going home tomorrow and I am spending the night at the hospital. I'm hoping that the storm will be long gone when we hit the road. Knowing the warmth and love that will be waiting for us makes it all the more enticing!

Kevy looks wonderful, and enjoyed a visit with the boys this morning, and some friends this afternoon. Life is good.

Will update after we get home.

Love Kim

January 20, 2012 11:20 pm

By the time I post this entry, it will have been 520 days since I had to utter the words "they found cancer" to a peacefully resting Kevin immediately following his colonoscopy back on August 20, 2010.

515 days since I was able to see him in the ICU, and almost scream from the top of my lungs "they cut it all out... Dr. says you are Cancer Free!"

What a long, difficult, arduous journey this has been. At the time of this writing, 14,722 visits to this caring bridge journal have happened, 129 entries have been posted, and the guest book has been signed 932 times.

But the number that is most impressive is the number of times we have heard the word love. Kevin and our family have been inundated with new friends, the rekindling of old friendships, the rediscovery of family, and the renewal of our faith. We have said "I love you", heard "I love you", and been shown love in a plethora of ways. We have said time and again that we are almost embarrassed from the over abundance of love, but I am realizing tonight that there is no such thing. The love shown to us has transformed us as individuals, as friends, as a family. I also believe that this " love fest" has transformed many of you, probably in ways you don't realize.

So we are left with a few more hours until we are home once again, bringing with us 1/2 a liver less, 55 staples, and a million blessings.

520 days of love.

January 22, 2012 11:54 pm

Our first full day at home has come to a close, and I have to say how relieved I am. Kevin slept pretty well, with bathroom visits numbering about three throughout the night. There were some really good stretches of time where Kevin was able to join us in watching some tv, a little conversation and companionship.

Today, Brian was back in town and stopped by for a few hours before making his way downtown on business for the next week. This brother of Kevin's has been incredible. He has been with Kevin from the beginning, and even with going through his own bout of cancer, has bounced back and has been there for us whenever we needed him, and many times before we knew that we needed him.

Teri Truty and her son Ty Estes came by today with some goodies, and a little visit. Always enjoyable. Not sure if I mentioned here but we put out an APB for a recliner for Kevin to use during his convalescence. The Matthews family answered the call and delivered a chair yesterday that Kevy has been using nonstop.

Early this evening, our very dear friends Steve and Julie arrived from Milton, Ontario to see Kevin, and to pitch in and help me out here. It's great to have them. Kevin has been friends with them since elementary school - I've known them since high school. Steve was our best man, Julie a bridesmaid, and both Kevin and I stood in their wedding. Kevin is also godfather to their youngest son Brad.

I have been having an emotional meltdown over the last few days. I suppose it makes sense considering I have had to keep it together for the last little while. It seems that now is my time to lower my guard, and sleep for hours on end. Crying happens too, as does prayers of thanks and extreme joy at being able to play footsies with Kevy again.

So I'm off to sleep, having tucked in Troy and Liam, said goodnight to Steve and Julie, and kissed my Prince goodnight.

My toes can't wait for the dance to begin!

Love, Kim

January 24, 2012 11:48 pm

Enjoy when you can, and endure when you must.

~ Johann Wolfgang von Goethe

So we have passed the one week mark, and Kevin is doing amazing. The key, we are finding, is to keep his feet up, and keep up on the pain meds.

It has been so wonderful having Steve and Julie here for the past few days. They are heading home on Wednesday after back to back days of taking care of both Kevy and I. They have cleaned, shopped, cooked and laughed with us. Steve also did some repairs around the house... our doorbell finally works after years of being silent. Come to think of it, I wonder how many angels we kept from earning their wings until the bells were ringing. :)

Kevin is an incredible man, and his courage in facing this down is beyond reproach. He has been solid from the get go and every day I see a little bit more of his old self shining through. He is asleep beside me, and looks peaceful. I have to tell you though, that the pain meds make for some hilarious conversations in the middle of the night. I am now starting to answer him, and seeing where he takes it.

May God continue to bless all of you who have made for yourself a permanent place in our hearts.

Love, Kim

155

January 29, 2012 2:01 pm

What lies behind us and what lies before us are tiny matters compared to what lies within us.

~Henry S. Haskins

Well just when I think I have seen it all from Kevin, especially during the last year and a half, I am once again amazed.

Kevin has persevered through such a difficult time, both physically and emotionally. I have been in awe of his strength of purpose, and belief that he was going to make it through, although I have to confess there were a few blips along the way that may have been void of such belief. He has never wavered in his faith for one second, nor in the knowing that it was going to be a tough battle through to the end, whenever that would be.

Kevin has a unique ability of lighting up a room when he walks in to it, or for that matter even when he is in a hospital bed, with those god awful gowns, wide open at the back showing one and all what a cute behind he has. The essence he has is too big to be ignored, and frankly not many want to ignore it.

Kevy has an innate ability of making everyone he meets feel like they are the most important person. He cheers relentlessly for the underdog, and will do what he can to carry them on his shoulders if it means they make the finish line.

The outpouring of love and support that has come his way is phenomenal, and perhaps one good thing that comes from having an illness like cancer.

Too often we don't take the time in our daily lives to reach out to those around us, and let them know how much they mean to us. We may just assume that the person knows how we feel about them, or we may label ourselves as one who is uncomfortable with sharing our feelings. Words are not as scary as you think, and once you start sharing them with those around you, it almost becomes a way of life.

I think many who have known me for many years, would be quick to say that I haven't always been this open and sharing of my feelings. But things happen in life that make you stand up and feel compelled to speak.

Kevin loves God, he loves his wife and children without reproach, loves his siblings, his friends, coworkers, players, neighbors, everyone. He cares for those he knows, and those he doesn't. He gives of us heart and soul to those who want it and to those who need it. Kevin would do anything for anyone of you, and he would be there for you even before you knew you needed someone.

Kevin is healing well, settling into a little slice of peace, and being ever so thankful for the incredible doctors and medical staff who have given him this second or third chance at a cancer free life. He is thankful for all of you for your support of him, and your support of us, his family. He is strengthened by all the prayers and masses that have and are being said for him, and he is awestruck that a guy from Brantford, Ontario who led both his hockey league and lacrosse league in penalty minutes, would be worthy of such love.

I for one, am not surprised at the love. I know what lies within Kevin Troy Griffin, and no matter what he has come through, or what lies ahead, the essence he has inside will continue to lead us all to a happy ending.

I Love You Kevin!

Kim

February 3, 2012 7:07 pm

On Thursday Kev had all 55 staples removed, and took it like the trooper that he is. He is now covered with tiny steri strips.

The doctor told us that all of the margins from the resection were negative!

So now we turn our attention and adoration back towards Dr. Hantel. Kev has an appointment on Tuesday and we will be getting blood work done as well. We will probably receive a CEA number (please God keep it low). Our next steps with respect to chemo will be the topic of the appointment. That is, after Dr. Hantel looks at Kev's incision, and says "what did she (Shoup) do to you? :)

Kev is slowly but surely gaining strength, and is looking better every day.

Thank you for your continued support and love for Kevy. He is so awesome, and I love to see what an impact he has had on others.

God Bless and may you feel the love that we are sending out to one and all.

Love, Kim

February 8, 2012 12:00 pm

Rejoicing in our joy, not suffering over our suffering, makes someone a friend.

~ Friedrich Nietzsche

Dear friends,

It is with profound joy and utter relief that Kev and I share with you the results of his latest blood work. He went to see Dr. Hantel yesterday to meet and kind of plan out the map of next steps. We weren't sure if he needed more chemo, and if so, how many treatments. We also were going to find out if the liver was functioning okay.

Drum roll please:

Kevin's liver function is in the normal range....and

Kevin's CEA number: 2.0 Normal range for CEA is <5.0 !

The doctors are absolutely thrilled with these results and couldn't be happier for Kevin.

We have been crying since getting the call about a half an hour ago. We are staring at each other and in utter disbelief. Joy. Joy. Joy

So for all of you who have been on our journey of suffering, it is now time to truly rejoice in the greatness that is GOD and modern medicine. Your never ending support has been what has carried us through the good days, and especially the bad days.

Kevin stated it best when he turned to me and said that we are surrounded by the best people in the world. God knew what we needed and sent his best foot soldiers in all of you.

We are so happy, although we have some trepidation. But for today, just today, we are going to throw trepidation to the wind, and bask in the pure joy of 2.0 and normal liver function.

YOU + NORMAL LIVER FUNCTION + 2.0 = PURE JOY!

Love to all of you for your steadfastness.

We will update after Kevin's Feb 28th appointment to let you know what's next.

Kim

March 1, 2012 5:59 am

Kev met with Dr. Hantel on Tuesday, but had to wait for all the blood work to come back before finding out where he stands. Well, it can be stated very loud and clear that Kevy stands on the side of NO CANCER!

His CEA was 2.1, well within the normal range. He does not need chemo, but will have blood work done once a month in the foreseeable future and will have a CT scan in April.

Perfect news at a perfect time because as many of you know lacrosse season is officially underway! Oh, yeah, today also happens to be Troy's 18th birthday!

Loving all three of my guys big time!

Thank you God for today. We are truly blessed.

Love, Kim

April 13, 2012 5:06 pm

As mentioned in the last entry of more than a month ago, Kevy was going to be having a CT scan in April. Well, Kev had the scan yesterday and he just got off the phone with the doctor's office....

ABSOLUTELY CLEAR. NO SIGN OF CANCER. ANYWHERE.

This is the first time during this journey that we have had back to back scans that are clear. We have always found something on the second one, so this is incredibly gratifying for our family.

He has an appointment on the 17th with Dr. Hantel, and probably blood work, but we move forward today with a profound sense of relief and joy.

Let the weekend begin!!!!!

April 25, 2012 5:18 pm

Just when you think it's safe to go back in the water.....

Boy do I hate writing this entry. Kevy had blood work done today as a regular follow up to the CT scan he had a few weeks ago. He met with Dr. Hantel after the labs were done today and was told that his CEA number is 12.1. The last work up showed his CEA at 2.1.

Dr. Hantel is working quickly to get a PET scan done so we can determine where this newest enemy is hiding. He has scheduled it for Tuesday, May 1 and typically I think we learn the results within 48 hours. As the doctor says, the best case scenario will be that it has metastasized in one location, and is not in multiple locations.

We are all shocked, but the boys and I are doing a better job of handling it right now. Kevy does not want phone calls, and has asked for some alone time in our room.

Please pray for Kevin and that we are able to once and for all find this nemesis and eradicate it from his precious life.

We need the strength of all of you to help us once again walk this journey. While comfort is usually found when walking through familiar territory, I never wanted to see this place again. But, for now, it has been decided that we will start our trek here one more time.

Love one another and please make sure you tell everyone you know to get checked for colon cancer. Early detection can save lives.

Love Kim

May 2, 2012 4:50 pm

Kev had his scan yesterday morning, and by dinner time Dr. Hantel had called us with some updates. The scan did not show anything which is frustrating. Dr. Hantel wants a repeat colonoscopy which is being scheduled. He also wants an MRI of his liver.

We are left scratching our heads and no closer to an answer than before. If we find out anything we'll let you know.

Kim

May 8, 2012 5:46 pm

I was looking back on the last few entries and realized that when I made the pronouncement about "Just when you thought it was safe....", I failed to mention how the news was given to me.

Kevin had the doctor's appointment and labs set for that day and went on his own. I was at work in the school, dealing with mixed fractions and haiku poems. Kevy very nicely offered to pick me up that day as the boys had my car and were going to be staying after school for practice. When I entered the car, Kevin was finishing an email on his phone and set it down. We exchanged a quick kiss, as is usual when we see each other at the end of the day. Kev was the first to inquire as to how my day had been. I mumbled something like OK, nothing new or exciting. I then asked him, and for a moment he said nothing. I looked at him and finally he responded by saying "it's back."

Now here is where the whole journey takes a rather quick and scary turn. I struggled to register what he was talking about. What was back? Did he find a lost item? Was it the sneezing from allergies? I could not fathom what was back. Then, in an instant, I read his face and knew. It was back...the cancer. How could I have actually gone a day without thinking about the cancer, forgetting about a doctor's appointment, void of all thoughts related to the cancer?

And in that instant, I knew something that I had heard before, but truly did not think would ever apply to me. I had moved on with life, and was living again. Cancer wasn't the first thought in my head, and to be honest with you, not at any time of that day. How dare I leave the dark nemesis on the stoop and move on? The drop in my stomach upon learning that "it" was back was magnified tenfold because I had let my guard down and forgot. Forgot. Forgot.

I think that is the reason that this time around, I am dealing with a lot of angst, anguish, guilt and anger. The problem though is that I am directing those feelings toward myself. I am feeling overwhelmed lately and in desperate need of being cared for. I feel unheard, unnoticed, forgotten and mad at all those around me that I love the most. I am making my home a very bristly place to be.

It's like I don't feel that I should have the right to complain about my own ailments, or my fears and stresses. I am feeling like I should be stoic and give way to Kevin and "It" when it comes to the catastrophe's scale. And finally this morning, I couldn't pretend. Poor Kevin, who had agreed to drive me to work, had to hear my pity party by himself, surrounded only by the steel frame of the car, and a radio that I insisted be turned off. He was his incredible self as he maintained a quiet acknowledgement of my babbling monologue. When I was done, he told me that he had heard me, and that he was going to try to be more aware. He didn't try to fix it, nor suggest that maybe I was wrong.

Right now I am home alone, with the boys and Kev at Marmion running a lacrosse practice. It was a good time to take note of my rather fragile emotional state and here is what I have determined:

Life does go on, and you can live again after a diagnosis of cancer.

My aches and pains and stresses and anxieties are valid and can be shared with my husband.

I have a right to be annoyed, angry and fearful of the cancer.

And I have come to realize that perhaps I have been feeling this way over the last little while, because I know that I have to steady and ready myself to get back up on my feet, put on my armor of support and determination and lead our next crusade to remove, or at the very least, have the cancer retreat.

This is my time to regroup, rejuvenate, reinvigorate, and realize that cancer does not mean that living life is over, and that yes it's scary and full of crappy feelings, but that I have and will once again rise to the occasion because of the support I do have. My sons, my husband and of course each and every one of you who have taken the time out of your own hectic lives to reach out to us in ways big and small to say "You are not alone", have sustained me this far into this journey. Surely I am not going to let anyone down, least of all Kevy. He is too precious and incredible to feel alone.

So, once again thank you for allowing me to share my heart with you, and for being my support as I begin to prepare for my role of "life partner" and best friend to Kevin Troy Griffin.

I will never FORGET all of you.

Love, Kim

May 10, 2012 11:30 pm

Kevin is having two MRIs on his liver; one without dye and one with dye on Monday. We can only hope that if there is anything that it is together in one spot, and can be burnt out.

All I can say is that I'm glad it's lacrosse season so Kevin is busy with the team. Keeps his mind occupied.

Will update results as soon as we get them.

Kim

May 13, 2012 12:18 am

Almost twelve years ago we moved our family down to the United States, and truthfully, I thought we might only be here for four or five. I can't believe that we are still here! But let me tell you one thing, I am grateful that we ended up sticking around this long because we have developed some incredible friendships along the way.

Today was a difficult day emotionally for Kevin, me and the boys. Kevin was really wanting a win for his varsity lacrosse team today, but it was not to be. I cried through half of the game knowing how much it meant to him. Enter our Marmion friends: Laura, Bob, Teri, Don, Renee, Randy, Diane, Gary. We were invited to a games night tonight and I tell you, it was exactly what we needed. We laughed, and laughed so much tonight, that I have a sore stomach. We shared drinks, food and "Catch Phrase" and had a blast.

Thank you to our friends who enveloped us tonight with their love and friendship, and made us want to face tomorrow with renewed vigor and fight!

We love you guys.

Kim and Kev

May 15, 2012 11:20 pm

When a dog runs at you, whistle for him. ~ Henry David Thoreau

I'm beginning to think that we have walked in to a nightmare that has no end.

We are coming up to the second anniversary of Kevin's cancer diagnosis and we are still fighting the damn disease as hard as we were the first time. A little grayer, some scars both visible and those that lie underneath a facade of "normal" living, but once again being told its cancer. This time it has taken hold as two suspicious spots along the incision on the liver itself.

The MRIs and other recent scans have been sent to Dr. Shoup who did the liver resection back in January to get her take on what she sees. Kevin is facing some sort of treatment, whether it's the "full monty" or some knock off of it. Surgery, radiation, ablation, chemotherapy are all out on the table.

One thing the doctors seem to have a consensus on is that the CEA marker in Kevin is very sensitive and is a good predictor for the doctors to follow. They say this is good in that we find the cancer at an earlier stage, and can fight it down before it becomes too big.

Kevin is having his colonoscopy on Monday, and has a doctor's appointment on Tuesday to find out what play is going to be called.

Life is funny. While we are being faced with this information, we are in the throws of the lacrosse season for Marmion winding down, Liam getting his driver's license and Troy graduating from high school. We have family coming down to celebrate with us on Friday and Saturday, a lacrosse game Saturday morning, Troy's graduation party Saturday afternoon, graduation mass Saturday night, and Troy's actual graduation on Sunday. Did I mention that Kevin is flying out to Tampa tomorrow morning? Life is funny.

I just don't know how far down we are going to have to dig to fill up our reservoir. I have a feeling that journal entries will be beginning again in earnest.

Here doggy……..;)

May 22, 2012 8:46 pm

When the world says, "Give up," Hope whispers, "Try it one more time."
~Author Unknown

Dr. Hantel met with Kevin today to map out a plan for this most recent recurrence of his cancer. It was confirmed that the two spots are cancerous and located in the liver, although this time around in a slightly better position; although the word "better" and "cancer" appearing together really don't add up!

Kevin's CEA number shot up from 12.1 to 21.6, which made the decision pretty easy as to what we are going to do. Kevy will start chemotherapy on Friday morning and will go through six treatments, every other week. After a respite of six to eight weeks, Kev will have another liver resection surgery followed by a few weeks of recovery and finally another six rounds of chemo.

After today's news, Kev's lacrosse team had their first playoff game since being crowned conference champions. We were losing 6-3 in the fourth quarter and because of perseverance we came roaring back and WON 7-6! It is the first time in Marmion Lacrosse history that we have won a playoff game. Kev kept telling the boys not to give up, never back down, and believe.

So this will be the theme that we will take and use in this most recent round of cancer. Perseverance. Hope. Success.

Love Kim

May 27, 2012 3:55 pm

Kevy is resting comfortably after having his pump removed this afternoon. He had his first chemo treatment Friday and was escorted by Troy. It was a grueling five hours to complete but Kev, ever the trooper, went on to host our lacrosse awards ceremony that night. He is undoubtedly a great role model of perseverance.

Kev has already noticed what a big role the mind plays in this illness. As we were heading to the hospital to have the pump removed he could feel his heart start racing, and he began to have dry heaves. It's going to be a long haul, but no other choice.

Enjoy the rest of your weekend and big prayers going out to Tom McNally as he faces a recurrence of his cancer.

Love Kim

June 1, 2012 2:48 pm

Kevin has been suffering from nausea, fatigue and headaches since his chemo, but that was the easy part. The anxiety leading up to today's colonoscopy was overwhelming. Sleep did not occur last night as Kevin was quite fearful of something being found.

We are home from the hospital, and Kevin is resting comfortably. Dr. Joo seemed satisfied that everything is okay with his colon, although where the resection took place is narrow. To put everyone's mind at ease, he did a biopsy of the area, and we should have those results in a week or so.

Kevin continues to battle mightily.

Happy 21st Anniversary to my husband, Kevin. "I promise to be true to you in good times and in bad, in sickness and in health. I will love you and honor you all the days of my life".

Love Kim

June 10, 2012 4:08 pm

Kevy had chemo number 2 on Friday and had the pump removed today. The treatments hit him faster and harder now, and he is sleeping a lot which truthfully is a good thing.

His CEA number went up this time from 21.6 to 24.4. We will have to see where it stands next treatment to see if we should be concerned. Dr. Hantel has told us that there is another med we can add to his cocktail, but we don't want to have to do that. It's been described as our backup plan, and once that is used, we do not have another option.

Now that lacrosse is over, Kev is missing some passion. His attitude, though, is good, and he is hoping to get out to the driving range perhaps next week to see if he can still hit the ball. I've got a feeling that it won't be a problem.

Enjoy the sunshine and maybe some watermelon, and say a few prayers.

Love Kim

June 17, 2012 12:50 am

Ugh! After a sleepless night last night because of intense shooting pain throughout his body, Kevy relented and we visited the Emergency room at the hospital this afternoon.

Kevin's best description of the pain was to say it compared to the screaming pain of shingles. Up and down his spine, radiating through his arms and around his torso, Kevy fought it off as long as he could. When they were checking him in at the hospital, he rated the pain a 10. That's saying something considering what he has been through.

They were able to make him comfortable with an IV of meds, and after a battery of tests and no explanation, we headed home. We will be putting in a call to Dr. Hantel Monday morning. Our best bet is that it has something to do with the chemo and the previous neuropathy events he has had.

I will say it again and again. I have never met a stronger man. Kev is so busy at work, and continues to put his best foot forward, even when it gets hard. He is the personification of perseverance.

He is getting the pains again... I'll try to help him doze off for a while. Thank you for your prayers.

Love Kim

June 22, 2012 4:48 pm

PHEW!

We were so anxious and nervous about today's appointment because we would find out if the CEA number dropped or if the cancer was showing itself becoming resistant to the chemo.

Well the CEA did in fact drop 4 points to 20.4 so at least for now, we are staying the course. Relief poured from every part of our body when Dr. Hantel told us we would not have to use our back up plan.

Good news continued with word that the biopsy done during the colonoscopy was negative - no sign of recurrence of cancer. Yeah!

As for the pain that Kevin was in last weekend, Dr. Hantel is convinced that it has to do with the injection Kevy gets to increase his white blood cell count. He has given him a prescription for pain meds in case it rears its ugly head again.

Kevin is resting now, as with each treatment, the side effects come on harder and faster and seem to last longer. He looks so peaceful sleeping.

Thanks for your continued support and love. Pretty sure that napping is going to consume a lot of this weekend. I can't wait!

June 26, 2012 8:23 pm

Kevin is having a hard go this time. Almost from the start of his treatment he started feeling ill and it continues. He is sleeping close to 20 hours a day. The good about that of course is that it helps his body heal and prevents him from feeling crappy for too long.

Some of the other odd side effects include a change in his voice. He sounds like there is gravel in his throat. He is also experiencing mouth sores, and of course the infamous hair loss. He is missing his hair a lot.

While this is going on, however, he is still able to dig down deep and bring out the smiles and loving words. He gets very mushy which I like, and emotional. And no matter what, Kevin Troy Griffin never gives up. He tells me everyday at least once that he is going to make it and I remind him that he is in fact already making it.

I'm grateful to be able to be home during the summer so I can help Kevin when he needs me. My biggest job most recently is keeping him in V8 juice, watermelon and ginger ale. These must be chemo cravings……thankfully not asking for pickles and ice cream!

Just wanted to remind all of you that we are so grateful for your support from far and wide. Your prayers continue to sustain us and your comments, cards and calls are welcomed with open arms. Never doubt for a minute that you are making a difference. Thank you.

Love, Kim

July 6, 2012 1:50 pm

Chemo #4 is just underway but we are happy to report that the CEA number came down 25% to 15!

Dr. Hantel is happy with how things are going. He is going to stop the Avastin med after this treatment in preparation of his planned surgery. Kev will continue through six treatments and then rest for four weeks before surgery.

He has had a rough ride, with a lot of anticipatory gagging and nausea. He is resting now which is a good thing because we will probably be here for at least 2 more hours.

Thanks for all of your encouragement! We feel the love!

Love Kim

July 9, 2012 8:43 am

ANGUISH. Pure and utterly debilitating.

Last night marked the absolute worst I have seen Kevy throughout his almost two year battle. He spent half the night on the bathroom floor, alternating between diarrhea and vomiting episodes. Peppered in between all of this were tears and muscle pulls. It is so hard to stand by and feel helpless while the love of my life suffers so.

The treatment is truly cumulative and can only imagine how the next two will play out. But in order to get through today, I can't worry about tomorrow. He is fitfully sleeping beside me, surrounded by pillows, towels, a pail, cans of Gingerale in various stages of fullness and temperature, and a wife who wants nothing more than to kick cancers ass.

Who's with me? Please God let this suffering bring with it a complete and permanent recovery.

Luv Kim

July 17, 2012 10:29 pm

This is worth writing about!

It has been over a year since Kevy last played golf. For those of you who know him, please do not adjust your monitor. One year! Unbelievable.

But today was the day that Kevy was able to pull out his brand new Nike golf bag that had been gathering dust in the closet, strap on his golf cleats, slather himself with sunscreen, and head out to play in a tournament. He joined Rich his friend/boss, and two friends/clients Tom and Georgia.

Kevin couldn't rave enough about how all three took great care with him, making sure to park the cart in the shade, and bring cool packs and drinks to keep him hydrated. With the heat here reaching something like 109 with the humidity, Kev figures he went through close to a dozen Gatorades and water.

Not only did he have a great time, but THEY WON THE TOURNAMENT! They shot 8 under and proudly accepted the accolades and adulation from all in attendance. Okay, maybe not that, but certainly a little applause.

When he got home, he was soooooo happy to have been able to play and not let the group down. He was proud of himself for making it happen, and he promptly lay on the couch and fell asleep while receiving a foot and leg rub. A few Aleve later and his nausea meds, he crawled into bed where he has been for the last 3 hours!

181

He claims that it was worth it! And I will second that.

Sure glad for the ups after some crappy downs.

FORE!

Love, Kim

July 20, 2012 3:34 pm

A pessimist sees the difficult in every opportunity;
An optimist sees the opportunity in every difficulty.

~ Winston Churchill

Well I found this quote and thought it appropriate to add to the journal entry for today.

My hero Kevin Griffin received his fifth treatment today after getting news that the CT scan he had last week looked good and in fact provided proof that the tumors are shrinking in the liver and that no new disease was found anywhere! The CEA moved from 15 to 12.7 which is still going in the right direction.

Dr. Hantel has spoken with Dr. Shoup who did Kevin's liver resection in January and they have agreed that after chemo number 6, Kevin will have his liver resection scheduled, probably during the last week of August. It is exciting to know that we are getting closer and closer to having this disease eliminated, hopefully once and for all.

Now, back to the quote. I took a picture of Kevin during chemo and it shows that he is holding a black thingy to his ear....yes his cell phone. If you were able to see through the phone, you would see that Kevin was conferencing in on the sales meeting at work. This proves conclusively that Kevin is an optimist, not that it was ever in doubt. Here during his difficulty, he was taking the opportunity to be involved and included in the sales force and management at work. It is perhaps one of the only meetings that Kevin was willing to take a back seat and primarily listen in to a meeting, and not prolonging, um I mean enhance with his knowledge and suggestions!

Things are definitely hitting him harder but he keeps on going. My little energizer bunny. While we are somewhat celebrating how far Kevin has come, we would like to take a moment to ask for your prayers for our dear friend "R" who is battling just as hard, if not harder than Kevin. His battle is intense, and we want all the love and good thoughts that we can muster up to go his way. We love "R" and his family and wish we could take some of the burden from them. This is the best thing we could think of doing. Knowing how much love and faith we are surrounded with, lets us know that the warmth it will bring our friend will definitely be felt.

July 26, 2012 12:18 pm

Surgery has been set for Kevin's second liver resection for Monday, August 20, 2012 at Loyola Hospital. How ironic that August 20, 2010 is the date of the original findings of cancer in Kevin's colon. I am deciding to take this as a good sign and that we will be victorious this time.

Dr. Shoup has explained that the location of these two tumors is consistent with remnants that were microscopic in size and left behind unseen by the doctor or the ultrasound. She is optimistic that because of where it is, she will be able to remove more liver, leaving a cleaner margin behind.

We are very confident with our doctors, and are truly grateful for their expertise.

Hope this summer finds you doing random acts of kindness, and embracing your loved ones a little longer and tighter. Even through this incredibly hot and dry time.

Love Kim

August 3, 2012 7:52 pm

Sadness is almost never anything but a form of fatigue. ~ Andre Gide

Chemo number 6 started this morning at 8:30 am with blood work and a meeting with Dr. Hantel. He has signed off on surgery for August 20, and is happy with Kevin's vitals. Kev is now 220 lbs, and his blood pressure was perfect. His port cooperated today, allowing the nurses to take blood from there as well as being the main entrance for the chemo. Dr. Hantel did increase anxiety and nausea controlling meds today to a higher dosage because Kevin has been experiencing symptoms right up until today, having no respite from his last chemo.

The meds kicked in right away and Kevy slept through most of his 3 1/2 hour appt. Great news was ours when we received the blood work sheet. Kev's CEA went from 12.7 to 9.8! Very happy with that.

Kev has been dealing with the usual suspects: nausea, dry heaving, gagging, cold sweats, headache, pulling muscles and weakness. He has been craving watermelon and cucumbers, I am guessing because of their high water content, as well as iced tea and ginger ale. When he got home, he went right to sleep and awakened to a snack of his cravings, topped off with a leg rub and affirmation to his questions of whether or not he was handling it okay.

Friends, people you pick to love and who in return love you, are vital in everyone's life. While we had been breathing cancer and having it

fill every nook and cranny of our daily living, our friend Rik Martorano had been courageously fighting his own battle. Pancreatic cancer had taken hold of him and he had been given a dire prognosis. And still he was fighting. With everything he had, Rik was fighting.

During this time, the boys went home to Canada to visit family, enjoy the beach at the cottage and see Uncle Rik. Troy made arrangements to go and see Rik on our family's behalf. Troy was able to sit with him and hold his hand while Rik moved in and out of consciousness. He would ask about Kevy and wonder where he was. Troy talked with him, comforted him and shared his love and prayers with him.

While sometimes difficult, we were forced into everyday life by things such as this. Loving friends and family is so important. You don't know what you've got until it's gone.

August 10, 2012 7:33 am

We received word a few moments ago that our friend R passed away earlier this morning at home surrounded by his family. One of Kevin's closest friends, Rik Martorano struggled valiantly through his diagnosis of pancreatic cancer, never giving up. He leaves behind his with Kathy, and their two children Brittney and Jordan.

Thank you all for your prayers for Rik and please keep them coming for his family as they need them now more than ever. God Bless you Rik.

August 11, 2012 8:06 am

We had to make some decisions about going home for Rik's funeral and after much discussion, I will be going while Kevy stays home and rests and prepares for his surgery. Kev wants to go so badly but realizes that for his own good, the stress of attending would be detrimental at this point.

Going in to his surgery, Kevy has to be in a good mind set, and while the sadness he is carrying now will be there, the similarities of circumstances hits a little too close to home.

So I fly home tomorrow and will be surrounded by family and friends as we celebrate Rik's life and all the laughs we shared. Kev will have the boys but would love to have friends around too.

Thank you all for your support as we continue this almost two year journey toward a positive outcome... eradication of this horrific unwelcome and hideous disease.

August 17, 2012 2:58 pm

Here is the game plan for Kevin's surgery.

Kev had his pre-op appt today for blood work and a meeting with the anesthesiologist. Everything is set and good to go.

We have to be at the hospital for 7:30 am on Monday with the surgery slated to begin at 9:00 am. They anticipate 4-6 hours for surgery.

A little of the anxiety that Kev has been dealing with recently has been put to rest as he continues to prepare himself mentally for this next step. He draws on the prayers of all of you for strength, so thank you.

I will update on Monday and be excited to pass along what I'm sure will be great news! Thanks for your support.

Love, Kim

August 20, 2012 10:36 am

Just got word that surgery has started. After two failed attempts at starting an epidural for pain control, they had to forgo that option and will use their backup plan of inserting a catheter into his abdomen to deliver pain meds.

Will update when I know more. Keep those prayers coming!

August 20, 2012 1:17 pm

Kev is in recovery after having ablation done to the liver instead of complete resection. The location of the spots and the lesions from the last surgery made Dr. Shoup decide the best plan of action was ablation.

She is happy with the result. He has a drain in his abdomen which he didn't have last time.

We will be able to see him in about an hour and a half. Once I get a visual on him, I'll fill you in. Thanks for your prayers. Love Kim

August 20, 2012 9:23 pm

Just spoke with Kevin's nurse to get an update on how he is doing.

He is comfortable, no pain to speak of and his vitals are good. Apparently he is looking forward to getting some sleep and to top it off the nurse said that he was PLEASANT. Kev is such a caring, thoughtful and agreeable guy that to hear he is pleasant only hours out of surgery does not surprise me. However, hold me back if he wants to dance her around the room!

I feel good knowing that he is comfortable and resting. I will hopefully be doing the same tonight.

A big thanks to Renee for coming with us and a special note of love and admiration for my son Liam who stood up and helped me through today. Liam, your dad and I love you very much and are so proud of the young man you have become.

Good night all. I will update as necessary.

Love, Kim

August 21, 2012 1.48 pm

Sitting in Rm 4907 at Loyola Hospital looking at my beautiful, strong, incredibly brave husband as he gently sleeps. While the pain meds might seem to the outside world the cause of his visit to dreamland, I am pretty sure it had something to with the sponge bath I just gave him with extra care rubbing his back.

Vitals are great, he was up walking already, and had green Jell-O for lunch.

His pain is harder to control this time without the epidural. He has catheters going into his abdomen to deliver meds directly where he needs them. Rating the pain about 5-6 right now.

Thanks for your constant support. It has kept our whole family going.

Love Kim

August 22, 2012 10:16 pm

Kevy looks fantastic! He has great color and was up walking around quite well. He is being told there is a good chance he is going home tomorrow!!!! I'm so excited. He is exhausted and in pain but his smile is radiating everywhere and even makes the hospital room look inviting.

Your unending support and care for Kevin and our family has been tremendous. You know the saying "What Would Jesus Do?" He would be doing exactly what each and every one of you has done for us from the beginning. Random acts of kindness, prayer after prayer, meal preparations, gift cards, hugging your loved ones a little tighter, doing for someone who can't do for themselves, loving each other. Jesus is in all of you who have been with us.

Thank you God.

Love Kim

August 30, 2012 10:23 pm

It is so true when they say that the more things change, the more they stay the same.

It has been almost two weeks since Kevin had his surgery and he is recovering nicely. We were blessed to have had Brian and Anne come down for a week to take care of us so life could go on. Yes, that's right Brian and Anne....here....again.

Life or "moving on" has sometimes become a difficult thing on this journey that started over two years ago.

The newness of a diagnosis that came out of nowhere and was so destructive to all who witnessed it is profoundly sad and overwhelming. When we decided to use CaringBridge to keep family and friends informed of Kevin's situation, it was a source of comfort for all, especially us. The prayers, good wishes, advice, guidance, and love that have embraced us from the beginning was essential in "moving on".

So now we find ourselves sitting in a familiar place, even after 3 surgeries, 2 radiation rounds, and 4 plus chemotherapy treatments behind us. Shouldn't we be in a different place? Shouldn't we be in a neighborhood or setting we haven't seen before, or that holds exquisite beauty?

We go to see both the surgeon and oncologist next week to firstly remove staples and get a better explanation of the surgical procedure that was done; and to find out if there will be yet another chemo treatment.

Speaking for myself, I am becoming fearful and anxious about the near future, and what it may hold for Kevy. Are we finally going to be able to look around and not see the same old same old? Will we be able to make plans, even on a small scale, of venturing to a hotel for a weekend getaway? Or ridding our medicine cabinet of pill bottles with names like zofran? Or how about being able to just be.....normal?

I am feeling so crushed and finding it hard, at least right now, of finding the silver lining.

Two tickets to paradise please, or at least a spot a little further down the journey's path.

September 5, 2012 6:56 pm

Throughout this 2-yr journey I can count on my one hand how many times Kevin has been down, tearful and afraid. Today was one of those days.

Our appointment to get the staples out is tomorrow, not today, and Friday we go to see Dr. Hantel. Hopefully some of the angst that Kevy is carrying around will be put to rest.

Having time on his hands, and pain all over his body has given Kevin time to pause and reflect and he isn't too happy with what he is seeing in the reflection. He hates his frizzy hair, his dry skin, and all the scars. While he tells people he has been in a fight with a shark, which is so Kevy, the reality is really starting to take a bite out of his optimism.

So, if you notice that you haven't heard back from Kevy, or that he seems subdued, know that he has retreated somewhat while anticipating the outcome of these upcoming appointments. We can only hope that the shark attack scenario ends up being the lead story, and nothing else.

Hold on everyone, Kevy is going to need a bigger boat. Love Kim

September 7, 2012 4:16 pm

"It is good to have an end to journey toward; but it is the journey that matters, in the end."

~ Ernest Hemingway

No more staples. No more chemo. No more. Kevin had blood work done today, and the results are amazing. His CEA is 3.3 which we all know we want below 5.0, and his liver function is in the normal range. The only lagging numbers for him right now are his red blood cells which are 8.2 of which a normal reading is 13. We will go back next week and the week after to have blood drawn to check his levels. If they do not climb higher, he may face having a blood transfusion. This information though helps to explain Kevin's incredible fatigue. Sleeping 19 hours yesterday just shows you how tired his body is.

You know in getting to this point, after having been here before, we are cautiously optimistic. We have come to the realization that on this cancer journey there really is no final destination. There is always going to be a possibility of the cancer returning, which is what every cancer patient faces. So this time we have altered our thinking and have truly realized that as Hemingway said, it is the journey that matters in the end. Right now at this moment, the view we have is breathtaking and full of all that is beautiful in the world.

We see all of you, surrounding us and adding to the beauty of the view. Every imaginable color and every incredible sound is resonating around us, and if we are still for a moment, we hear laughter and cheers and feel the joy coming from all of you. We will take this spot on the journey as our destination for now and reap all that we can. We will do for others, stand up for others, pray for others, and be the support that others need during their times of sorrow or angst. We will never give up our faith that Kevin will heal completely and most importantly how Our Lord has never failed us.

So please feel free to join us as we celebrate this stop on the journey. We may not have streamers and balloons up, but as said before, the beauty that is surrounding us right here, right now is spectacular, and only adds to the celebration.

Thank you all and God Bless.

Kim

October 14, 2012 9:35 am

The wise man in the storm prays to God, not for safety from danger, but for deliverance from fear.

~ Ralph Waldo Emerson

Monday, October 15, 2012 sounds like just an ordinary day, a day that will bring with it a sunrise, possibly obscured by clouds; a gentle breeze to move the changing leaves, possibly enveloped by a bold wind; and everyday tasks of living, although for Kevin it will be shrouded with a dark, doom like feeling... of fear.

You see, Kevy has a CT scan on Monday as well as blood work to check his CEA numbers. This will be the first scan since his liver surgery. While he has had two blood panels done right after the resection, it is this one that we are fearing. Kevin's cancer journey has followed a pattern we are hoping will be broken, yet afraid will be a repeat. It has been with the first post surgery scan and blood work that we have found a recurrence ... four times.

Optimism and positive thinking can only take you so far when you are facing odds such as these. I would have to admit that we have typically faced these parts of the journey with a certain degree of optimism but that this time for some reason, it is full of doom. Has Kevy had any symptoms to make us feel this way? No. In fact quite the opposite. He is feeling stronger than ever before, enjoying time with his sons more and more, and is expressing his love to me through songs, conversation and the best hugs this side of the Mississippi. Right now everything seems normal.... and I guess that is the problem.

Normal, and I'm using the term loosely, is something we as a family have not felt for over 2 years. We have been anything but normal. Or should I say that we developed and formed a "new normal" that took us from day to day. You know the saying, "You don't know what you've got until it's gone"? It is so true. Seeing Kevin partaking in life full of energy, enthusiasm and with a renewed sense of purpose, brings such joy to the hearts of all who know and love him. It also brings fear.

Logically I know that fearing this makes no sense, but from an emotional level, it makes complete sense. Seeing how alive Kevy is and feeling how "normal" our family is right now, makes me fear the results.

We have shared some late night pillow talk about tomorrow's tests, and tears have joined in on it as well. Kevin does not want to go back to cancer's lair and have to fight all over again. Don't get me wrong, he will fight like the dickens but he really doesn't want to.

If I can ask all of you who have been with us to please take a moment for a group prayer tonight (Sunday) at 9:00 pm EST or 8:00 pm CST for Kevin. Stop for a brief silent moment and bring Kevin to mind and ask God to protect him and give him the strength to face tomorrow head on. I believe that a barrage of prayers at roughly the same time will definitely get Our Lord's attention and propel him to give Kevin whatever he needs.

We need all of you to pray. In return, we will be praying for all of you and thanking God for putting you into our lives. Thank you and much love, Kim

October 15, 2012 5:06 pm

Well, it appears that we are back on the cancer roller coaster. While we have not received the results from the CT scan, the blood work that charts Kevin's CEA number came back at 6.9.

Normal range is 5 and under.

Kevin's CEA count has always been a precursor to finding the cancer. His body is so sensitive to this reading, that the cancer isn't usually visible on the scans even though the CEA has risen. Last time we had this recurrence, the CEA came through first, a CT scan showed nothing and we had to have an MRI to tell us where the little buggers were hiding.

Dr. Hantel wants the blood tests redone in 2 weeks to see the rate of increase.

Thank you for your prayers last night. We felt like we had a blanket wrapped around us keeping us safe. While we know that you are all with us in prayer, we want to ask again if you will please pray for Kevin and that a miracle finds its way into his life and cures him of this horrific disease.

Will keep you posted.

Love, Kim

October 18, 2012 10.44 pm

The results are in for Kevin's CT scan. Dr. Hantel told him that there is no sign of cancer on the scan, but more importantly it shows that Kevin has a liver infection. There is a pocket of fluid and air showing on the scan that Hantel has started treating Kevin for immediately with two antibiotics.

Thus, there is a slight possibility that the increased CEA numbers are indicative of the infection and not a recurrence of cancer. Kevy is having his appointment and blood work with Dr. Hantel moved up a week to next Friday. Please pray that it is the infection and nothing more causing the rise.

While not jumping for joy, we are at least for now holding our tears.

To be continued...

October 26, 2012 1:19 pm

Had our appointment with Dr. Hantel today and while the CEA number nudged up from 6.9 to 8.4, the good doctor remained firm in his belief that because the number was under 10, it is presenting as the result of the infection and not cancer. NOT cancer.

Kevin is uncomfortable when he was examined around his abdomen and side which is where the infection is located. Dr. Hantel wants Kevin to continue his antibiotics and will repeat the CT scan next Thursday and meet with him at 8:00 am on Friday to see if the scan shows the infection decreasing in size. If it remains roughly the same size, we will most likely move toward having the infection drained.

All in all a very POSITIVE AND HAPPY appointment.

Thank you for your prayers and good thoughts! We are continuing in the belief that all is or at least all will be well.

Love and a wicked little smile, Kim

November 2, 2012 2.02 pm

Stop me if you think you have heard this one before...

Met with Dr. Hantel for blood work and to discuss the scan and what it showed with respect to the infection. The infection has reduced in size which is a good thing, but because it has not disappeared completely, Kev will be on a stronger dose of antibiotics for another two weeks. We will meet again at the end of November for another scan and blood work.

Unfortunately the scan also showed one, possibly two spots on the liver. While we were there for the appointment, the CEA number had not come back yet, so Dr. Hantel was referring to the spot(s) as suspiciously unknown entities. He did tell us if the CEA marker went up, it would indicate cancer.

The CEA went up to 11.9. Therefore the spot(s) are cancer.

They are located in a totally different area of the liver, and based on their placement, treatment will probably consist of radiation or ablation through a tiny incision in the abdomen. Definitely good news as Kev would rather not have major surgery again! It would be an outpatient procedure.

We will know more about treatments at the end of the month after the next scan. At least for the near future, Kevin will be able to exist in the realm of normalcy which means that, for the first time in over two years, he will be able to enjoy the U.S. Thanksgiving and the set up and decorating of the Christmas Tree.

Thank you again for keeping us in your thoughts and prayers.

November 4, 2012 5:21 pm

3mm.

That is how big the one spot on Kevin's liver appears on the CT scan.

A little more than 1/10th of an inch.

And yet it has become the big white elephant that is weighing on Kevin's shoulders, totally unbearable in its weight and size and it is slowly changing us all yet again.

First found in his colon, removed, chemo and radiation.
Returns in a lymph node in his abdominal area; radiation and maybe chemo, I forget.
Found in liver; chemo and liver resection.
Found in liver again; chemo and liver resection.
Found for a fifth time, in the liver, ...treatment TBA.

How will we ever get ahead of this thing? Just when we take a breath, and begin to exhale it churns up again. I have never hated something so much before. Normal will never be a state of being for us, for Kev, and hope and optimism are not coming to our aide as quickly this time.

We will wait until November 30 for another CT scan to make sure the infection has gone, and now I suppose, to watch the spot(s) that have shown up. I'm afraid of what we will find then. How much bigger will the spot(s) be and will they have brought along some of their friends who have been so good at hiding out for 807 DAYS.

2 years, 2 months, 15 days… looking more and more like a life sentence of grueling treatments and holding our breath. Sad. Very sad.

November 15, 2012 7:21 am

Happy Birthday to my best friend.

A man who is caring, loving, smart, witty, kind, eager and above all a fighter. May you have an incredible birthday today and know how much you are loved. Thank you for the almost 30 years of being the biggest part of my life. Thank you for making me your wife, and for giving us two awesome sons.

May all your wishes and dreams come true.

Shoes.

November 30, 2012 9:15 pm

Slight not what's near through aiming at what's far. ~ Euripides

It's been a while since I have opened with a quote and this one is bang on.

Kevy had his CT scan yesterday, and today we met with Dr. Hantel. Kevin's CEA levels have gone up to 19.1 from 11.9 which confirms cancer. However, the scan was less forthcoming.

The spot(s) that were seen in the liver from the last scan have all but disappeared, the bigger one only a tiny tiny blip. So good news, but not good news. Nothing showed up on this most recent scan, making the cancer "Waldo" from "Where's Waldo". So where do we go from here?

At the end of December, Kevy will have a Pet scan, which covers his whole body—from the tip of his head, now covered in hair that is slightly different in color, but still as sexy as hell, to the bottom of his feet. So if Waldo is thinking he can hide out indefinitely behind a shopping mall, or mail box or a pretzel shop, it's wrong. We will most likely find the bugger and then set upon a path of attack.

Until then, however, we are going to enjoy each and every day that we have in front of us. Kevin is feeling great, excited about the holidays, and for the first time in three years, will be able to join us Christmas morning as we celebrate the birth of Christ and relish in our small family circle. Honestly, who could ask for anything more?

209

As the quote states, for any of us to be looking too far ahead into the future about what will happen, we miss out on what is happening right now. Like right now Kev is awakening from a snooze on the couch after a great scalp rub from yours truly, Liam is laughing his head off playing computer games with friends and I am truly smiling ear to ear because right now, at this moment, life is good, joyous, and tangible. I can see and feel the love we have inside these walls and beyond.

During this hectic time of year, don't forget to remember to be in the moment; take in the sights and sounds and smells of things around you. Don't worry about the small stuff; grab it and put it away. Love on each other even more right now and know that Kevin and I along with the boys thank God every night for all of your prayers, good wishes and thoughts. We are soooooo lucky. I wouldn't want to change places with anyone! Love Kim

December 10, 2012 12:33 pm

Last night was a tough night for Kev.

I think the fatigue of dealing with such a serious illness for almost two and a half years has reached its tipping point. He is feeling so overwhelmed at the prospect of fighting it again, especially since he has not had treatments or surgery since August. Physically, he is feeling the best that he has since August 2010 and the thought of the cancer somewhere within the confines of his battered and scarred body is enough to make him wretch.

Last night Kevin felt so alone and sad, realizing that for the moment, cancer is somewhere in his body, and nothing is being done about it. Now granted, if we can't find it, we can't treat it, but all that does is make Kev feel like he is standing still, waiting for it to creep into deeper and darker pockets.

Two plus years ago, when this diagnosis was new, everyone was so on top of the results, questioning Kevin continuously on how he was doing and offering their love, support and prayers. Jump ahead two years, and what was once new and shocking, has become the norm and almost expected... by almost all of us. However, Kevin's perspective remains focused on the "new" findings and "shocking" CEA results yet again.

While he is rocked again with this news, the rest of us have been living on the periphery since the beginning, and the cancer has sadly made itself at home in the fabric of our lives. What was once a very obvious, glaringly bright colored piece of thread that did not belong, has almost seamlessly been interwoven, losing itself among the many threaded hues of everyday living.

Now no blame is being placed here, merely noting how life goes on, and time does not stand still, even for cancer. We move to new homes, get married, have children, win yet another lacrosse season (wink), land a big piece of business, go off to college, breathe.

Kevin has gone on, barely stopping in between his surgeries, chemo treatments, and radiation. He has landed new business, had another winning lacrosse season, renewed our wedding vows (his idea), said good bye to a very dear friend who lost his fight against pancreatic cancer, and had to begin a new reality of having only one son at home. Oh, yeah, and he also breathed now and again.

My desire to write today is to remind us all that life is so precious and goes by so fast, that we have to remember to slow down, and take in all that there is to see, hear, smell, taste and touch. Reflect on what makes us tick, how we are contributing to each other's lives, or realize that maybe we have to kick it up a notch and be in the moment.

Sleep finally came last night for Kevy but only lasted a few short hours before he was back up to face the world anew. Tears do tend to cleanse and helped to release some of his built up anxiety.

While it sounded like a good idea at the time, Kev scheduled his PET scan for December 24, and a meeting with Dr. Hantel on December 26 to find out the results. The thought was that maybe we could have Christmas day, just 24 hours, of believing that we were living a normal, happy life, uncomplicated by illness and financial burdens.

Looking at it though, waiting for another two weeks before we know what we are dealing with is making the fabric that Kevin is cloaked in appear to be thinning in some spots. Please help strengthen the fabric of any and all family and friends who need to be reminded that they are thought of, and cared for, each and every day.

I may have shared too much here today, but you have all added to our own fabric, and want to make sure you all know it. Our love for you is immeasurable.

December 26, 2012 4:39 pm

Here is hoping that all our family and friends had a wonderful Christmas. If I'm being honest, I'd have to say that ours was less than perfect. I think it's safe to blame it on the anticipation and anxiety of finding out today if Kevin's Pet scan showed any signs of cancer. We all seemed to be a little on edge. Thankfully by the evening, we had released some of the pressure with tears, and hugs and ended the day in a good way.

Dr. Hantel was straight up with us in letting us know that there is a spot in the liver that is for sure cancer, and a lymph node outside the liver, near what he called the celiac axis and the pancreas that is "involved". At this point, he is saying 50/50 likelihood that the node is infection from his liver infection, which would make sense, seeing as Kevin had to go back on antibiotics within the last week because of symptoms reappearing. Of course, the other chance is that the node is cancer and this would produce a whole new mix of problems.

So, starting on Friday, Kevin will undergo IV chemotherapy with two drugs, one from previous chemos called irinotecan and a new drug called Erbitux. He will receive a total of four treatments, one every other week, but will not have a pump this time.

We meet again in two weeks, and then in four weeks, we will redo the PET scan to see if the lymph node presents as infection or cancer.

Thank you for your prayers and know our love for all of you is unsurpassed.

God please keep Troy and Liam in your warm embrace, and help me to find the strength to support Kevin. I am very weak right now, and don't know how I will rise to the occasion. Keep Kevin close, and continue to feed his optimism.

Love Kim

December 29, 2012 12.04 am

Kevy had his first new chemo treatment today, and was grateful to have his best bud Steve with him. Steve and Julie along with their sons came down from Canada yesterday to spend some time with us.

The new cocktail caused Kev's private room in the Cancer Center to be rushed by four nurses, as he broke out in hives, and began having trouble breathing. I'm kind of glad Steve was there, and not me. The incredible nurses got his reactions under control, with Benadryl and oxygen. He slept for some time, and for the most part feels pretty good.

We are concerned with the CEA as it went up from 19.1 to 36.7, the highest it's ever been. We won't know for sure until Kev has at least two treatments as to whether the number is because of infection in the lymph node or cancer. PLEASE pray and pray.

Love to all.

January 8, 2013 2:21 pm

As the caregiver of someone with cancer, you begin your journey with a single focus and determination and that is to get your loved one through the horror and mess, and get them to the other side where cure and pure joy reside.

Through the days that turn into weeks, then months, and finally years, the objective is clear, concise, and easy to maintain a focus on. Easy that is, until you reach a spot along the journey where you are frozen in place, not unwilling, but unable to take the next step.

I am at a precipice that to me right now is so insurmountable, all I can do is kneel down and cry. Where has my strength gone? Why can I not pick myself up like so many times before, and just keep moving?

Surely Kevin deserves to have someone beside him to help him through this most trying of times - someone he can lean on and be cheered on by. Why in Kevin's darkest hour am I unable to muster the strength to even want to breathe?

I can't breathe at times; at others I feel so tired, I can only turn my pillow over and pull my blankets up high over my head. I want to do all the things a good partner should do, and yet, all I can do is cry and feel sick to my stomach. I need help, but I don't know what to do with it.

I can't.

January 11, 2013 11:25 pm

Let me start out by thanking all of you for your love and immediate response to my emotional letting. It was powerful and meaningful. Various means of help have been offered, and I have started taking some of you up on them. I do need all of you to keep me afloat. Know that I can't thank you enough.

Treatment number 2 is in the can for Kevy, and thankfully with no significant reactions. It was very long today, almost 6 hours, partly as a precaution and attempt to avoid another harsh reaction.

Kevy has developed a significant rash on his face, neck and back, as well as increased dry skin. Nausea is present, cold sweats and aches. Thankfully though, only two more to go.

The infamous CEA went from 36.7 to 26.4, a fairly big drop, which Dr. Hantel wasn't anticipating. He actually suggested that it may go up, and show no decrease until after this treatment! Very encouraging!

Quietly watching Kevy drifting in and out of a light sleep, thinking about how lucky I am to be able to join him. Good night and God Bless.

Love Kim

January 25, 2013 6:01 pm

Treatment 3 is over, and Kevin is sleeping on the couch. For the most part, he is only experiencing fatigue, although not at the rate he was during previous chemos, rash on his face, chest and back, and extremely dry skin on his hands. Some nausea creeps in now and again, but tolerable.

Of course I'm saving the best bit of information for last because it truly is awesome. Kevin's CEA was 26.4 two weeks ago at his last treatment and today's number is 11. Yep, you read it right.....11. We were told not to expect another big drop, so we were gobsmacked when they told us. Very happy and more hope seemed to envelope us.

I want to thank all of you for your offers of help. I have taken some steps to help myself, and slowly but surely will get there. Kevin continues to tell me how much he loves me, and how glad he is that I'm going through this with him. I wouldn't want to be with anyone else, anywhere else. I love him to the woods and back.

Thanks.

February 8, 2013 12:33 pm

Do not fall before you are pushed. ~ English Proverb

We have just finished meeting with Dr. Hantel and have a mixed bag of news to share. First and foremost : Kevin's CEA went from 11 to 6.2! If I can quote the good doctor he is thrilled with how Kevin is responding to the treatment. So we are very happy!

Now for those of you who know me, you know I live to use analogies. So as mentioned, we received a mixed bag of news. So while the 6.2 would be considered the corn or broccoli in the mixed veggie bag, (i.e. the good veg) the Lima beans represent the news of four more treatments. Yep, after coming today thinking this was it, we were told four more treatments over the next eight weeks. We both teared up a bit but it is what it is.

Now I know when you eat all the veggies together it's the best, so we are trying to take all this in at the same time. Kevy will also have a CT scan within the next week or so and then will have a PET scan after the last treatment. The CT will give us an idea of size and may be able to tell us if the abdominal lymph node is involved or if it was infection.

Dr. Hantel has made a slight adjustment to the erbitux med, the newest drug which causes Kevin severe dry skin, rashes and acne. A slightly lower strength is now being given to help with the side effects. He takes an antibiotic and uses a steroid cream, but to no avail. He is

219

having to call clients ahead of meetings to give them a bit of a warning so they don't go running the other way! Ha ha. Only slightly kidding though.

I want to thank all the incredible people from Brookdale Elementary (where I work) and Marmion Academy as well as our friends who have all stepped up to give us a helping hand. My sister told me it takes a lot of strength to ask for help, but let me tell you it takes even more humility to be the recipient of such tremendous outpouring love. Amy Hausman you are wonderful.

For our family in Canada, stay safe and warm during the storm. Random acts of kindness for all, and thank you all as you continue to sustain us through our journey.

Love and gratitude, Kim

February 21, 2013 9:20 pm

I just emailed Michelle Obama and asked her to wear the blue star - the symbol of the eternal memory of those we've lost to this disease and the shining hope for a future free of colon cancer.

This is a cause I care about - please join me by taking action yourself and then spreading the word!

Visit Colon Cancer Alliance to send an email to the First Lady and remember that March 1 is the first day of Colon Cancer Awareness Month. Wear blue and get the word out to friends and family alike....

What's Up Your Butt?

Get screened and make a donation to help eradicate this horrific disease that has Kevin in its hold for over two and a half years.

Love, Kim

February 22, 2013 7:32 pm

Courage doesn't always roar. Sometimes courage is the little voice at the end of the day that says I'll try again tomorrow.
~Mary Anne Radmacher

Kevin had his treatment today which means he only has three more or six weeks of chemo. I was very fortunate to have our friend Randy join Kevy today at chemo which I think was good for both of us. This is only the second time I have missed a treatment, I think, and there was a definite lessening in my anxiety today. Kev said he and Randy had some good conversations (more likely Randy listening to Kevy...) and have almost finalized their lines for the lacrosse teams. By the way, the season officially starts Monday. Go Marmion.

Kev's CEA went from 6.2 to 4.0, a drop of 33%! He is now officially in the normal range. If only we can stay here forever, that would be great.

Kev was shown the CT scan and said that you can't see the spot in the liver anymore. The lymph node located smack dab center of the body near the celiac axis also shrank 25% making us hopeful that with the low number, the node is strictly the remnants of infection. We will, however, not know that until the PET scan which will happen after the remaining three chemos.

This chemo, Erbitux, really plays havoc with Kevy's skin. Brutal rashes and acne and his skin has never been drier. Let's add here that Kevin is one person who absolutely hates skin cream or lotion. Unfortunately he has to be coated from the tip of his head to the bottom of his feet. But, this too shall pass.

I have learned that no man is an island and you need to surround yourself with help and let me stress right now that from day one we have been completely surrounded. We couldn't be more thankful for all that has been given and done for our family. Know that we continue to pay it forward, as there is no possible way to pay it back.

So, a reminder that March is Colon Cancer Awareness month, not to mention the holder of many of our family's birthdays. Please have yourself checked, and bug anyone you know to make sure they find out "What's Up Their Butt". Kevin's brother Brian, who was diagnosed only after going for a colonoscopy because of Kevin has been given a clean bill today. He is cancer free!

Have a wonderful weekend. We will be laying low, hunkering down, being together, listening to the little voice saying to try again tomorrow. Thank God for tomorrows.

March 8, 2013 11.42 pm

Kev had his treatment today and saw the CEA go from 4.0 to 3.2!

He was accompanied today by my sister Karen who is down from Canada for a few days.

Doctors are happy with results but concerned with the toll it's taking on him. It was suggested that he skip a session to which Kev replied with a resounding NO!

Kev's skin continues to show incredible irritation. However he is determined to see the treatment through to the end which by the way is only two more chemos!

Thanks for checking in here and remember to count your blessings.

Love Kim

March 22, 2013 9:18 pm

Sticks in a bundle are unbreakable. ~ Kenyan Proverb

I've always wanted to go to Africa, but perhaps, at least for now, this is the closest I'll get - a Kenyan quote that I think speaks volumes.

Today Kevin received his seventh treatment, at the end of the week that was home to St. Patrick's Day and the week of the first lacrosse game of the season. Luck is in the air. Maybe, just maybe it's this exact treatment that is kicking the final cancer cells out of Kevin for good and forever.

Kevin's CEA went from 3.2 to 2.8, which shows the chemo is still doing the trick. Believe me when I say that it is a true attitude changer. It truly makes our two weeks, before the next treatment feel hopeful and lighter.

Skin issues are still part of the daily battle, with Kevin taking antibiotics and steroid creams to help control the acne and rashes that make a home for themselves on his face, back, and chest. His skin is so dry that we are going through lotion like nobody's business. Stomach issues are back and with a greater vengeance, causing Kevy to have to bow out of life for large parts of days.

One newer side effect that Kevin is dealing with is anxiety and panic attacks. They are apparently "normal", although I don't think there is anything normal about cancer. There have been at least 4 times over the past two weeks where they have got the better of him. He is being given some meds to help, and our hope is that after all this is over, he will be free of these truly immobilizing spells.

The reason for the quote is because I have to give credit to where credit is due. Many people have recently been asking me if I am doing better, because I appear to be happier, smilier, and engaging in more creative works than I have in the past two and a half years. And the answer is a resounding Yes!

While I have been doing some self help work, making me a better caregiver and all around nicer person to be around, I have had resounding support from co-workers at Brookdale Elementary School. The staff held a fundraiser for us last month and presented me with a card and a monetary gift that was very generous, and very welcome. They had administrators offer teachers an opportunity to buy "time" out of their classes, meaning that if a teacher wanted 25 minutes to catch up on paperwork, plan, grab a snack and check email, they could have an administrator come and cover the class for that time. This was only one way that they found to raise money for us.

On top of my coworkers, we have been lucky to have had families from Brookdale, and Marmion join together and keep us covered for dinners, work lunches for me, and fruits and veggies, water and V8 and Gatorade for us all. They have also been sending care packages to Troy who is away at school in Iowa.

Troy is doing well at school, and will be a Resident Advisor next year. Liam is excelling in his Jr. year at Marmion, and is gearing up to play Varsity lacrosse for the second year. They practice every night M-F for an hour and a half, and have a couple games this upcoming week. Kevin is pumped about lacrosse which has always been the carrot that he looks for through the various treatments he has received.

While he missed practice tonight, and who could blame him, he is resting up to lead his team tomorrow in their first game. He may have to sit through part of the game, but I know that only after the game has finished will he let himself feel the fatigue and stomach cramps that are part of his everyday world. Lacrosse is truly the best medicine for him.

Having our family as one stick in the bundle surrounded by many, many more is making us all stronger. I'd like to say we are even more than that....we as a whole are a force to be reckoned.

So, time for jammies and to tuck Kevin in for a good sleep. May you all have a great night and God Bless.

Love, Kim

April 6, 2013 10:05 pm

Kevin is finished with his chemotherapy!

The blood work shows that his CEA remained at 2.8, the same from two weeks ago. Good news as it didn't go up.

We will wait to hear from the hospital early next week as to when his pet scan will be scheduled. We will be meeting with Dr. Hantel on April 19 to talk about the results from the scan. Have no idea what to expect, but hopeful that there will be a reprieve from doing anything.

Thank you for your continued support of our family both with prayers, acts of kindness, food, cards, but especially for checking in here to see how things are going. Kev looks so forward to reading the notes left.

He is such a trouper. The acne and rash are bothersome, his hair has thinned, and stomach cramps pop up, but through all of this, as well as battling fatigue, I can tell you that Kevin is an incredible role model to his sons, his friends, me, and to all his players - he has never given up. Ever.

Enjoy the rest of your week, and remember to compliment a loved one, pay for the person behind you at Dunkin Donuts drive-through, and to know that everyone is carrying a heavy burden.

Love and God Bless,

Kim

April 10, 2013 12:53 pm

Kevin is scheduled for a PET scan on April 16 and we have a follow up appointment with Dr. Hantel on April 19 to discuss the results and the plans for the future. That is when we will learn what procedures or treatments will have to happen, if any.

Our gut feeling is that there will be some sort of maintenance plan put in place, which could likely include taking meds indefinitely. We will let you know when we find out.

I have to tell you that through this journey, there are numerous trips to the pharmacy to pick up prescriptions for Kevin to help with pain, nausea, reactions to drugs, you name it. This one instance brought some confusion with the prescription amount, so I was stalled slightly at the counter.

As I was watching the pharmacist working to correct the problem, it hit me that he (Anthony the pharmacist) knows Kevin by name, but doesn't know him. That thought hit me like a punch to the gut and I got upset.

With thousands and thousands of people that come into our lives for the brief time we are here on earth, only a handful get to know the real us. I was sad to think that there are people who will never know Kevin beyond recognizing his face, name or connection to someone.

Many will never know how much Kevin fights for the underdog in all realms of life. How he loved being a young uncle to Tiffany, coaching her t-ball team while he was a teen. He enjoyed being the uncle to Courtney who showed up with chocolate bars in his back pockets, pretending not to know they were there, and having her find them. He dressed up as Santa for my niece Cara's preschool celebration when she was 3-ish. And how cute he looked when he dressed up as Barney the purple dinosaur for Courtney, wearing black dress socks underneath.

How many won't know that Kevin asked my step-father for permission to marry me; would take me to visit my Babcia; play racquetball with my dad; introduce me to Woodland Beach; mini golf at BenMar and have a frolic or two in Glenhurst Gardens! He also made my childhood complete by taking me to Disney World in our first year of marriage.

Kevin's heart is bigger and softer than any other. When he took the job down here in Chicago and had to be here for 8 months without me and the boys, he found he had a lot of free time on his hands. His evenings and weekends were empty, and he was offered an opportunity to do some painting at his boss' house making a cement floor look like the Chicago Blackhawks home ice. It didn't take long for Rich's sons to go running past their dad to hug Kevin when they walked through the door.

Kevin is a team player and very very loyal. He doesn't take his commitments lightly, and he has an incredible ability to build and maintain relationships with elementary school friends to this day. He has remained friends with people from high school, university, summer jobs, and co-workers from his first job after he graduated. But by far, I think what really says a lot about Kevin is his ability to have developed friendships on a deeper level with clients from throughout his 25 plus year career. That Anthony the pharmacist doesn't know how many young men Kev has coached and who have told him how grateful they are to have had him as their coach and mentor, is a loss for him (the pharmacist). And how many days over the last 2 and a half years that Kevin has been in pain, nauseous, fatigued and desperately overwhelmed emotionally, but has met each day and everyone in his days with a smile or kind gesture. I'm so grateful that Troy and Liam have such a wonderful role model to look up to. You all know now. It's time I let Anthony in on it too.

April 19, 2013 3:43 pm

Cancer is a word, not a sentence. ~ John Diamond

We met with Dr. Hantel this morning at Edward Cancer Center and got to review the Pet scan........

NO SIGNS OF CANCER..NO LIT UP AREAS...NADA

Yell, scream, cheer, cry. That's what we did and that was only in the first minute!

After we came down off the ceiling, we got down to brass tacks. Kevin will be on a maintenance program for the next three months. This means that he will be receiving IV chemo every two weeks as he has been, but only Erbitux, not the other chemo drug as well.

Erbitux is the drug that causes the skin rashes, drying and acne, but that is all. The nausea, stomach issues, and fatigue should be a thing of the past. Kevy's hair should come back full and beautiful as it was before.

After three months, another Pet scan will be given, and the results will hopefully be the same. At that point, a determination will be made as to whether we are done with chemo, or if we will do it for another three months.

So, suffice it to say, we are grateful to God, modern medicine and of course all of you who have stood with us from day one. It's a lot of standing:

974 days
or
139 weeks
or
23,352 hours
or
1,401,120 minutes
or
24,705 visits from you on CaringBridge

So wonderful, gracious warriors, rest your weary feet and give yourselves a hug from me and Kevy. God Bless, and keep checking in here as I will post if we have any news, or if anything incredible is going on. Our heartfelt love to all. Kim, Kevin, Troy and Liam

April 24, 2013 4:14 pm

So how would you celebrate hearing cancer free?

Probably a lot differently than Kev.

Friday he received his first maintenance treatment and went home smiling because of the results. Good night Friday.

Saturday was the start of a two day lacrosse tournament that had Kev coaching the boys to 3 wins and 0 losses! Yeah. Went home that night not feeling great.

Sunday, after a sleepless night Kev got up and went to coach the second day. He lasted the first game and came home heading for the bathroom, followed by bed... alternating between both ever since.

We did have to renew our green cards on Tuesday, thankfully in Naperville. It was a set appt. and if we didn't show, they would consider our request null and void. We went but Kev was so ill he ended up lying down on the floor in the waiting room. He couldn't care less how many people were there.

Fevers, vomiting and ghastly BMs have been nonstop. We contacted the cancer center to inquire if it could be from the treatment on Friday. They went ahead and prescribed antibiotics and wanted a record kept of his temperature every hour.

Finally today, they told him to come in to the hospital. So they did blood work and hooked him up to an IV to bring him back from

233

dehydration. They are giving him potassium and anti nausea drugs too. Will be here a while longer. Still has the fever that we thought was gone, but, hopefully, it will be gone soon.

Thinking my idea of dancing and dinner was a better way to celebrate!

Thanks for checking in and prayers.

April 25, 2013 2:56 pm

Antibiotics are starting to do their job, and Kev is feeling better. No fever, and the vomiting has finally subsided. Other side affects still hanging around, but the stomach pain is under control.

Prayers were answered it seems, and for that we are grateful.

Now back to the business of living!

Love Kim

May 6, 2013 2:15 pm

Any fool can criticize, condemn, and complain but it takes character and self control to be understanding and forgiving.

~ Dale Carnegie

As we get closer to the three year mark of Kevin's diagnosis of colon cancer, I have been reflecting. Kevin and I are at a crossroad and the uncertainty and unknown are even more forefront in our minds.

Kevin received his second maintenance chemotherapy treatment on Friday, and spent the weekend essentially sleeping. Of course that is what his body needs, not to mention his mind.

I notice at times that we are all unsure of our role as we move forward. This applies to Kevin as well. When we use the term maintenance, it presents the idea that all is well, nothing more is wrong, life should be getting back to normal, if not yet, maybe tomorrow. Labels begin to slip, and "Kevin the patient" is now being labeled more often without "the patient". While that is, of course, what we are after, everyone, especially Kevin, has to remember that chemotherapy is chemotherapy no matter how it's labeled.

He is still receiving poison through the port that was inserted into his chest almost three years ago. It's not a quick injection like a vaccination. No. It has to be given intravenously and over a designated amount of time. It cannot be rushed, cut in half, or mixed with the other IV meds he is given. One med is given at a time and the pattern and time frame have to be followed.

It would be wonderful if cancer would just give up and go away permanently, without having to be monitored and forefront in our minds. As Kevin begins to recover from his three year ordeal, our expressions of joy and elation have to be tempered with the inconvenience of appointments, and the possibility of feeling crappy for a few days or more.

We all want Kevy to be healed and healthy and able to carry all the loads that he had before. But nothing will ever be the same. Especially Kevin. He will have gained much, but he will have to let go of others. As he learns his new way of "living", we have to take our cues from him and put expectations of him off to the side and wait until he tells us he is ready to take them back and strong enough to carry them.

Our take away from this has to be to make sure our understanding and ability to forgive are in tune. He is going to forget things that he would have no problem remembering before. He is going to drop something because of the loss of feeling in his hands. His ability to accomplish some physical things will be tested because of years of chemical abuse on his body which has not only killed off the cancer cells, but healthy cells as well.

So while Kevin may not look like a "patient", those around him who love him and care for him now have to wear the mantle of "patience" as he slowly resumes his former self. Hopefully this time for good. Love and best wishes for a great day!

May 18, 2013 2:40 pm

What a great start to the weekend! Kev had his treatment yesterday and aside from his magnesium levels being low, his numbers were great.

We had been told that the chemo drug that he is no longer taking would still be affecting his results for a few cycles. Its nickname for us was rhino, can't figure out the real name at the moment. So the CEA number this time would be a reflection of the drug erbitux alone.

Looks like it likes Kevy as his number went from 2.8 to 2.1! Again logically we know all numbers under five are essentially the same, but emotionally it puts us in a good place.

After we got home, Kev napped for an hour and ever the coach, got up and went to coach his team! It was a tough loss, but the boys played with so much passion, thanks to their role model.

So if everything goes well, Kev will have his first vacation at home in three years. He can't wait to get to the cottage!

Thanks for the prayers and good thoughts. Enjoy the weekend.

June 1, 2013 6:50 am

Things are going great! Kevin had his treatment yesterday and found his number at 2.0, down from 2.1.

He had relatively minimal discomfort from the chemo, and was able to get by with just a short nap last night. He is sleeping soundly right now and I'm so grateful.

Today is our 22nd Anniversary and I'm so blessed to be married to my best friend, a man who makes it his mission to make those around him smile, laugh and be glad they know him. He is an amazing person and I'm very proud to be his wife.

We meet with Dr. Hantel in two weeks, and perhaps we will have an update on what will be happening next for him.

I do, in the meantime, need all of you to add Anne my sister in law to your prayer list. She has found out someone near to her has been given a very dire diagnosis of cancer. Anne, as you will recall is married to Brian, Kevin's brother and has been a warrior of this disease for almost 3 years. She has been there for not only her husband when he was diagnosed, but for Kevy and our family from the first moment. I love Anne so much and am hurting for her. I know that prayers will help to comfort her as she steels herself to once again do battle for her loved one.

Thank you for your prayers for Anne.

Love, Kim

We were at the Cancer Center today for Kev's treatment, the fifth of six. While we were in the waiting room, a couple sat down across from us and appeared to be pretty young - maybe late 30s. The wife was the patient and her husband was there to support her. It reminded me so much of the first time we were in the waiting room almost 3 years ago. I could tell by their faces that they were probably thinking a lot of the same things we did. That they were too young to be there. Is this a bad nightmare that we are going to wake from? Can we just turn around and run?

I so much wanted to say something to them, but what? For whatever reason, primarily trying to respect their privacy, I didn't reach out with words, only a smile. But, if I could have mustered the courage this is what I would have said.

You have every right to be afraid. It is scary to sit there looking at the other patients and loved ones who occupy so many chairs. You will have a tough battle on your hands... BUT... you are in the best place for your cancer treatments. You will meet incredible nurses and doctors, and you will begin your journey of healing. You are not alone. We will pray for you.

July 7, 2013 7:35 pm

I didn't realize that it has been a while since I posted something. What that tells me is that we have been living life! Imagine that. Kevy has been out to golf a few times, and is getting better with every round. What is kind of interesting though, is that Kevy told me the other day that he is feeling good, but is feeling guilty about feeling good. I guess having been a cancer patient for three years will do that to you.

Kevin had his sixth maintenance chemo June 28th but no blood work or meeting with the doctor. We meet with Dr. Hantel on July 12 for a blood draw, hoping of course that the numbers have remained below 5. We will also be discussing our next course of action. As of right now, we will be holding off on having a scan until sometime in August. I think their reasoning is to allow the body some time to acclimate to being free of any chemotherapy drug. I suppose that way, if something is still lurking in there, it will make its appearance more definite and obvious.

So as not to get ahead of ourselves, we are super uber excited about having a family vacation for the first time in three years! Liam and I will be heading home next weekend, and Kevin and Troy will be flying up to join us a week later. A week at the cottage on Georgian Bay is just what the doctor ordered! We are going to be swimming and walking and talking and playing games and swimming some more and having naps on the beach! We can't wait.

As is very obvious to all who have followed this, we don't know what the future holds. Therefore we have to enjoy and take advantage of the time we do have together. Even if it's raining all week it's going to be great. Kevin is surviving cancer. He is living. We are living. And we are loving it!

Please remember: If you have a family history of colon cancer; are 50 yrs old; have symptoms such as bleeding, change in bowel movements, unexplained weight loss, abdominal pain; or are in the age range and have been afraid to go for a colonoscopy....please book yourself for one. Find out what, if anything, is up your butt! It can save a life. It can save YOUR life.

And when you get in there for the exam, tell them Kevy sent you.

August 13, 2013 9:23 pm

We enjoyed our time in Canada - going home is always a time of laughs, love and fun. It was great to see family and our friends Steve and Julie surprised Kev with a party full of good friends, some of whom we haven't seen for years.

Kevin had blood work done on Friday, and we found out yesterday that his numbers have risen to 7.4

Dr. Hantel has ordered Kevin to have a Pet-Scan before the end of August. It will once again be our road map of where to find this disease that will not let go.

Kevin did not want to talk last night, so we had a quiet evening, just the two of us as Troy has gone back to school, and Liam was away with his friend Jake and his family in the Wisconsin Dells.

Tonight Kev is feeling very defeated, and sad. I'm taking a different stance - at least today. I'm feeling ready, willing and able to fight until this leaves us alone for good. Now tomorrow may be a different story, but all we can do is live one day at a time. And while we do that, we will once again ask for your prayers to surround Kevin and the doctors working hard to eradicate the cancer.

The boys have been told, and it's incredibly hard for Troy being so far away from home. I know if he could, he would be here right now. But the best thing and the one way to help Kevin is to keep on keeping on. Liam is taking it in stride and has gone to a friend's house for the night.

So Kev and I have the place to ourselves, and quite honestly, sometimes the quiet is truly deafening. We will use the time for quiet reflection, prayers and refocusing ourselves to the fight at hand. Thanks for checking in, and if you haven't heard it enough, we truly couldn't put one foot in front of the other without your support.

Love and peace, Kim

August 27, 2013 8:28 pm

We met with Dr. Hantel today, and while we don't have the complete puzzle figured out, we have been able to put some of the pieces in place.

Dr. Hantel is encouraged to see that the areas that lit up are the same ones that lit up in December. So, to him, it hasn't spread.

He will be presenting Kevin's case in front of a board of specialists at Edward Hospital tomorrow morning. Here they will have numerous specialists from all aspects of care who will evaluate the scan and blood work, and help to come to a conclusion and blue print for a plan of action.

The good news is that the lymph node that is involved has been reviewed on the scan by the radiologist who has said that he WILL be able to use radiation on the spot. We are truly thankful for that because surgery specific to this location is out of the question, and chemo doesn't seem to be enough.

So we will wait until sometime tomorrow to hear from Dr. Hantel to find out exactly what steps will be happening first. Of course we don't want to be singing this tune again, but if we have to, we like seeing the good doctor being so upbeat.

If you are finding yourself getting a little short with the sales clerk, or trying to rush past an elderly person who might not be walking as fast as you would like, or are complaining that you have had an absolutely miserable day, try and remember one thing. Life is precious, and the small stuff is so not worth getting upset. Kevin is facing his cancer for at least the fifth time, and while it is weighing heavily on him, his sole focus is on getting better for himself, his family, friends and coworkers. He will be facing some pretty crappy days and weeks ahead, but you would not know it by looking at him. He is incredible. He is my hero.

I'll let you know what we find out tomorrow.

August 31, 2013 10:05 am

Kevin spoke with Dr. Hantel yesterday and finally Dr. Shoup had an opportunity to view the scan. After viewing the scan, everyone agrees that radiation will be the first attack. It will be used on the lymph node only. Dr. Hantel also wants Kevin to take Xeloda, an oral chemo that he has used before when he was on radiation.

Dr. Shoup wants to a more thorough and specific scan on the liver and lower lungs after radiation. It is her opinion that there is a minute spot on the lower lung, although at this point Dr. Hantel is not in complete agreement.

Kevy did blood work on Tuesday before our appt. with the Dr. and the CEA came back at 19.1. So after finding out all the latest info, there has been a transformation in how Kevin is feeling. He is usually truly hopeful and resilient. Usually. But, I have to say that he is feeling quite defeated.

My friend Jean brought a song "I Won't Let Go" by Rascal Flatts to my attention some time ago, and it is exactly what is our life. If you can listen to it, even better.

Please pray and pray for serenity for Kevin, for a sense of safety for the boys, and for strength for me to do the only thing I can for Kevin - Love him totally and completely and forever...

September 3, 2013 9:26 pm

We now have a game plan to start the ball rolling. Kevin met with the radiation oncologist this morning, and had a cast and CT scan done this afternoon. He has been told he will receive 28 treatments, beginning on Monday. He will go Monday to Friday, and on those days of radiation, he will take eight pills of oral chemo called Xeloda.

Kevin can look forward to a greater likelihood of nausea and vomiting because the location is higher up in the abdomen, and therefore may not be hammered down with diarrhea as well. He will take a medication, zofran for the nausea but of course it causes really bad headaches.

I'm so angry today, and so is Kevin. We are both just looking to pick a fight with anyone who crosses our path. We know that the anger is misplaced if we take it out on anyone, including each other. We are angry at the cancer; the stupid, dumb, gross, ugly, unwanted cancer.

At the same time of being angry, I'm totally saddened and crushed. I want to crawl into bed and cry and cry and cry. But that's not going to do anything. So, instead, I will laugh at Liam's jokes, rub Kevy's feet, and read a book. Maybe when the lights are off, I'll shed a tear or two. Or three…

September 16, 2013 7:13 pm

Kevin has started his radiation and oral chemo. Actually he is 6 down, 22 to go. Fatigue is hitting hard as is nausea. He is taking his zofran to help with the nausea.

His strength and determination are admirable. I am in awe of him as he faces this thing yet again. I'm having some difficulty with this round, feeling down and overwhelmed. But the great thing about our partnership is that we are rarely both down at the same time.

When he is done the radiation we'll reconvene with Dr. Hantel and see what's next.

Until then, hold your loved ones close and pray for serenity and peace.

Love, Kim

October 2, 2013 1:28 pm

Typically I so look forward to this time of the year. It is officially fall, the leaves are turning to beautiful shades of gold and orange and red. The temperatures are usually lower, having you in need of grabbing a comforter or sweater for the evenings. Apples and apple pie. Pumpkins and pumpkin pie!

Sadly, this year the season brings with it sadness and a sense of dread. We have sadly been informed that a parent of one of our past varsity lacrosse players passed away on the weekend after a valiant fight, first against cancer and finally infection. Kevin coached his son for three years and we have been buoyed by the family since Kevin's diagnosis. Our hearts are truly saddened.

Kevin's Aunt Sue from Ottawa, who is an oncologist and has been our 2nd opinion with respect to Kevin's treatments was also diagnosed with lung cancer and has just undergone surgery. She is resting and recovering well.

Kevin is right in the middle of his long stretch of radiation. He has completed 18 of his 28 treatments and the culmination of the treatments and the oral chemo that he has been receiving is taking its toll on him. Rarely do I get to spend much of the evening with him. He is so fatigued and nauseous that it takes everything for him to enjoy even an hour or two of the evening.

We are also gearing up for the next phase of Kev's treatment. We think it will involve blood work, scans and then ultimately a decision on the next form of treatment.

As they say, when it rains, it pours, and I truly feel like I'm drowning. Worries from all facets of our life seem to be culminating in the perfect storm. If only Calgon could take me away...

Your prayers are appreciated, as is all of your support. While I know this will pass, I truly can't see the forest for the trees.

Love Kim

October 8, 2013 9:05 pm

What a whirlwind the past few weeks have been for Kevin and his trips to the radiation department of the Cancer Center. First of all, it continues to knock the heck out of him, making him want to nap for a couple of hours. It does take a lot for him to get through the days, but he is doing it.

Then one morning last week, he shows up for his treatment, and much to his surprise, he comes face to face with....wait for it.....THE Stanley Cup! It seems that a patient of the cancer center had close ties to the Black Hawks and was given the opportunity to have the cup delivered to his home for him to see it. Instead, the selfless man decided to have it delivered to the cancer center so that all the patients facing their own high stakes game could enjoy the win!

What an incredible thing to do. It made so many people happy that day, many of whom don't have many things to smile about. As you can see from the picture, Kevin sure did smile. Kevy was so excited to show the boys, and you can guess how they reacted. They were ecstatic! A true piece of history that will forever bond the three of them together.

On the down side, Kevin had blood work done last week, and was having incredible "pinching" in his left arm, the side where his port is implanted. The doctor immediately ordered an ultrasound of his arm to make sure there weren't any blood clots. Turns out that the port has moved since it was implanted three years ago, and is partially behind the clavicle bone. The position is causing inflammation and would explain why he is getting pain. For now, they are leaving it as is, but if it gets worse, they may have to do something for him.

Also, the blood work showed a CEA marker the highest we have ever seen - 73. The doctor is not sure what to make of it, saying we have to allow for the disruption that the radiation is causing, essentially having dead tumor cells rocketed through the blood stream. CEA also marks for irritation, and, lord knows, there is a lot of that happening.

So for now we continue on the path of completing the radiation, and of Kevin resting when he can. But no matter what comes Kevin's way, he is an inspiration to so many, me especially, and no question, hands down is the winner of the Conn Smythe trophy in our eyes.

A silver lining to a rather yucky looking cloud.

October 15, 2013 5:33 pm

Today Kevin met with Dr. Hantel after he finished his second to last radiation treatment. Tomorrow he is done with radiation! Yeah!

I was at work, but they put me on speaker phone so I could hear the Dr. talking about what's going to happen next. He ordered blood work for Kevin to do this morning and he booked a CT scan for him for October 28, 2013.

After the scan is done, and it was determined that the CT scan is the better choice, as it apparently gives a clearer picture of the sites in question, Kevin and I will be meeting with Dr. Shoup. We will be discussing what surgical procedure will be used to get a handle on the cancer that continues to avoid complete eradication. Knowing Dr. Shoup and Kevin, I think they will book his surgery rather quickly, probably before the end of November.

Kevin's CEA numbers just came back and they are at 72.4, a mere smudge down from last weeks. Dr. Hantel isn't saying much about the number, wanting to have the scan to refer to before he makes any decisions. He did, however, talk about chemotherapy (IV type) as still an option.

So, Kevin is stressed about what is to come, because he knows what to expect. The surgery will most likely be the rather invasive type, even if they use ablation because of the position of the spots. However, I am jumping ahead of myself as we truly have no idea precisely what is going to happen. It's like trying to find a street by looking at the globe.

I am putting this request out now, as my ability to have time off of work is considerably more difficult this year because of my new position.

IF Kevy has surgery, and IF it is the rather invasive kind, I would be looking for help with Kevin once he returns home. It would probably be over lunch time. If I remember correctly from last time, I was able to get him up and medicated and fed breakfast, then we had some coverage at lunch time, and finally Liam would arrive home mid afternoon.

But again I'm getting ahead of myself. For now, let's pray that the options we have available will make a difference.

Love Kim

October 20, 2013 9:44 pm

Love is a symbol of eternity. It wipes out all sense of time, destroying all memory of a beginning and all fear of an end. ~Author Unknown

Kevy, we have been part of each other for so long now. I know you as well as you know yourself. You know me better than I know myself. You have a way of being one step ahead of me, in knowing what I want, need or desire.

What has caused this weekend to be a difficult time? I have been in desperate need of your voice, your smiles, your tender embrace. I want to be close to you, but I want to be alone. I watch you from across the room with a smile on my face, and when you see me, my eyes fill with tears.

We are perfectly imperfect for each other. You see only beauty when you look at me, and I see only love when I look at you.

Your broad shoulders are still there, carrying the weight of the world on them. Yet you never complain. I complain. You don't.

You wipe my tears as they fall. You hold me when I sob. You never shudder. I do. You don't.

This waiting game we are playing seems to be going on forever. It gives me time to worry, be fearful, and to pray. It gives me time to miss "before cancer". It gives me time to miss "normal". Time is marching on so slowly and so fast. I want to get to the scan and the results and the next steps, but I don't want to lose the time. I want as much time with you as I can.

Could we make time stand still? Make the noise drift away? Could we go back to you and me? To you?

I love you to the woods and back. Always and forever. Shoes.

October 24, 2013 9:27 pm

If God had wanted me otherwise, He would have created me otherwise.

~Johann von Goethe

Never let it be said that Kevin keeps who he is a secret.

CaringBridge became part of our life over three years ago, and it has been a true godsend. It has allowed us to keep family and friends, coworkers and clients informed of Kevin's progress and at the same time, allowed Kevin and our family to feel the love of said family, friends, coworkers and clients.

As I looked over the messages that have been left it is amazing what kind of picture evolves. You see, there are Kevin's family members who have known and loved Kevin longer than anyone else on this earth. They encourage him with their love, their prayers, their thoughtful words of encouragement.

His extended family has not known him as long, but has sustained Kevin with their love, their prayers, their thoughtful words of encouragement.

Kevy's friends mean a great deal to him. He has heard from friends from elementary school, high school and university. He has also repeatedly heard from friends he has made through lacrosse and at work. They have once again encouraged him with their love, their prayers, their thoughtful words of encouragement.

Kevin has been a very loyal employee since beginning his career way back in 1988. He is dedicated to his job and coworkers. He has been with his most recent employer Reebie Storage and Moving for over 14 years. I think it's safe to say that he has developed some strong friendships there, and perhaps some "family" relationships as well. No surprise that they have all encouraged him with their love, their prayers and their thoughtful words of encouragement.

Finally there are the business associates that Kevin has befriended over his 25 years of working. I look among the messages and see some from clients he had when he first started in the business back in Toronto. There are clients from Brantford, Kitchener, the whole greater Southern Ontario area. He has befriended clients here in Chicago and throughout the United States and around the world. From Africa to Thailand, England to British Columbia. They have encouraged him with their outreaching of love, prayers, and thoughtful words of encouragement.

So, God created Kevin as he is: a loyal, funny, loving, caring, devoted, educated, dedicated, determined, fighter of the underdog, passionate, compassionate man who has touched so many lives. Family. Friends. Coworkers. Clients. ALL OF YOU have been impacted by Kevin and he by ALL OF YOU.

This is a very difficult time for Kevin right now as we gear up to his scan on Monday and results and discussion with the surgeon on Tuesday.

PLEASE RALLY KEVIN WITH A MESSAGE OF HOW YOU MET, AND WHAT YOU THINK OF WHEN YOU HEAR HIS NAME.

He needs you all. Right now.

October 29, 2013 8:15 pm

Kevin had his CT scan yesterday.

2 spots in liver have increased in size.

Lymph node that was bathed in radiation for 28 treatments has shrunk in size, but it is too early to tell if it is completely irradiated.

Earlier today we had scheduled Kevin for liver resection for Friday, November 8, 2013 after meeting with the surgeon, Dr. Shoup.

Kevin did all the pre-op stuff: EKG, blood work, 3-phase CT scan of Kevin's liver. We were given the presentation on the hospital, as it will be the first time for Kevin to have surgery there.

Came home, had late lunch. Rested.

Phone call from Dr. Hantel about 3/4 of an hour ago.

2 spots in his lower left lung that were seen (barely) at the last scan, have grown exponentially to about 1 cm in size for each.

Therefore:

Colon - lymph nodes - liver - lymph nodes - lung.

We are now, as per Dr. Hantel, moving forward with the scheduled liver resection, but he will be talking with Dr. Shoup the surgeon and Dr. Das Gupta, the Radiation Oncologist and within the next 24 hours we will figure out if there will be a change in our plotted path.

What an absolutely crappy, horrific, sad, grief filled day. Please pray to thank God for all that he has given you. Thank him for our beautiful friendships, and memories.

And let's all rush heaven with the most profound and powerful prayers for Kevin that we can. Please.

November 3, 2013 8:29 pm

There is a sacredness in tears. They are not the mark of weakness, but of power. They speak more eloquently than ten thousand tongues. They are messengers of overwhelming grief...and unspeakable love.

~ Washington Irving

Five
Five more sleeps until Kevin faces his liver resection surgery. Using sleeps is what we used to do when the boys were little and we were counting down to something exciting, like a birthday, Christmas, trip to Disney World. I suppose in a weird and twisted way, we are also counting to something exciting....another chance at eradicating cancer from Kevin's liver which will make him stronger and better able to get through the probable lung surgery that will quite likely follow in quick succession.

Four
Four people who make up our immediate little family. Kevin, Kim, Troy, Liam. The bond that holds us together is stronger than anything man made or naturally formed. We are united together forever. Period. I love us so much and when one of us is down for the count, the other three are right there with them.

Three
Three times for liver resection is crazy. I remember asking the surgeon at one of our first meetings how many times you could do a liver resection. She answered she had done 5 on one patient. Her resident who was doing rounds with her told me not to jinx myself by asking. Jinx. Buy me a coke. (SNL reference here).

Two

Two is the number of times that Kevin and my path crossed before realizing that what we had was meant to be forever. When I think of it literally, it makes me picture a beautiful path with flowers and willow trees hanging down while the sun peaks out from behind a small cloud. Butterflies and birds fly through the blue background and I am walking toward the man that I love more than anything. The smile that Kevin has on his face while waiting at the end of the path, is only bettered by the smile that breaks out on my face.

One

One life is all we are given. We can make it the most beautiful experience, or waste it away on viewing such things as cancer as something that controls us. We get one shot at looking at the glass for the first time and seeing it half full, not half empty. One chance to make a good first impression. One time to have that first kiss.

Treat others as you want to be treated. Look for the good in all. Never go to bed angry. And never forget to count yourselves among our truest and purest signs of love. We need your love. We need your prayers. We need you. And hopefully, you need us too.

Kim Griffin

November 8, 2013 1:31 pm

Surgery just underway. Will give updates as able.

November 8, 2013 5:13 pm

No resection. Ablation on three spots in liver. Third one was found using internal ultrasound. He was stable throughout, and did not require any blood.

Dr. says Kev's liver is looking rough which she would expect with all the chemos and surgeries he has had. Wants him back in a few weeks to do cauterizing of the blood supply to the areas where the tumors were.

She said she is throwing everything at him to keep him around. She would not speak about the spots in the lung but did say she does not like the path his disease is taking.

Waiting to see him in ICU.

November 8, 2013 11:16 pm

Kev finally got to his ICU room around 7:15 pm tonight. He looked great. Good color, all vitals were good and he was not as agitated as last time coming out of the anesthesia.

He has tubes everywhere! Both arms, his nose, his neck, not to mention the catheter. His legs are wrapped in cuffs that keep his blood circulating. And hospital issued bright yellow socks!

I stayed until 8:30-ish and came home.

Thanks to Liam, Randy and Renee for staying with me today. You are troopers every step of the way. A great surprise was meeting up with Sally at the hospital. A super lady whose husband works with Kevin, they have become friends! Awesome people in my life.

A great ending to the day was pulling into the driveway to be met by another dear friend Sharon and her daughter Abby with hot chocolates and chocolate croissants.

But the best was calling the hospital for an update on Kev and his nurse being able to hand the phone to Kevy so we could say I love you and goodnight.

After a very stressful day, a smile has crossed my face. And it feels right.

Thank you for your prayers and good thoughts. We truly feel the love!

November 11, 2013 1.48 pm

Discharged.

Long drive home.

Tucked in bed with a glass of icy clamato juice.

Snuggling.

Resting for now.

Appointments to book and meds to pick up.

Happy.

November 13, 2013 6:24 pm

Patient:

Able to accept or tolerate delays, problems, or suffering without becoming annoyed or anxious.

A person receiving or registered to receive medical treatment.

Kevin is only five days out of surgery and he is off pain meds, and sleeping for long stretches. He embodies a perfect patient. But of course he doesn't want to be a patient anymore. The definitions above show us how seemingly ridiculous it is to have such different explanations for a word. Yet, in a way, Kevin is both.

We met with Dr. Hantel today to do blood work. Kevin's labs came back and were looking really good. The numbers that needed to be up had in fact gone up, and the number that we wanted to go down, the CEA, has gone down to 39.7. While that is definitely lower than prior to surgery, we have been told that it is still too soon after surgery to be a completely accurate indication of what is happening inside.

We did talk about the spots in the lung, one 6 mm and the other 9 mm in size that are in his left lung. While Dr. Hantel did speak about the three options we have with respect to the lung spots, he emphasized again and again that the most important part of handling the disease that has enveloped Kevin is focusing on the liver and preventing it from occurring there again.

Dr. Shoup, the surgeon who has operated on Kevin three times, has scheduled an appointment for November 26 for removal of the stitches from his boomerang like incision and for a consultation with Dr. Stanley Kim who was the interventional radiologist who assisted with Kevin's liver surgery.

Dr. Kim will most likely be performing an embalization procedure designed to cut off the blood flow to the area of the liver that keeps housing the tumors. The thought is that this will starve any cells that are left behind and prevent them from becoming tumors. This will be confirmed at our meeting at the end of the month.

The weight of this disease is crushing. It crushes dreams, hopes, thoughts of normalcy, and the ability to wake up and not immediately go to that dark place in your mind. It certainly feels that way when you have all the pieces (or at least all that we know of) to the picture of where the disease is living.
That is when to me it becomes almost impossible to be patient. We have to wait to see how the liver heals. We have to make sure the lymph node continues to shrink. We have to wait for the next procedure. Wait. Wait. Wait. And all I think about is that we know it is in the lung right now because we can see it. What about the small cells that we can't see? What happens if we are patient and wait?

Lord, grant me patience....but hurry.

Sleep well. Kevy looks so comfortable right now, sleeping among his pillows and blankets with no sign of being a patient. But he will be. We will be. Patient.

November 15, 2013 9:39 am

Happy Birthday to the strongest man I know. You are a true inspiration to all who know you, and especially to those who love you. Keep fighting the fight as you look forward and enjoy this great gift you have been given... perseverance.

Love you!

November 28, 2013 11:22 pm

Kevin has been trying to heal from his surgery earlier this month, although I think he is doing a pretty crappy job with respect to taking time to rest. He wants to be back to "normal" and working and living normally, but that seems to be something just a little out of reach - at least for now.

Since the ablation surgery on the 8th, he has had very little true pain originating from the incision site. He is, however, experiencing incredible "referred pain" in his shoulder.

We met with Dr. Stanley Kim at the hospital on the 25th. He assisted Dr. Shoup on the surgery and is an interventional radiologist. It was he who told us about the referred pain and how when the diaphragm is irritated as Kevin's was during surgery, it sends pain signals to the brain. As the diaphragm has no nerves or pain receptors itself, the pain message is sent to the shoulder. Kevin is having a very difficult time with this pain. He is taking pain pills along with Aleve to help with the irritation and inflammation. So far, not much change. That is why it is so important that he rest - completely - so his diaphragm can heal completely.

Now back to Dr. Kim's appointment. He is very soft spoken and very highly recommended. He has said that he and Dr. Shoup agree that Kevin would be a good candidate for chemo embolization. One of the advantages is that it sends chemotherapy directly to the liver, full strength as opposed to the other chemo that becomes dissipated as it travels throughout the body. However, there will be side effects to this treatment as there has been for every chemo treatment. The side effects from the chemo embolization will be nausea, fatigue and some local pain.

The following information is from the American Cancer Society website:

Embolization is a procedure that injects substances to try to block or reduce the blood flow to cancer cells in the liver.

The liver is unusual in that it has 2 blood supplies. Most normal liver cells are fed by branches of the portal vein, whereas cancer cells in the liver are usually fed by branches of the hepatic artery. Blocking the branch of the hepatic artery feeding the tumor helps kill off the cancer cells, but it leaves most of the healthy liver cells unharmed because they get their blood supply from the portal vein.

Embolization is an option for some patients with tumors that cannot be removed by surgery. It can be used for tumors that are too large to be treated with ablation (usually larger than 5 cm across). It can also be used with ablation. Embolization does reduce some of the blood supply to the normal liver tissue, so it may not be a good option for some patients whose liver has been damaged by diseases such as hepatitis or cirrhosis.

Chemoembolization

This approach, also known as trans-arterial chemoembolization (or TACE) combines embolization with chemotherapy. Most often, this is done either by using tiny beads that give off a chemotherapy drug for the embolization. TACE can also be done by giving chemotherapy through the catheter directly into the artery, then plugging up the artery.

It was suggested that this is not to be considered a cure. Rather this is more of a maintenance treatment or an attempt to control the cancer. It will happen a minimum of 2 times, with a chance of 4. Each time it is done, they will do one lobe of the liver. Three weeks later Kevin will go back in for the next treatment, and they will do the opposite lobe. So he is looking at treatments over 12 weeks.

In the meantime, all doctors associated with Kevin i.e.) Hantel, Shoup and Kim are discussing how best to proceed with the lesions in the lung. While both are less than a cm in size, they will have to be addressed. The determining factor will be if they can wait the twelve weeks for the liver treatments, or do they want to do the lung treatment during this time. So, we will hopefully have a better idea of a time frame for everything early next week.

While we are slightly down trodden from this last appointment, we have unfortunately been touched by the loss of two people, one of a young woman in her early thirties, and another in a heartbreaking way. Please offer prayers for any and all who are hurting because of the loss of a loved one.

It puts things into perspective, and makes us realize that there continues to be hope and where there is hope, you are sure to find Kevin and his supporters. We will continue the good fight, giving it everything we have and continue to be in awe of the strength and perseverance Kevin has. He is amazing. And for that I am thankful.

Take the time NOW to show your loved ones how much they mean to you. Tell them. Tell them again. No one knows what is going to happen next so never leave any good thing unsaid or undone.

Love Kim

December 3, 2013 7:39 pm

This morning, Dr. Kim the Interventional Radiologist took Kevin's case to the "Tumor Board" at CDH to discuss his case and come to a decision on how to proceed with the embolizations and with the lesions in the lungs. For now the lung has been put on the back burner and we are moving ahead with the liver surgery.

The chemo embolization has been scheduled for Friday, December 6 at 9:00 am. We have to arrive at CDH for 7:00 am for them to get Kev ready for the procedure. After all that Kevin has been through, it is this surgery that he is dreading. The doctors have assured him that they will give him something for his anxiety. He is very grateful for that.

It takes about an hour and a half to complete, barring any unforeseen roadblocks. He will be staying overnight to be observed and to make sure his pain is under control. As mentioned before, depending on which side they are doing first, he will experience pain either in the center of his abdomen, or under his right ribs and around the back. Fatigue and nausea will be along for the ride too.

We have both been feeling out of control of this situation, although really who is ever in control of something like cancer? Is there too much lag time between treatments? Are the lung spots growing exponentially? Will this finally be the answer we have been waiting for?

The way we are looking at it, Kevin has never had this procedure done before, so perhaps this is the golden ticket. Maybe bathing the liver in chemotherapy and starving off the cancer cells will finally put an end to three years of absolute agony, pain and fear. Someone has to be the ones they write about in the medical journals right? The ones who overcome incredible obstacles? My vote is for Kevin to be the poster boy for beating the odds.

When you tuck in to bed tonight, make sure you have told at least one person what they mean to you. Never ever waste an opportunity to be heard. Love is the one thing we all need in order to thrive.

At this time of the year, we begin to reflect on the past 12 months and what we have seen, heard, achieved, learned and passed on. Kevin and I have seen endless acts of kindness, heard many I love yous, learned that patience must accompany all steps in this process and have hopefully been successful in passing along our deepest thanks and appreciation for all you have done for us. Our family is indebted to you all, and we will never forget.

You are in our prayers always.

December 6, 2013 5:47 pm

Well the procedure is over and after a rather difficult day, Kev is resting in his hospital room.

Dr. Kim delivered the chemo irinotecan directly to the liver. It was applied to the right lobe and caused incredible pain. Kev was rating his pain a 10 for quite a while, but after some trial and error they found the right combo for control and he is finally saying it's a five.

They said that 90% of the drug went to the right lobe and the remainder spilled into the left lobe. The doctor said that was good because one of the lesions was close to where the liver divides into each side. Dr. Kim said that they could do the next procedure as soon as two weeks from today.

Kevin doesn't want to come back... at all. Right now, his mind frame is, "Why do I want to go through this pain if it's not a 'for sure' cure?" While I know it was the drugs talking, he said he wanted to die. And he cried. This has been by far the hardest thing he has been through.

I'm going to go home now as Kevy has only been awake long enough to have a Popsicle. Hopefully after a good night sleep, we will both feel better about everything. Because honestly, right now I am completely overwhelmed with agony for the love of my life.

Everyone, love your loved ones and hold them tight.

I'm going to go home and cry... for a little while anyway.

Love Kim

December 9, 2013 10:04 pm

Today was perhaps the worst day that Kevin has ever endured during this very long 3 year battle.

He had his procedure done on Friday and spent the night as they were having a very difficult time controlling his pain. He came home Saturday afternoon and rested for the remainder of the weekend.

As I'm trying to be sensitive to my new job, and live up to my commitment at work, I went in today just before Liam left for school. That left Kevin alone with the dogs. Little did I know that it would be hell on earth for him.

Mya, our Newfoundland puppy became sick, and Kevin tried his best to clean up after her. It became almost impossible for him to do which is absolutely understandable. But perhaps more importantly, Kevin was fatigued, nauseous, feverish and in extreme pain, both physically and emotionally.

I think being alone, feeling as poorly as he did, gave him time to reflect on everything and begin to fear the worst. Lord knows he was feeling it that's for sure. The day was very long for him, and he couldn't wait for me to get home.

As I entered our bedroom, I could see Kevy sitting on the side of our bed sobbing uncontrollably. He was racked with so many feelings, and physical battles, that he was beyond exhausted. All I could do was hold him and wipe away his tears. He wouldn't let me go as he was so happy to have me home. Of course I cried along with him, but with his head buried in my neck, he couldn't see the tears. I held him forever, until he was able to take a breath.

He said he couldn't do it anymore. He didn't want to go on. He wanted to crawl into the covers. He wanted to stop. Everything.

Luckily our friend Randy came to take Mya to the Juriga's Veterinary Hospital (River Heights) to have her looked at, and to stay for a bit so she gets the care and attention she needs so Kevin can get the care and attention that he needs. Before he left, Randy stayed with Kevin for a while and let Kevin lean on him. It was a good release for Kevy.

Once they were on their way, Kev climbed back into bed, and right beside him climbed Liam. He threw the tv on and put the newest Family Guy *on. I went and heated up dinner from the Truty's and brought it upstairs so all three of us ate dinner in bed. We laughed at the show, and inside my heart grew 10 times larger, almost bursting because of the incredible pride I have for Liam. He is an incredible young man.*

I realized after I returned home that while my job is incredibly important and I hate putting anyone out, what is most important for me right now, in this exact time is for me to be here at home, with Kevin, loving him into wellness. I'm headed to bed, to cuddle with him, rub his back, bring him ginger ale when he asks, hold his hand and whisper to him that he made it through the day. One day at a time.

Sweet dreams to the most amazingly strong man I have had the honor of knowing. I love you Kevy.

December 19, 2013 9:47 pm

This past Tuesday, Kevin and I met with Dr. Hantel to discuss the overall handling of his ongoing treatments, specifically the tumors within the lung. We had a later appointment that same day with Dr. Stanley Kim, the Interventional Radiologist who is the one who is using the procedure of direct saturation of the liver with chemotherapy.

Dr. Hantel continues to put our minds at ease as he explains and questions everything that is suggested for Kevin. He told us that he wasn't convinced that Kevin needed four treatments on his liver and that he would be discussing it with Shoup and Kim to have them justify the reasoning.

He also went on to tell us that he is surmising that Kevin will receive Stereotactic Body Radiation Therapy on the tumors in his lung. It has also been referred to as CyberKnife and Gamma Knife. The process uses multiple narrow radiation beams that target small, well-defined areas with precision. It gives high doses of radiation safely and accurately over just a few treatments (usually one to five sessions overall). Kevin will first have to undergo a scan to confirm that the spots are attainable.

We then went to meet with Dr. Kim. We discussed in great detail that we needed to have a better plan in place to handle Kevin's pain. Dr. Kim has assured us that while it will still be painful, he is going to start Kevin on pain medication in the operating room before he is alert enough to use the pump to receive more pain meds. They are also going to look at having Kevin sedated longer in the twilight zone if you will so that he has less recall of the pain. Unfortunately, Dr. Kim did reiterate that the chemo being used is a very painful one, and there will not be an ability to prevent it from happening.

Kevin is going in tomorrow for his treatment at CDH. He has to be there for 7:00 am, with his treatment scheduled for noon. It should be about an hour and a half, recovery for about 2 - 3 hours, and then he will definitely be moved into a room for at least one night. I have to be at work, although I desperately want to be there for Kevin. The fortunate thing is that Troy will be accompanying Kevin and will be there for him. As soon as I am done with work, I will be making my way directly to the hospital. I can only hope that once I arrive, his pain will be under control, and he will be alert enough to see the love around him.

We have heard back from Dr. Hantel, and he has had the other doctors agree that Kevin will only receive this one more treatment to the liver. The planned number of 4 has officially been cut in half. We are very happy about that.

Prayers are great appreciated and a few swear words directed toward the cancer cells in the liver are quite acceptable as well. Of course these may want to be said under your breath!

December 20, 2013 8:31 pm

Kevin had the second, and hopefully last chemo embolization today. I was unable to be there as this was the last day of work for me before Christmas break. One of the great things about working for an elementary school. We had 22 Christmas parties going on today and it was crazy - in a good way. Thankfully the good Lord gave us Troy and Liam who stepped in and were their dad's advocates.

The procedure lasted about an hour. They treated the opposite side of the liver, although they only injected half of the chemo into that side. They injected the remaining chemo back into the other side that has been the home of the tumors and recurrence. They were satisfied with the saturation that took place.

Kevin's pain was intense again for about three hours. They did increase sedation and pain meds, and he was on oxygen this time. He slept a bit more during this time, which was good. They were planning on moving him to a room for the night, but they began weaning Kevin off the pain pump and after a few hours, when his vitals were consistently stable, they agreed to let him come home. BUT, they have insisted that he rest, rest, rest. The oral meds are keeping the pain at bay, however the nausea is incessant. He has thrown up 3 times since coming home only a few short hours ago.

So now Kevin will rest this upcoming week and hope that he has been a good boy and that Santa will bring him something for Christmas. He will rest, sleep, rest some more, and then maybe watch Going My Way *which is THE movie of the season for us.*

After a slight reprieve, we will connect with Dr. Hantel to find out when he will schedule the scan for Kev and determine how much the spots in the lungs have grown. While we expect that they have grown, we are hoping they have been on a slow path.

Kev's CEA as of last week was 33, which is down slightly from the 39 before the resection and ablation. We continue to hope that this number goes down, but it will take some time.

In the meantime, thank you to all who are helping us through this time with your gifts of prayers, healing thoughts, and food. Your generosity is unsurpassed only by the love we feel from all of you. Love can move mountains, and we are so grateful that for right now, our seat is right on top, at the highest peak. The view is spectacular, and we continue to know we are blessed and lucky.

During this very hectic time, if you can stop for just a moment and find a small moment of silence or quiet and let it envelope you and make you feel the love that is from within and from the Good Lord. We are all blessed, especially Kevin. Thank you for making him remember that he is in fact a tough guy and that he is and can get through this, with your help.

January 4, 2014 4:15 pm

Hope everyone had a great Christmas and New Year. It was just the four of us and honestly, it was very nice and enjoyable. Watched some movies, played some games, slept in, and slept some more.

Kevin has had a slow recovery from the last embolization. Nausea and vomiting have happened consistently and have lingered a little longer than we would have hoped. Emotionally, this holiday season was a tough one for Kevin, and for the first time in the three and a half years of his battle, heard him ask, "why me" and that he doesn't want to go on. He is too tired to fight. He was very angry on New Year's Day and truthfully was looking for anyone to engage him in an argument. Who could blame him? He has been so stoic and strong for so long that finally he had to yell Jenga.

Tears are definitely a good release and I know that I speak for our whole family that we were all privy to releasing pent up anxiety, fear, sadness and desire for "normal". A day or so of puffy eyes that even cucumber slices didn't help :) and the fighting Griffin's are all back on their game.

Kevin had blood work done Friday and the results were given to us today. The Liver appears to be functioning quite well despite all the torture it has been through. His white and red blood cell counts are down, but expected. Unfortunately the CEA is up to 41 from 33 just a few weeks ago. Dr. Hantel has stated that it is not an out of control jump, and is pretty sure it's because of the lung lesions.

Kevy is scheduled for a CT scan with and without contrast on Wednesday. Luckily for him, his eldest brother Jack is going to be around and has graciously offered to take him for the tests. He has then promised Kevin a sushi lunch which seems to be what he craves after a visit to Edwards.

Once the scans are complete, we will have the doctors come up with a final game plan for treating the lungs. We are still holding out hope that the "Gamma Knife" radiation can be used and eliminate Kevin from undergoing another surgery. The scan will also tell us if the lymph node that was treated with radiation a while back has finally succumbed to the treatment. As of his liver resection/ablation surgery at the beginning of December, it was still obvious to the eyes of Dr. Shoup, who said it looked like it was decreasing in size. But, as we have learned, radiation takes some time to complete its execution on the cancer cells.

We have had many offers of help throughout our ordeal, and have appreciated them all. It is with mixed feelings that I share this next information with you. Some parents of Kevin's lacrosse players wanted to do something for us, and help us in a way that hadn't been done before. Two of the parents work for hospitals, and have done fund-raising for different events and people. They wanted and have set up a website that accepts monetary donations to help us offset some of our incurred expenses. Please understand that we are humbled/overwhelmed/embarrassed and blessed to have had these wonderful people put this into action.

January 10, 2014 7:32 pm

God has not called us to see through each other, but to see each other through.

~Author Unknown

Kevin had CT scans on Wednesday, one with contrast and one without. He was met there by his brother Jack who then took him out for what else, sushi. Kevin said they had a great visit. I guess on the way out of the Cancer Center, Kevin gave Jack a tour of where he has been going for the last three and a half years. Of course, with Kevin's personality and length of his illness, he was waved to, called out to, greeted by name. As Kevin said to Jack, this is not the place you want as the one "where everybody knows your name". Got quite the laugh.

So we heard back from Dr. Hantel yesterday with a very preliminary reading on the scan. The liver looks good - as good as it can anyway, and this was good news. The previous lymph node in the abdomen region that was treated with radiation some months ago still lit up but was smaller, so for now there is no cause for alarm.

As you would expect, the two spots in the lung have grown, although we did not get an official measure. Dr. Hantel said they have "obviously increased in size". The kicker.....and you knew there would be.....is that a lymph node near the aorta that feeds into the lung lit up and is enlarged.....cancer. The question now is can we still have radiation as an option for the spots, or is the lymph node in a spot too precarious for this kind of treatment. No definitive answers.

Dr. Hantel told us that he would be talking to the radiation oncologist Dr. Das Gupta for his opinion about next steps the next day (Friday - today).

Today, Dr. Hantel got back in touch with Kevin to say he did in fact speak to Dr. Das Gupta. It just so happens, and truly I think a greater power is at work here, that Dr. Das Gupta is attending a medical convention on Wednesday of next week that deals with the lungs and radiation and surgery options for patients. He will be taking Kevin's case (hope he has a roller bag, or an assistant to carry it) to the board at the convention and have a plethora of specialists who deal in cases like Kevin review his file, and weigh the pros and cons of any and all options. So while we will have to wait for the end of the week to find out what steps will be happening for Kevin, it's good to know that from the beginning of his journey, Kevin's case has been presented in front of so many different boards filled with all kinds of medical professionals, and we have been able to pick the minds of a larger number of specialists.

Since New Years, Kevin has been very weepy. He is very emotional at every turn, and finds it hard to say or hear anything loving. He has been quite fatigued and nauseated. However, he keeps getting up every day, and every day is a new day that may hold an answer to some of our questions, concerns, or needs.

We continue to be blessed from all around. Coworkers from both Patterson Elementary and Brookdale Elementary have risen to the task of meals. Marmion lacrosse parents, new and now retired Marmion parents wrap us in gifts and food and Kevin's coworkers at Reebie step up with constant affirmations, a couch in his office for him to lie down, and rides to and from work so as to keep him from using his little found energy on just getting to work.

God is so good to us, and while others who may be looking in from the outside may think we are nuts (we are nuts) when we say how lucky and loved we are. We live so many miles away from our family who send love and prayers constantly and it truly helps them feel better knowing how much love surrounds our family, our Kevy.

Thank you to those who have so graciously donated to the fundraiser that was started by some of the lacrosse players parents to help us defer our costs. We continue to be astounded (but not really) with the support. It is truly needed, and truly appreciated.

Thank you for seeing us through.

January 16, 2014 6:25 pm

We finally heard back from the radiation oncologist today and things are in place for Kevin to receive the CyberKnife radiation treatment to both the spots in the lung and the lymph node nearby. We have a 2 1/2 hour consultation on Tuesday at Elmhurst Hospital where the CyberKnife is located. His treatment will be occurring here as well. We will know more particulars after our meeting on Tuesday, but here is a blurb from the CyberKnife website that explains what makes it so different from regular radiation. It also explains the implantation of gold seeds around the tumors prior to the radiation treatments. They have tentatively told Kevin he will receive his via the camera down the esophagus.

The challenge that doctors face with tumors in the lung is that those tumors move as the patient breathes. Radiosurgery devices, such as the CyberKnife® Robotic Radiosurgery System, offer patients a new option for the treatment of lung cancer. Unlike traditional radiation therapy, the CyberKnife System precisely identifies the tumor location as the patient breathes normally during treatment and can be used, in some cases, to treat lung tumors non-invasively.

Some tumors may require the placement of fiducials within the lung to help the CyberKnife System pinpoint the tumor's exact location. In that case, the patient will be scheduled for a short outpatient procedure beforehand in which three to five tiny gold seeds -- called fiducial markers -- are inserted into the tumor or surrounding lung tissue. These markers may be placed by putting a small needle through the chest, guided by CT scan or an ultrasound. Alternatively, a camera might be passed through the patient's mouth and into the airways or into the esophagus to allow access to the tumor. If fiducials are required, the patient must wait approximately one week before CyberKnife treatment planning can begin to ensure that fiducial movement has stabilized.

We understand that they want to move quickly on this as the spots have grown, so I'm sure the placement of the seeds will take place as soon as possible, and then it looks like we will have to wait at least a week before they can begin the process. They have told Kevin that because of the involvement of the lymph node, he will most likely face five treatments, instead of three. They will be longer in length than regular radiation, perhaps an hour or more each time.

It has been a very difficult and stressful beginning to the new year. Kevin's fatigue from the prior treatments still grabs him and won't let go. He is doing his very best to get to work or work from home as much as he can. His outlook is slightly tainted, and he has more "blue" days than ever before.

I do want to take a moment and thank everyone for their unending support of our family. We are constantly reminded how lucky we are with the people that are in our lives. I know things happen for a reason, and at some point, the Lord knew that we would have to be surrounded by pure love and caring. And all of you are a part of that. Please know it is never taken for granted or assumed. We cherish our time together with you, whether in person, over the phone, or through prayers.

We truly could not do it without our team. You allow us to pass the ball off now and again, which gives us time to catch our breath and call the next play.

Once we know more specifics after our Tuesday meeting, I will update. In the meantime please know prayers are offered for all of you every day. If there is one thing I could ask it is this. Please ask for strength and stamina to be given to Kevin so he can face this upcoming treatment with a reservoir of faith, hope and determination.

Always in our hearts! Love Kim

January 21, 2014 9:26 pm

Today we met with Dr. Das Gupta, the radiation oncologist who will be using the Cyberknife for Kevin's radiation to the lung. The machine itself is pretty incredible, and if you are interested there is a video on youtube that shows you how it works.

The two spots in the lung are both 9x9 mm in size and probably 3-4 cm apart from each other. The third spot, is called the hilar lymph node which almost looks like a grape hanging off of the pulmonary artery. This is where it gets tricky. Dr. Das Gupta can never say with 100% certainty that there will be no complications. It's a possibility that treatment could cause damage to the artery, but it's probable that it will continue to grow and puncture the artery itself if left untreated. Therefore we are going ahead with treatment.

Kevin meets with a doctor tomorrow who will implant gold seeds into the lung around the tumors to help guide the radiation laser. He is then scheduled for a scan on Thursday and we should know before the end of the week when Kevin will have the outpatient procedure. After a week or so which is time to allow the seeds to settle into their new home Kevin will begin the radiation.

As soon as we know more, we will share. Until then please think of a random act of kindness that you can do tomorrow. It not only makes someone's day, it in fact will truly make you smile all day.

Love, Kim

January 25, 2014 5:01 pm

It was a very busy week for Kevin. As mentioned, we met with Dr. Das Gupta on Tuesday and Kevin followed that up with meeting Dr. Greenhill who will be implanting the gold beads around the tumors to enhance the precision of the Cyberknife.

Dr. Greenhill explained to Kevy the procedure will take about an hour and the biggest potential risk is a collapsed lung. She seems pretty confident that there will be no complications. Once the beads are in place, they will remain for good. We have their assurances that Kev will be able to walk through the airport security check points without setting off the alarms!

The week finished out with a scan and Tuesday, January 28th set for the procedure. It will happen at CDH and be an outpatient procedure. After a week or two, radiation will begin. Please continue the prayers. They help to ease this incredibly long journey.

Love Kim

January 28, 2014 11:19 am

We have all been there. The popcorn is popped and in the bowl. You have a drink beside you. Blankets are thrown over your legs to keep your toes nice and warm. Lights are off.

DVD is loaded into the player and just when you are about to push the start button... The power goes out.

Only for us, we got a call just moments ago canceling Kevin's procedure that was scheduled for 2:00 pm to have the gold beads implanted around the tumors, the first step toward radiation with Cyberknife.

It appears that they are having technical difficulties themselves.

The scan that Kevin had this week was a certain kind which is used by their equipment as a kind of GPS, allowing the doctor to be guided to the exact locations in the lung for the implants to happen. They apparently were having trouble lining the scan up with their software, and therefore it had to be canceled.

A couple of things are racing through my head but I will censor myself. I don't know how many more sleepless nights we can go through. Kevin and I tossed and turned all night long and both of us have bags under our eyes to prove it. The anticipation of the actual procedure, the thoughts of having the cancer in the lung, of having to go through another round of radiation, and the mere logistics of arranging our schedules to allow me to have the time off, and for Kevin to schedule appointments with clients around treatment days is absolutely all consuming.

It has been rescheduled for Friday at 8:00 am. Crap.

January 31, 2014 3:37 pm

No hiccups this time.

Kevin and I arrived at CDH Hospital around 7:30 this morning. We got checked in by two of the most awesome nurses ever. Mary and Mary were great and of course Kevin had them laughing and laughing.

So for those of you who love learning medical jargon, here is one for the ages. Today, Kevin had a Navigational Bronchoscopy and Fluoroscopy with fiduciary marker placement.

His procedure started with a nebulizer treatment that acted as a numbing agent and a way to relax his lungs. They took him to the OR shortly after 9:30 am. Now they did take a little while to get started but once they were in it was completed with no complications.

He came back to recovery after about an hour and a half and declared that it had been awesome! He remembers five tv screens in there but nothing else. Typically the process can cause coughing, but up to this point, he has coughed three times.

We have to watch out for fever or any pain in the throat, chest or neck.

We had to wait two hours before he could have anything to drink to make sure he was able to swallow correctly. He passed with flying colors and enjoyed some ginger ale and soup.

He will sleep off the anesthesia (which he is doing right now, here beside me) and should heal nicely.

Now the waiting starts for the ok to begin radiation. Probably in a week to ten days.

Thanks for checking in, and for the great vibes!

Love Kim

February 4, 2014 7:29 pm

DENIED

That is our word for the day.

Kevin got a call today from the CyberKnife Center letting us know that our insurance carrier Blue Cross Blue Shield has denied coverage.

They said yes to the Bronchoscopy to place the gold beads in Kevin's lung. A step that is in preparation for the CyberKnife radiation treatment. A procedure only done to assist in radiation and not to decorate his insides. They said yes.

They said NO to the radiation treatment from the CyberKnife.

We will learn more tomorrow about why, but in the meantime we sit and wait. Wait and wonder. Wait and wonder how much the cancer is spreading. Wait and wonder if we will be given a chance to try and keep up with the cancer. Wait and wonder how medical treatment can be denied to someone who has been fighting for three and a half years.

Wonder who makes those decisions to say yes, or more importantly those who say NO.

Lord, help me to understand.

I am shattered.

I am broken.

I am grieving.

I AM PISSED.

February 6, 2014 5:00 pm

APPROVED.

Thank you to Dr. Das Gupta and his team for getting Kevin's radiation with the CyberKnife approved.

Kevin goes tomorrow to be fitted with his own personal body pillow that will be used every time he has radiation. He will rest on the pillow like a mattress and it will keep him in position.

We hope to find out tomorrow when they will begin radiation. Perhaps Monday.

Keep praying friends. Thank you for your love and support.

I am drained.

I am relieved.

I feel like we are back to fighting the TRUE enemy.

I AM GRATEFUL.

February 15, 2014 5:02 pm

Valentine's Day started out like any other day except it wasn't. It was the first of five radiation treatments Kevin will be receiving to his lung.

Well Cyberknife has made its first appearance and after two hours of Kevin being strapped down and unable to move, it has left its mark, although not to the human eye. That sucker hit all three spots letting the cancer know "hey loser, game on, and oh yeah, there is four more where that came from".

Kevy said it was tedious, and truthfully more difficult to be unable to move for two hours than you would think. Not knowing what to expect as far as side effects go, Kevin was grateful to have his coworker and friend Steven go with him. Steven has been an incredible help to Kevin and me as he has made it possible for Kevin to get back and forth to work over the last few months. It has allowed me to focus on my job and make sure that Kevy is getting to where he needs to be.

So, Kevy did it and went to work. A real trooper.

Valentine's Day ended much nicer. Dinner with two of my three favorite Valentines, Kevy and Liam. A heartfelt shout out to Troy! We enjoyed the time together and the love.

One down, four to go.

February 19, 2014 12:38 am

The strain of a disease like cancer can be debilitating. In this instance, it's me, the wife and caregiver of a cancer patient who feels like I can't go on.

I find myself wishing time would go by faster so we knew if the cancer has spread. At the same time, I don't want to lose a precious moment of time with Kevy. I want to believe he will beat this, but after such a long journey, my faith in this being a good outcome is being tested.

I feel beaten down. Defeated. Alone.

I came home from work today and could barely function. I gave everything I had at work, and there was nothing left when I got home. I was met with my husband holding open his arms to give me a hug and a shoulder to cry on. He listened and changed his plans for the evening. Instead of going to conditioning with his lacrosse team, he asked Randy to cover for him so he could stay here with me.

I had a small bite to eat, as my stomach is in knots, drew a warm bath, and went to bed at 6:30 pm. I awoke at 11:00 and cannot fall back to sleep. I know I am depressed. I know I am questioning my confidence in defeating this disease. I know I am lonely, even when surrounded by many who care for me.

I want to crawl into a warm bed and bring the covers up over my head and sleep forever. Or at least until they say the cancer is gone. I can barely get myself together for work, let alone being pulled together for my family.

I want to scream. I want to kick. I want to cry. I want my husband to be free of cancer. I want my sons to not worry about their dad. I want my sons to think that I am strong, and will always be there for them.

I don't want to wall myself off from others, but I am. I sure could use some prayers. And Kleenex.

Love from a beaten down Kim.

March 5, 2014 6:23 pm

The last CEA number I could find in the journal was back in January and it was 41. That was after the chemo embolization treatments that attacked his liver directly, but before the radiation to the tumors in his lung.

Fast track to today and the CEA is 104.

104.

We have to wait until the middle of April before they can do a scan on Kevin. So, we have to wait, and know that the radiation while it may cause some irritation, could not hike up this number alone. Nope not alone.

It's there. Somewhere. Still.

We are in hell.

April 7, 2014 5:59 pm

We have anxiously awaited the time out before Kevy could have his blood work done. Today was the day and it was preceded by immeasurable angst and nervous tension.

Kevin got the call around 2:30 pm.

His CEA has been a clear indicator for him and the true north on our compass for what lay ahead.

It is with utter knee dropping sadness that we share that his number is 229.

We are truly in hell and have to wait again for the scan. We are hoping once Dr. Hantel finds out (he was out of town today) that he will move the scan up to this week.

If tears could put out the flames that surround us, there would be tranquility and no heat at all.

Please pray for Troy and Liam. They are heartbroken. Ask God to watch over his son Kevin in this darkest time and for me to find the strength to put one foot in front of the other.

Love Kim

April 16, 2014 11:33 am

Just asking for extra prayers today and tonight as we are meeting with Dr. Hantel tomorrow to discuss the blood test and scan results. We are not looking forward to it. As you will remember, his CEA which normally should be in the 0-5 range was a staggering 229.

You know, through this journey, a very common response that I have received is to stay positive. What I have come to find is that people have different definitions of being positive.

Here is my definition or idea about being positive.

When confronted with a situation or experience, it is human nature that you have a reaction. Sometimes that reaction is to smile, scream, appear shocked, angry, fearful, feel sadness, laugh or cry. Those physical reactions happen almost immediately, and it is very difficult to curb or even stop them. Here is where my explanation of being positive begins.

When I receive or hear bad news, my usual response is to begin feeling bad quickly followed up with tears. From the time I was little, I was looked at in my family as the sensitive one, or emotional one because I cried easily. If I did something wrong, all my mom had to do was say my first and middle name together in a tone that told me I was in trouble, and the tears flowed.

Now, as a grown woman, who has a husband living through an almost 4 year battle of Stage III cancer, I become emotional and cry when I reflect on news we receive, or see Kevin and how he has been affected by a treatment, or look at my sons, and see the anxiety that washes over them.

I ALLOW myself to feel the tears streaming down my face, encourage the guttural cry from the very tips of my toes, and embrace, yes embrace the total feeling of fear/loss/pain. I may even lull there for an hour or more. And then, I crawl back up to the top, and take a breath. I cautiously begin moving again and start to readjust my vision.

And I move. I gather strength from my faith, my family, and my friends. Just because I stop and allow my feelings to be expressed, does not mean for a moment that I have given up being optimistic. Perhaps the re framing could be that I am being emotionally healthy because I am not suppressing the sad feelings. Just as I laugh when I hear a funny joke, or get angry when I see injustice being handed out, I cry when I'm sad.

I think some confuse crying and admitting our sadness as being negative.

If I don't get rid of any of my feelings, I am lying to myself and to others. If you look at it, how can you limit your laugh at a funny joke or situation. I am unable to cut it off mid laugh. Heck, the more I try to stop, the more I laugh, and quite frankly the funnier sounding I get as well!

It is important to express yourself as you deem necessary, provided of course that no one else is being hurt.

As we hold our breath for tomorrow to come, there may be tears and sadness. There will undoubtedly be some laughs and smiles. There will also be a belief that we will continue to move forward and do all that we can to bring strength to Kevin as he most likely starts a new treatment plan.

God bless you all, and please hold Kevin close. Heck, hold all of us close.

April 17, 2014 11:53 am

All four of us went together to meet with Dr. Hantel and to face the news as a family.

The news was a mixed bag. No signs in the liver -yeah. Spots in lungs have decreased in size. Great.

BUT

A lymph node that lies between the vena cava and the duodenum in the abdomen has blown up in just over 2 months from nothing to over 2 inches in width. Very aggressive.

It is in a location very close to where Kevin has received radiation before, thereby making radiation unavailable as a treatment option. It's a precarious position also makes surgery unavailable. As the doctor said, the risk of surgery near the vena cava outweighs any positive gains. So now we have one option left which is a combination of chemotherapy drugs.

Kevin is starting chemo again next Friday, and every other Friday indefinitely. He will be there for four hours each time. After the first one, blood will be taken and providing it shows some response, he will continue for four treatments at which time they will do a scan to see if there is any change.

Kevy has had the drugs before, and will face nausea, diarrhea, fatigue, facial rash.

The bigger thing that Kevin is facing is that the cancer is popping up very quickly. This lymph node is so very close to so many things, that it has left us in tears and anguish.

Yes, we do have a treatment available, but it is not a "clean up in aisle seven" treatment. It will remain. In some form or fashion. In some place.

So very sad. The boys are sad. Kevin is very sad. And he cried.

As I am crying.

April 25, 2014 11:00 am

This morning Kevin started his first of at least four chemo treatments.

We were told that the regiment Dr. Hantel wanted Kevin on consisted of three drugs, which in the world of treatment options is considered more experimental, even though there has been great success. We of course were told we may have difficulty getting it approved through insurance, and if that were the case, we would use two of the drugs.

The GREAT news is that they approved the use of the three drugs. We now have the best possible fighter in the long and arduous fight against Kevin's cancer.

Liam is joining him today as he is still on his spring break.

The treatment will be about 4 1/2 hours long, and hopefully Kevin will sleep through most of that time. Liam said that they have given him Benadryl and anti anxiety drugs already, so he is well on his way to a relaxing (if that's possible) treatment.

Keep the prayers coming. We feel the warmth of them and they continue to sustain us at this lowest point of our journey.

Love Kim

May 9, 2014 12:50 pm

Treatment 2 is underway and Kevin got some really good news today.

During his meeting this morning, Dr. Hantel told Kev that he had spoken with Dr. Shoup (the surgeon who has done Kevin's 3 liver resections) and she has stated that IF the lymph node responds well enough to the chemo, and gets small enough, she thinks she would be able to do surgery and remove that node! Needless to say we are elated with that door being unlocked, if not open.

The second part of the news is that we always look to the CEA number which tells us if the chemo is working. His number went up before his first treatment to over 430, which was expected. Now that Kevin has had one treatment, and only one so far, the number is now 293!!!!!!!!!!!!!!!!!!

This tells us the chemo cocktail is working! Glorious news.

Keep praying and smiling... God is good and you, all of you are amazing.

Kevin would want me to remind all of you who are in the area, that if you have a free day tomorrow, make your way over to Marmion Academy (1000 Butterfield Rd., Aurora) where we are holding a lacrosse tournament with over 18 schools from around the state attending. It is a day full of lacrosse games on five different fields, silent auction, concessions, and incredible family fun!.

Kevin will be there, although with a lot of rest in between games. He would love to see you out there!

Have a great day... we are!

May 23, 2014 6:36 pm

Kevin had his third treatment today and received not only the poison that is killing the cancer cells and a few healthy ones along the way, BUT incredibly good news. The CEA number which last chemo was at 293 is now residing at 162.3!!

Dr. Hantel was ECSTATIC with the number. He reiterated to Kevin that he is looking forward to having Dr. Shoup look at the scan after his fourth treatment and quite likely performing surgery to remove the lymph node.

I have mentioned it before, but this time it's true. This round of chemotherapy is kicking Kevy's ass. Every imaginable side affect he is experiencing: nausea, fatigue, headaches, aches, pains, runny nose, runny eyes, break out of acne all over his face and scalp - they actually appear at times like blisters. Very often they begin to weep without any invitation to do so. He has been trying to pull himself into work and life itself, but has had no "feeling good" time this go. Even yesterday he was experience nausea, sweats and headaches.

So of course we are thrilled with the results, but the day to day living with the impact of the chemo can be downright draining for Kevy. He is trying so hard to be there for everyone, that he runs himself ragged. If you are visiting this site, then you know how stubborn he is. It's certainly hard to keep a good man down.

The thing about cancer is that it stops for no one or nothing. Kevin has to deal with his job, his family, his health, and too often that is tied to dealing with others expectations. Liam graduated yesterday from Marmion Academy and it was a very special time for our family. Kevin being the strong person he is, fought his way through his fatigue, nausea and excruciating headache to be present for his son's accomplishment. It was not lost on Liam. Liam was so happy to know that Kevy was there. It's kind of ironic but Liam started high school within days of Kevin's diagnosis of cancer in August 2010. Here we are four years later and Kevy is still fighting like a trooper to gain the upper hand on this disease. He now has two sons who are college students, two dogs who drive him both nuts and happy, and a wife who is throwing her hat in the ring to take on a year round full time job. He has a job that he loves, friends whom he adores and of course all his lacrosse players, both past and present who go out of their way to let him know they are praying and thinking about him.

Kevy is resting now in bed, quietly moaning and occasionally coughing as he had to fight through an infection these past two weeks as well. Lacrosse season is over, and his team finished with a winning record. He is now gearing up for the end of year awards banquet for the team and, hopefully, an Alumni vs. Varsity game. The word has been trickling out there about this game and Kev is super excited about it. He would love to see some of his old players come back and suit up to face off against the varsity team. It's the carrot he is most focused on right now.

Thank you for your continued prayers and for checking in here when there is an update. For our American friends, Happy Memorial Day Weekend. As for our long weekend, we plan on spending it together, most often resting in bed, or watching some TV. There will be a lot of time to take care of Kevin as the boys are home in Canada this week, and our big puppy has gone to play at the kennel.

Kevin + me + your guest book signings = a very memorable weekend.

Love and Blessings.

May 28, 2014 9:04 pm

Strength does not come from physical capacity. It comes from an indomitable will.

- Ghandi

Kevin is the epitome of this quote. This chemo treatment has totally taken the physical strength from Kevin and replaced it with weight loss, cramping, shooting nerve pain, a weakened voice, diarrhea, bloody noses, runny eyes, severe nausea, incredible fatigue... and an indomitable will.

As a man who is carrying so much responsibility around, it's easy to understand how he can be totally empty of strength and ability to move forward. Yet everyday he tries to get up and move through the day as if it were a regular day. Sadly, though, these are now "regular" days. His attempts have not been completely successful, yet he tries.

He sleeps rather fitfully when he is able to fall asleep. While totally fatigued, he sometimes is unable to drift off to the place where he has complete peace and serenity. It is truly a complete joy to behold. It is during this time that I know he will not cry because of his scaled down existence. He will not share a guttural cry because of all he is unable to do. He will not wince because every part of his body hurts beyond belief.

No. He will attempt everyday to move forward, get up and try to make the most of his day. Sometimes the most of his day is making sure he drinks enough water and ginger ale and has something to eat in an attempt to regain some strength and to ward off the nausea that is all encompassing.

Yet he has the will to carry on. The will to keep trying. The will to keep living.

I love him. And he loves us.

June 6, 2014 6:39 pm

Today was treatment four and we needed someone to go with Kevin. Enter Ty. Tyler Estes, a Marmion Alumni player who played for Kevy as our top notch goalie and is now going into his sophomore year at Regis College where he has continued his playing.

Kevin was so grateful to have Tyler there. The comfort of having someone that you trust, feel comfortable and safe with makes the difficulty of chemo bearable.

Kevin's numbers have dropped yet again. It is now 99. Dr. Hantel was very happy and is continuing on the path of surgery. He wants Kevin to have his PET scan on June 17, followed by a meeting in his office June 20. That will give the doctors enough time to review the scan and make a plan. Kev was told that the surgery is going to be tenuous - very delicate but necessary to overcome the disease.

These chemos are incredibly strong, like always, and this one has not disappointed. Kevin says it feels like the 3rd or 4th day after treatment, not the first one. He is quite down and feels that he should be able to mentally walk himself through this and will away any negative impact. While I think he is all that, even Kevin Troy Griffin is not powerful enough to do that. He has shed some tears tonight, and keeps wondering aloud if it's worth it.

Of course it's worth it. It is for you sweet Kevy. And for all of us who love you. And at last count, that was quite a big number.

Keep the prayers coming, and love one another. Take the time to kiss your partner. Hug your sister. High five a friend. Just always, always pay it forward and love, love, love.

God Bless.

June 18, 2014 7:15 pm

I ask not for a lighter burden, but for broader shoulders. ~Jewish Proverb

So Kevin had his scan yesterday at Edwards Hospital and we were supposed to meet with Dr. Hantel on Friday to discuss the results. Key word here is supposed.

Dr. Hantel called and spoke with Kevin today and revealed the results of the scan.

The lymph node that is located smack dab in the middle of everything and near the vena cava has shrunk which is good. If it has shrunk enough for surgery is another question.

Hantel sent a disc with the scan to Dr. Shoup so she could review and determine if she thinks it is small enough to operate on. We are anticipating hearing from her tomorrow or Friday.

A gotcha moment however, is that another lymph node near the psoas muscle which is near Kevin's left hip/groin area is lighting up. This will have to be addressed, whether with ablation or surgery. I believe it is in the area where Kevin has had radiation before, and therefore it would not be an option.

So about Friday.

Kevin has been told by Dr. Hantel that prior to surgery, he has to be off one of the three chemo drugs that he is taking right now for 6 weeks before he could have surgery. As of Friday, it will be 2 weeks. So, Dr. Hantel informed Kevin that he will be receiving two more rounds of chemotherapy minus the one drug (avastin). This will allow the cancer to be held at bay and not given a chance to repopulate while waiting out the time before he can have surgery.

Therefore, Kevin will be having his fifth chemo treatment on Friday.

As per usual, we have to hurry up and wait.

Kevin is feeling pretty good today, and seems optimistic after his talk with Dr. Hantel.

I think I will reserve my optimism until we hear from Dr. Shoup and if she thinks surgery is still in the mix.

Anyone know exercises for increasing your shoulders?

June 20, 2014 7:14 pm

In a very fast moving day, Kevin and I and Liam met with Dr. Shoup to talk about surgery. She has reviewed the scan and has agreed that surgery is what we should do. She has decided that she will go after both spots during the same surgery. What this means is that Kevin will have a very long incision straight down his abdomen to be able to get to the lymph node by the pancreas and the lymph node by the psoas muscle and bowel. It has the potential of being a fairly bloody surgery because of its location so close to main blood vessels. She has assured us that she will have her vascular team there ready just in case. She anticipates a stay in the hospital of anywhere from 4 days to a week, depending on recovery and any bumps in the road.

Surgery is scheduled for July 14, 2014 at CDH. Dr. Shoup also agreed that she wants Kevin to have two more chemo treatments without the one drug that he has to be off so healing is not impaired.

After her meeting, we went to Edwards and met with Dr. Hantel. He was happy to hear that Dr. Shoup said yes to surgery. He signed off on Kevin having chemo today and then on July 3rd. We got to see the last two scans side by side and you can see the difference in size of the tumors. It truly is remarkable. The one higher up in the abdomen is measuring about 1 1/2". We didn't get a measurement on the lower one but it is much smaller.

Blood work came back and the CEA has gone from 99.2 to 63. Another nice drop.

We got home around 6 tonight and Kevin has just woken up. He is so tired, and down. He is not looking forward to the two rounds of chemo. He wants to jump right in to surgery.

As always, your prayers keep us afloat, and Beth Beedles, you are right, the exercises for broader shoulders is to get down on your knees and pray and pray and pray. We are there right now!

Life of course goes on and both boys are working full time at the warehouse helping with moving household goods. They are so awesome. I love having them home this summer knowing that it will not be for much longer that we are all under the same roof.

I am now officially working full time as the principal's secretary and, therefore, do not have any vacation this summer. I will have to use a few sick days so I can be with Kevin on the day of surgery. The boys will be joining us too.

Pay it forward this weekend. Do something nice for your neighbor, or pay for someone's coffee behind you at Starbucks. Take time to love on each other, and to let the little things go.

Love to all,

Kim

July 13, 2014 8:18 pm

Kevy is scheduled for surgery tomorrow morning at 10:30 am at Central Dupage Hospital. We have to be at the hospital by 8:30 am. At this time, Dr. Shoup is anticipating a singular incision straight down the middle of Kevin's abdomen which will leave him with a rather funky looking scar, based on the other ones! Her plan is to go in after the two affected lymph nodes, one near his left hip and psoas muscle, very closely snuggled near a major vein. The second, and more tricky one is located near the vena cava and the duodenum/pancreas/stomach/liver etc. It's going to be a lot of digging and moving things around to get to the spot, but we know if there is anyone who can do it, its Dr. Shoup.

Dr. Shoup will have an interventionist surgeon with her who deals in surgeries that are at a greater risk of bleeding because of the location of the nodes so close to the blood sources. She has continued to reassure us that she would not have agreed to the surgery if she didn't think she could do it successfully.

He is expected to be in the hospital for about 4-7 days, depending on any complications or surprises. Kevy is pretty stoic tonight and looking at it like it's just another scar. I wish I could say the same.

Troy is trying to stay upbeat, although I know underneath he is stressing. Liam and I are having a more difficult time not showing how we are feeling. Liam has been very quiet the last two days and especially today. I know he is scared, and who could blame him. I'm grateful that we have this option which didn't exist a few months ago, but I am worried too. Will they be able to get it all? Will he do okay through it?

For those of you who are great believers in prayer, please continue to add some tonight for Kevin. For those of you who may occasionally pray, this would be a great time to start and ask for strength for our family and for the surgeons to have healing touches. If you have never prayed before, let me tell you it is comforting to both those you pray for and for yourself.

Thank you for your continued support. We are preparing tomorrow which will be Kevin's 6th major surgery since this whole thing started just shy of 4 years ago. His body has gone through so much, we just need it to hang on a little longer to get over this hump.

Lots of tears flowing from me right now and I am trying to get it out of the way so I can be a strong partner and mom. I'm beginning to think though, that my strength may take the form of someone who cries, collects herself, stays strong, and then breaks down again. I just wish firstly that Kevin didn't have to go through this again, and secondly and just as importantly, I wish that Troy and Liam didn't have to face this situation of seeing their dad face a relatively serious surgery. I would carry their burden all by myself if I could.

If anyone feels like reaching out to Troy or Liam, please do so. They would appreciate it. I will update tomorrow morning once things get started. Love one another, and thank God for today. Love, Kim

July 14, 2014 12:17 pm

First incision at 12:03 pm.

July 14, 2014 2:40 pm

Kevin is in recovery and surgeon is elated. Got both masses and said everything looks great. One week in hospital and a long recovery. Will update after I see him.

July 14, 2014 7:25 pm

Well my hero is resting more or less comfortably, with lots of tubes and a pump in his hand to control the pain. When I told him that Dr. Shoup got both masses, he made a fist pump... if only a few inches off the bed.

Did not see the incision, but told it is what will make his stay a little longer.

Boys are relieved, and I am ready to dance and cry! Thank you all for your prayers and love.

July 15, 2014 7:55 pm

Kevin is now resting in Room 203 at CDH. He has the tubes from his nose and neck removed, and is controlling his pain by using the button thingy (pretty sure that is a medical term). His color is great and he has even been up to walk a little bit.

He had family visiting him today, including Troy and Liam and he was quite happy. I worked and went there straight after I was finished my day. Turns out all the visiting earlier in the day made for a rather quiet, sleepy visit. Kevy slept for most of the time I was there BUT I was thrilled. I knew that they had gone in and removed all the bad ass stuff that they were looking for, and then some. Turns out they saw something close to the one in the abdomen that looked suspicious so removed it. Dr. Shoup said it was within striking distance of the original site. As I mentioned before, she was elated when she came into the consultation room to tell us she got everything.

We are so grateful right now, that tears that are flowing now are full of gratitude and relief. I am home now, having put cream on Kev's very dry skin, fed him ice chips and assisted him on a walk. I got a big smooch and he was snoring by the time I hit the door.

He is alive. He is healing. He is here. He is everything to our family and we couldn't be more grateful to our Lord for watching over the surgery. We know he will continue to watch over Kevin as he continues on his journey of healing.

Thanks for checking in.

Love and blessings, Kim

July 31, 2014 8:17 pm

Well two weeks and two days later, Kevin's 42 staples have been removed, and today he went back to work (okay a client function at Wrigley Field). He is moving slowly, and still hurting, but he is getting on with life. Energy levels still have to be replenished, but every day is better than the one before.

Your constant prayers and good wishes have helped our family through a very tough time. We can't thank you enough.

Tomorrow Troy heads back to school to begin his junior year, and second year as an RA (resident advisor). We are going to miss his company and hugs! In a few weeks, we will have to pack Liam up and send him off to school as well. Can't believe we will be empty nesters!!!

Kevin will meet up with Dr. Hantel in a few weeks, and probably have some blood work done to see where the counts are. We pray for good news.

Enjoy the weekend and hug your kids.

Luv Kim

August 5, 2014 6:52 pm

First visit with Dr. Hantel, and more importantly the first blood work since the surgery happened this afternoon.

5.2 CEA!!!

We are very happy with that number, although a few other numbers aren't so great.

Kevin has lost almost ten pounds in the last month. Hantel said as long as Kevin doesn't keep losing weight he won't get too concerned. So we hope he is able to maintain.

The other number they are watching is his hemoglobin. He is pretty anemic, with the number around 9. They will watch that number closely too.

So now what? Well, we go back in two weeks for follow up blood work and that will help Dr. Hantel decide if Kevy will be going back for more chemo. He talked about Kevin having 4-6 chemo treatments but it's not for sure. We will have to wait for another set of numbers.

Good visit, but there will likely be clean up chemo. Mixed feelings and blessings.

Thanks for checking in, and as always, for your prayers and good wishes.

Love Kim and Kev

September 5, 2014 7:27 pm

When I think of broken records, I think back to when I first purchased an album (vinyl) of Donny Osmond. He was wearing a purple cap and included the hits "Puppy Love" and "Go Away Little Girl". I was taught from the beginning that I had to handle it carefully, as it was easily scratched, chipped or broken and that would be the end of the music.

Reporting on Kevin's cancer battle is sounding like a broken record to me. Same thing over and over again. Cancer has the upper hand, and Kevin is fighting it harder than he has ever fought before.

Today was round 2 of chemo, with Hantel asking Kev to hang in there for 4, possibly 6, and maybe even 8. He had his first treatment two weeks ago and his CEA was 14, up from 5.2 immediately following surgery.

This second treatment started as usual with blood work to see how he is reacting to the chemo and if he is healthy enough to sustain the treatment. He was able to have the treatment and we got the new CEA number. 16.2.

16.2 is 2.2 points higher than 14 no matter how you slice it. Higher. Greater than. More. Moving upward. Fuck.

Now Hantel is telling us to not panic, that it does occasionally happen after a first treatment. (Although technically this is like Kevin's 100th treatment or close). He has told us to wait until the next treatment and blood work to see how the CEA reacts.

How much can one man endure? How much can one liver endure? How many tears can the body manufacture before running dry? We have to be getting close.

Kevin really struggled with the first treatment, having a rather long turnaround time. He had probably 3 days where he felt OK. And maybe 1 1/2 days of feeling good. Now he has endured another 4 hour round of chemo, and will probably experience the incredible side effects quicker, more intense, and longer. Yippee.

This man needs a reprieve from this Godforsaken disease that is torturing his body and soul on a daily basis. He talked to Hantel today prior to finding out the CEA results and asked him what he thought about the idea of a "Chemo Holiday"? Just so that the quality of daily existence would be slightly better. Dr. Hantel said that he wants Kevin to do at least 4 treatments before he will consider the holiday. With today's number, maybe there will be no holiday.

Please love on your family and friends as much as you can. Hold them close because you never know. Ever.

Overwhelmed, overloaded, over and out. Kim

September 19, 2014 2:59 pm

DOWN, DOWN, DOWN!

Kevy's CEA went down to 13.3.

It tells us the chemo is still working and fighting this disease and for that we are thrilled. Dr. Hantel says Kev will have treatment today and once more in two weeks. At that time Kev will have a scan and most likely start a maintenance program using one drug instead of three, which will bring a better quality of life to Kev.

We are relieved that we are on the back side of this treatment, and look forward to having a restful weekend.

Love to all, and thank you for your friendships.

Kim and a sleepy Kevin.

September 24, 2014 7:37 pm

It's been a while since I posted a journal entry that didn't just deal with statistics and blood test results etc. I have a need to share in the way that I have for over four years now. I don't think I would call it a pity party, but more of a reflective observance on some of the elements that make up our lives.

Kevin is struggling through this treatment, with incredibly difficult side effects. He has extremely debilitating abdominal cramping, nausea, constant shaking limbs, horrific skin rashes and acne that is covering his head, making laying down at night almost too painful. We now use colored pillow cases as we have to change them every morning because of the blood. He has diarrhea that is nonstop and makes it impossible to go anywhere without the proper undergarments. I have seen this man double over when we are out and have to cringe and "pant" to make it to a washroom. His voice is almost nonexistent sometimes, and the sores that develop in his mouth make it very difficult to eat and drink. But right now, the thing I have heard him say the most is that he misses his Mom.

For those of us who are lucky to still have our mothers in our lives, we know how comforting their words and arms can be during times of pure joy and utter failures. For those of us who are fortunate enough to be a mother know that whatever happens to our children happens to us 100 fold. And then there is the Holy Mother who is there always, without being asked, without a word being whispered.

I hope that Kevin's Mom is able to make it down here to see him as I know this would be a great morale booster.

I hope that both of my sons, who are carrying huge burdens of their own, can feel the love that I have for them, although this alone will not fix what is wrong. I am helpless in doing anything to lessen their load, although I have been trying for so many weeks to be supportive, lend a shoulder, let them bend my ear, and send endless prayers to the Holy Mother to help them both to find the strength to keep moving forward, and to know they do not walk this difficult time alone. Out of respect for their privacy, I am unable to share what is weighing on them, but please add them to your prayer list.

I am so very numb from things that are going on in my life that I'm sure those looking from the outside would be surprised at the massive, almost impossible-to-carry load that is my constant companion. Now I know that I do not stand alone in this life as having the worst, or largest set of problems. However, I have tried for so long to hold on to them and not discuss them so as not to appear weak, whining or self absorbed. I know that the good in my life outweighs the bad, but sometimes the bad becomes so bitter and all encompassing that I have to spit it out.

My husband is living with cancer and all its ugly side effects. My sons are suffering not only from this reality, but from their own. I have an incredible boss who took a chance with hiring me on with not a lot of experience for my job, and not once has she complained about my lacking. But I hold myself up in the mirror, and am so disappointed in my performance, that of making my boss's job easier, I wonder everyday if this will be the day that she sees it too.

I am numb. I am numb. How do I lift myself up?

I have never liked rollercoasters, and know I never will. It seems my life has been a constant ride on a rollercoaster, most especially these last 15 years. Moving to a new country and away from family was difficult. Missing out on being an aunt, a great aunt, a daughter closer to help her elderly parents has been hard. Missing lifelong friends has been at times unbearable. Having my best friend and greatest love be diagnosed with colon cancer was debilitating. Telling our children this news was terrible. Letting my sons go on to college, and be faced with surprising circumstances and not being able to change it has truly been the lowest point of this ride. Finally getting a chance at a job that I have wanted for so long and seeing that I am in fact making it harder on my boss because of my newness, saddens me to no end.

So as a mother who is so numb that even the rollercoaster does not make my stomach turn, I urge you to tell your Mum you love her, send her some flowers, talk to her on the phone or through the heavens. Make each day count, because you truly don't know how many you have. Don't let a day go by without saying at least one thank you and remember that sometimes people may appear to be okay, when in fact the truth is so very different.

Help one another. Smile at a stranger. Have a safe place to fall. Like a mother's arms.

October 3, 2014 8:31 pm

Kevin endured the 4th chemo treatment today, and is home resting on the couch.

His CEA dropped to 9.8 which shows the meds are still working on the cancer for which we are truly thankful.

Moving forward Dr. Hantel decided because of the incredible side effects that are all encompassing, to turn down the strength of the chemo to eighty percent strength down from one hundred percent strength. It we are told will not affect the result of the fight on the disease. It will though, lessen the side effects that Kevy has struggled with for the last two weeks. He should have less rashes and diarrhea should be minimized. You have no idea how happy we are to hear that.

A week from Monday, Kevy will have a CT scan and we will meet with Dr. Hantel on Tuesday to have blood work done and discuss next steps. This is when we will find out if we will continue with a chemo regiment, or move to a maintenance program.

We will keep you posted.

October 14, 2014 5:43 pm

We met with Dr. Hantel today and got to see the scan results and the blood work numbers. Kevin's CEA is still dropping and went from 9.8 to 8.6!

The scan is where we found the blurred lines. Side by side with his previous scan taken right after his surgery, we can see some of the areas of concern have shrunk which is great, but there continues to be a haze throughout the abdomen. His liver and lungs are clear which is great, but there remains a pocket of fluid (at least that is what Dr. Hantel thinks it is) very close to where the lymph nodes were removed from the stomach/pancreas area. We have been told that it could be a fluid pocket, or something else, but the haze makes it unable to be 100% accurate.

So after much discussion, we have a plan.

Kevin is going to have two more chemo treatments at the dialed down dose like he had the last time. He was off of work for three days, which tells you how much pain he was in, but the doctor and we want to give this thing everything we can. So Kevy will have chemo on Friday, and we will do blood work at some point as well.

Kev continues to be slightly embarrassed by the rash/acne that is a big side effect of the drug erbitux. He is very reluctant to be out in public, and has quite the skin regiment each night. Nausea and cramping and diarrhea will continue with these treatments, but we hope to get the CEA below 5. After these two treatments are done, we are truly going to visit the idea of a vacation from the chemo treatments, or stretch them out a bit more. We may also change up the cocktail, depending on the readings over the next few weeks.

Thanks for checking in, and for your continued bolstering of our spirits. The treatments are definitely wearing thin for all, especially Kevy, but he keeps insisting on getting back up off the ground and going after it. So blurred lines or no blurred lines, we are back in the fight, and plan to win.

Love Kim

October 22, 2014 8:39 pm

Let's jump back to Monday night when Kevin wasn't feeling great. He kept complaining that he was having pains in his lower abdomen which he thought was constipation. This would typically happen after chemo treatments but would then be followed by diarrhea. He was rating the pain Monday night around a 5-6 and spent a restless night tossing and turning. Every time he turned, he would wince in pain. Tuesday, we slept in a bit and Kevin was still having pain. I took his temp which was normal, and we called Dr. Hantel's office to make sure they didn't think it could be something else other than constipation. Based on our descriptions, they asked us to treat it with Miralax. Kevin wanted to wait a little while before doing that so we did. Around 3:00 pm on Tuesday, he agreed to the four ounce drink I gave him which had the Miralax in it. Kevin proceeded to vomit it up, and hit the ground before he passed out.

Now, he had felt like passing out prior to this, and ended up lying on the floor in the bathroom. None of this was out of the ordinary for the days after his chemo treatment. Also, considering that this was the fifth treatment, we expected it to be the same if not worse than previous treatments. No, it was the same... yet somehow different.

Finally he agreed to go to the hospital, and after making his way downstairs, he yelped in excruciating pain. He told me he didn't think he could make it to the car and seriously considered calling an ambulance. He caught his breath and made his way to the car where our ride was horrific because of construction, and every movement of the car brought another cry from Kev.

335

Once we arrived at the ER, they took him immediately. He was given a CT scan and we were told that he had a perforation in his colon. He would be having emergency surgery right away. He was given pain meds which dropped his number from 9 to a 2 and we waited to meet the surgeon. He painted a rather dour picture, and said that if we had waited until the next day Kev would not have made it.

His surgery lasted about 3 hours and when the surgeon finally met with me told me that there had been 2 perforations in the colon and that Kevy's abdomen was completely fully of contaminated waste. It was a difficult clean up and removal of the dead colon. He did however, tell us that he found a nodule very low in the pelvis area that was questionable which was removed. Everything was sent off to pathology, and we should get results within a day or two. Kevin was left with another surgery scar, and this time a colostomy bag. It will not be reversed. It is permanent. This is going to be a very difficult thing for Kevin to deal with.

He is in the ICU at Edward Hospital and as of late this afternoon, early evening, he was removed from the ventilator. He is breathing on his own, which is great and a big hurdle to get over. He has two drains in his abdomen, and all the regular tubes and wires. He is also experiencing a fever, which while not surprising, is definitely the focus of their attention. He is receiving a broad spectrum antibiotic and it will take a while for them to find the cocktail that will hopefully fight the infection and see him on his road to recovery.

Thank you to all who have been praying and sending messages. I have shared them with Kevin and he is very appreciative. Much love and thanks goes out to my coworkers who are so supportive. Thanks to Linda, Steven, Randy and Renee as well.

I will keep you updated as I find out more, but for now, he is still in serious condition and all prayers are truly appreciated.

Love Kim

October 26, 2014 12:50 pm

I don't even know where to begin.

Kevin is incredibly strong, and is fighting so hard to get better. He is being cared for not only by the staff of experts at Edward Hospital but also by all of you. Your prayers, positive thoughts and daily living of paying it forward are also elements to Kevin's healing.

He had a really rough day yesterday, with vomiting of bile almost nonstop. No amount of nausea meds, or any meds for that matter would curb the grip that was on his stomach. He didn't sleep much last night either. I was in contact with the hospital twice through the night, first around midnight and then 3:30 am. He was still throwing up and not able to sleep.

I got to the hospital this morning about 9:00 am and he had been up for a walk and sponge bath. However, he also threw up while I was there and the nurse contacted the doctor to determine what to do. He decided that he wanted Kevin back on the NG tube that goes through the nose, and into his stomach to give his bowels a rest. Kevin wanted nothing to do with it. He would not allow the nurse to do it, even after receiving some meds that made him sleepy. Fortunately for him, whether it was because it had passed, or because he willed himself, but he as of this posting had not thrown up again. Now, I am at home, but when I left at noon, he was still free of vomiting. I can only hope that this lasts.

337

He is unable to take anything by mouth, which is a step back from before, but sometimes through a journey you have stumbles and setbacks. We just need Kevin to continue to rally to whatever is placed in front of him. I will admit that his spirits are much better today than yesterday. He was very down yesterday.

Our family appreciates all of the love and support that has been flowing nonstop. I also know that many would prefer more frequent updates. Let me assure you that I am doing my best to keep everyone informed in a timely manner. And most of you know that Kevin is my first priority; Troy and Liam are my second. And last is me. It is when these three things are somewhat right with the world, that I am able to grab some time and share with all of you how incredible Kevin is.

So I am home right now, for a rest, and will head back to the hospital for the evening. Barring any major setback, I will be back at work tomorrow as Kevin is well cared for at the hospital. I do have an appointment there late afternoon with the team that will walk both Kevin and I through the new challenge of the colostomy bag.

I would be remiss if I didn't thank my brother Mike who drove down from Canada yesterday morning and spent all of yesterday at the hospital with Kevin. I am very lucky to have an incredible brother. I love him more than I could possibly tell you and it meant so much to us to have him here. He had to head home today to get back for work tomorrow.

Hope you enjoy this beautiful fall day. Pay it forward, for you truly don't know how much you have until you give it away.

Love Kim

October 27, 2014 11:53 pm

Kevy is fighting a fever that came on this evening. They are doing blood tests to try and figure out where the infection is located. He is not in pain, but incredibly down. It will be tomorrow night before they find out what is causing it. Love him so much.

October 28, 2014 7:36 pm

I thought this quote by Theodore Roosevelt was speaking directly to me. In turn, I hope it speaks to you as well.

It is not the critic who counts; not the man who points out how the strong man stumbles, or where the doer of deeds could have done them better. The credit belongs to the man who is actually in the arena, whose face is marred by dust and sweat and blood; who strives valiantly; who errs, who comes short again and again, because there is no effort without error and shortcoming; but who does actually strive to do the deeds; who knows great enthusiasms, the great devotions; who spends himself in a worthy cause; who at the best knows in the end the triumph of high achievement, and who at the worst, if he fails, at least fails while daring greatly...

For all who find comfort in visiting this site, thank you for your never-ending support. Be nice to one another. Kevin continues his fight and I will continue to let all who love him know how he is succeeding everyday because of your love and encouragement.

Love Kim

October 30, 2014 6:48 pm

Kevin was able to come home from the hospital this afternoon. He is very happy to be home. His only objective at this point is to heal, heal, and rest. Maybe some more rest too. We have nurses coming tomorrow to administer his IV antibiotics and to check on the dressings that he has on both drainage sites, as well as along the incision that is housing staples, and has been seeping a bit today. Kevin will be on the IV antibiotics as well as oral ones for at least two weeks, which is also the length of time that he will have the drains in. They will be emptied about twice a day by us, and we are getting used to the newest member of our household, Kevin's colostomy bag. If you have a suggestion for a nickname for it, let us know. "Bag" just doesn't sound sexy enough!

The doctors have suggested for Kevin to really focus on healing, and to do anything and all that he can to gain his strength. I am lucky enough to be able to stay home with Kevin tomorrow - Yeah Patterson Staff - and then we will have the weekend together. We have some plans in the works for next week with respect to supporting Kevin and me as I will be returning to work.

Your visits to the hospital, be it with a lunch for me or dropping by to offer a smile for Kevin, has been truly appreciated.

No fevers. No pain thanks to pain meds. Just a warm home and each other.

341

November 2, 2014 12.04 am

All who find themselves reading these journals have found themselves at one time or another under attack. No one, more so, than Kevin Troy Griffin.

Tonight, I have been lying beside the man who has been a part of me for 31 years. We have been together since we were 18 - my brother was twelve, Kevin's niece was 3, cabbage patch dolls were all the rage, as was Purple Rain and Prince. This man has fought through many things in his life. He would brawl in the corners on the ice or on the lacrosse field, leading both teams in penalty minutes so his teammates could make a shot or score a goal. At home, he had to fight off three sisters and two brothers for the one bathroom they all shared. He fought to get into university, convincing them that his street smarts were more valuable than his book smarts. And while he may have had to fight to get in, he rose to the challenge, and came out victorious.

Kevin appreciated his brother, Jack's, assistance in getting him an interview for his first full time job at Preston in Toronto. A door was opened for him, but Kevin lived up to the expectations of all and exceeded them with his determination to be nothing but the best. He was successful in his career from that moment on. As a son, brother, husband, father, boss, co-worker, coach and friend, Kevin has shown us all how strong a man he is.

The battle that is before him right now is the biggest fight he has ever faced. His body has been enveloped in poisons, cut into with scalpels, violated with radiation, ravaged by nausea, pain, neuropathy, diarrhea, headaches, horrific skin rashes and insurmountable fatigue. He takes one step forward, and three back. He was excitedly looking forward to completing six chemotherapy treatments, hoping that finally the disease that is wreaking so much havoc would be silenced for a while so he could rest. Rest. Rest. And then, he knew, would have to fight anew to continue to have the upper hand on cancer.

Best laid plans of mice and men.

His body was halted in mid-step by a perforated colon that nearly took him away. He has battled through yet another surgery, infection so large as to keep him in hospital for almost 10 days and send him home on IV antibiotics. He juggles two drains dangling from his abdomen and of course the elephant in the room - his colostomy bag. He is so sick, that sleep is a constant companion, and pain medications cause him to talk during his sleep. He wages a war against cramps, nausea and as of tonight a fever that peaked at 102. He is cold. He is hot. He is comfortable. He is afraid. He is defeated. He is unable to be alone. I can't move in bed without him reaching for me to make sure I'm still there.

I'm still here. Always. Forever.

Kevy. My Kevy. The man who has the most beautiful blue eyes and dimples. I fell in love with his sense of humor and tender heart. His broad shoulders and curly blonde hair didn't hurt either! I'm more in love today than I was 31 years ago. I love his scars, his tattoos for lining up his radiation treatments. I love the short cropped hair he now sports to help the medication for his scalp and skin be more effective in fighting the rashes. I love his rashes. I love his port. I LOVE HIM.

Always. Forever.

November 12, 2014 6:40 am

As this is a very impromptu plan, for any and all who are able, I am having an "Open House" birthday party for Kevin on Saturday, November 15, 2014 which just happens to be his actual birthday. He has no idea that I am doing this, but after everything he has been through, I thought the faces of those who are thinking about and praying for him and our family would be the best present we could give him.

The party will start around 6:00 pm - if you are able to come for only a short time, or are willing to camp for the night, we would love to see you. It's going to be very low key - just a few munchies and drinks - the most important thing is just to have Kevin see how many people love him and are wishing him a happy birthday. He is having a rough go right now, and finds himself pretty down. In the past, the most tried and true way of curing that is for Kevin to be surrounded by people, which is his way of recharging his battery.

So, please consider this your invitation to come and celebrate Kevin's day. The most important direction, however, is that it is Best Wishes Only. We only want to celebrate with you, and your time and effort to be there is gift enough.

For any Marmion parents, past and present, please include your sons in this invitation. They are so important to Kevin, and I think they also take away a sense of never giving up, and to keep moving forward, no matter what.
Hope to see you there!

Love, Kim

November 13, 2014 7.44 pm

Both Kevin and I have been lucky enough during the last month to enjoy the company and love of our mothers. And there is nothing better!

Kevin had been missing his Mom for some time, as she is in her eighties and travelling is not as easy anymore. Luckily though, for Canadian Thanksgiving which for our American friends was Columbus Day, Kevin's parents, his eldest sister and his youngest sister and her family came down to spend the weekend of thanks. Kevin was so happy to see everyone, but his eyes sparkled and he smiled just that much bigger when he saw his Mom.

If any of you have read "The Five Love Languages" you understand "love language". For those of you who have not had the luxury of reading a great book, find it on Amazon or at a used book store and get reading. It describes five different love languages and how we typically use our own love language to show how we care for someone else, when in fact their love language may be something totally different.

The five love languages are:

Acts of Service
Quality Time
Physical Touch
Gifts
Words of Affirmation

Kevin's love language is quality time, with physical touch not too far behind. So it seems that his Mom has always known that because once they hugged, it was hard to see Kevin without seeing his Mom holding his hand, or sitting and talking with him. Over the weekend, Kevin's spirits were lifted so much by the quality time that he got to spend with his family, his Mom. His whole family filled his need for quality time by sharing stories, jokes and laughs throughout our time together.

My love language is acts of service. It also appears that my Mom has known that all along because for the last four days, my Mom and stepdad Doug were down here under the guise of caring for Kevin. The truth however, is slightly more involved than that. Of course they were here to help Kevin with his IV antibiotics and other medications as well as giving him some of the best ever homemade meals. They also fed his soul and spirit by sharing time with him, and keeping him company. BUT, along with caring for Kevin, my Mom without missing a beat, was caring for me too.

Mom came down with a cooler full of frozen homemade food that more than filled out freezer. This act of service will, in and of itself, keep her love going forward for weeks to come. I could be at work knowing that my Kevy was in safe keeping. I also knew that when I got home, there would be a homemade meal waiting for me, with the table set, and my Mom, with some stiff legs and a slightly tired smile, waiting to show me what else she had been able to do for me. She insisted on cleaning up after dinner every night while I went and sat with Kev. She cleaned out my pots and pans cupboard, my Tupperware cupboard and my pantry! Who knew I had a few too many boxes of rice! My mom continued making me feel loved by doing laundry, and accompanying Doug to the hardware store to buy and replace a gazillion light bulbs in our house.

Once you determine your own love language, and that of your spouse, child or parent, you will unlock a plethora of wonderful feelings and unlimited blessings. I used to think that Kevin would love it when I cut the lawn, or tidied the garage for him. While he appreciated it, I was using my love language to tell him how I felt about him and all the while he would have rather had me sitting with him and enjoy a movie, conversation, or some music. He would have preferred to have me brush his hair, not organize his closet.

Thankfully we both learned each other's love language some time ago, and I haven't made the mistake of cutting the grass since!

In all, the love of a mother typically can't be beat. They know the deepest parts of you, and they want you to be happy, safe and loved. My mom is a lovely lady who knows what I need. And just as importantly she knows that I have in Kevin the person that I need. And love. And who speaks my language.

Thanks Mom and Mum.

November 15, 2014 12:53 am

Happy 49th Birthday Kevy! We love you truly and deeply. Enjoy your day and being celebrated!

Love Kim, Troy and Liam

November 17, 2014 9:12 pm

We were together. I forget the rest. ~ Walt Whitman

What a fantastic weekend!

To start it off, we had two doctor appointments for Kevin on Friday. Dr. S was the surgeon who performed the emergency surgery on Kevin met with us and told Kevin how good he looked. He told Kevin how truly lucky he was to have survived the surgery and its complications. I think it made Kevin really think and realize how far he had truly come in only three weeks. The doctor removed the two drains and took out all the staples, except one that I found when we got home. I got to play doctor and took it out!

After that first appointment, we met with Dr. Hantel. I shared with him that Kevin was putting so much pressure on himself, and felt that he should be further along in his recovery i.e.) back to full strength and able to leap tall buildings in a single bound. Dr. Hantel looked Kevin straight in the eye and said "You're nuts". This is why we love him so much! He said the same things about Kevin and how lucky he was and that he was doing great. Kevin is down to 200 lbs, and is only taking pain pills once or twice a day. He is still sleeping a lot but that is truly when his body can heal. We also did blood work on Friday, and got the CEA today... 5.6! Kevin is also gearing up for a CT scan tomorrow to make sure there are no pockets of infection left.

Friday night brought Troy and Liam home from Iowa, which was an amazing gift in and of itself. We love their company and we soaked them up as much as we could.

Then there was Saturday night. An impromptu party to celebrate Kevin's birthday. What a turnout. Thank you to all who were able to make it out during our first official snow event! It made Kevin's whole month. While he is physically healing, his emotional and psychological state needed some TLC and you all made good on that. For those who sent messages of well wishes, and prayers, you were part of the healing too. Kevin was humbled and overwhelmed with true joy and love. He was unable to fall asleep that night as he kept thinking about the party. We were also so very proud of Troy and Liam and how they assisted in being great hosts.

Once again you have helped out family to see the light. To feel the love. To share the happiness. Pay it forward everyone. 'Tis the season.

Love Kim

November 26, 2014 11:22 am

Worry never robs tomorrow of its sorrow, it only saps today of its joy.

~ Leo Buscaglia

As we gear up for Thanksgiving, I wanted to take a moment and pass along news and offer thanks.

Kevin saw Dr. Hantel yesterday, thanks to Liam who is home from college and was able to take him to his appointment. Dr. Hantel had ordered a CT scan which shows a pocket of fluid near Kevin's right hip which is measuring approximately 3" x 3". Consensus seems to be that it is most likely fluid that has been trapped from the surgery and healing process. Kev's white blood cell count is in the normal range leading the doctor away from thinking the pocket is infection. We also got a new CEA number, 14.4 which is up from not quite two weeks ago. Dr. Hantel did say that he expected the number to go up because as of October 17, Kevin had not been receiving chemo. So being out of the regimen has allowed the cancer that is chronic to start showing itself again. We have been told before that inflammation can attribute to the number increasing, but we know that the main reason is the cancer.

Dr. Hantel told Kevin he is not well enough yet to begin a treatment plan. Kevin is still fighting through fatigue, abdominal discomfort, depression, and an overall yucky feeling. Hopefully with me home for the next five days, I can make sure Kevy is eating, moving, resting and eating some more. We have to get him feeling human again so he can get back to living a relatively normal life. Once he reaches that summit, then he can begin a maintenance of this cancer. As I'm reading this back, I realize that the carrot of being well enough to get back to fighting cancer isn't necessarily that appealing. I mean, who wants to keep fighting, and fighting some more. Kevin does. And so do we.

So, as the quote says, worry only saps today of its joy, and there is truly an enormous amount of joy in our family. Moving into this incredible season of joy and celebration we will continue to focus on the good that is happening.

Kevin is here. Living. Loving. Healing. Smiling.

Our sons are home for a full week. What a wonderful feeling to have our home full of our most loved people.

We have been inundated with offers for this Thanksgiving.

My boss, Michele Frost and her family invited us for dinner. While I politely declined because Kevin is still not sure how he will be feeling from day to day, Michele would not take no for an answer. She gave me a turkey yesterday at work (just like the old days when companies handed their staff turkeys for the holiday) and told me that she and some others (whom I will name once I know) would be stopping by today with the rest of the dinner, including wine!

We have received a food box from a church that my co-worker Julie attends that contained all things needed to make a great meal for my thankful family.

Michele LMC as she is noted on my phone, gave our family a gift card to purchase a completely made Thanksgiving meal from Jewel. We will be holding on to that for Christmas!

My coworkers consistently check in with me and let me know they are praying for us, and sending their love, love, love.

Families from the Ashbury Subdivision, which is where Patterson Elementary is located (yeah prairie dogs!) have given food, gift cards, invitations to join them at their homes for parties, book discussions, a glass of wine... anything to keep me busy and give me some alone time which is truly appreciated.

WOW, a group of women who gather for bible study on Wednesdays took up a coin collection and added our family to their prayer list. Selfless and loving women.

The students of Patterson Elementary who have been collecting coins for Kim and Kev to help with finances as we are currently a one income family. Children have been coming into the office with baggies full of coins and even bills. I had one particular student who had received money for his birthday and when asked by his Mom what he wanted to do with it, he said he wanted to donate it to Mrs. Griffin's family. A fifth grade student gave up his money for us. Truly inspiring and a wonderful example of how great and incredible people are.

The Juriga family run River Heights Vet Clinic in Oswego which has been a second home for our puppy Mya. Mya, our 2 year old Newfoundland has had to be out of the home as Kevin dealt with his post surgery healing. They treated her like a queen, and were sad to see her leave. We, however, were very happy to have her back. She is growing up more and more, and less likely to want to jump up on Kevin for a hug!

Of course, once you start mentioning specifics, you are bound to forget someone. I do, however, feel it so important to share with you how much our community has come together to see one of their own through a very tumultuous time. If I have unintentionally not mentioned someone here, know that all prayers, thoughts, hugs, conversations, smiles, donations, and friendships have not fallen away. Each and every moment is adding to the blanket that our family is wrapping around ourselves, and every thread is needed to make this happen.

Thank you one and all and may God hold you and your family close this holiday season. God is Good, as he has led us to you.

Love and blessings,

Kim

November 30, 2014 11:20 am

When a father gives to his son, both laugh; when a son gives to his father, both cry. ~William Shakespeare

Well today marks the end of a great 10 days with Troy and Liam. They have been home for Thanksgiving, and it has made us both more thankful for these two beautiful young men. They brought back noise, and laughter, and presence, and pure rapture. Home has never felt so good. We know it's only a taste of the upcoming Christmas break, but the tears that are falling today don't care. That is two weeks away... and today is now.

Troy and Liam are quite simply the salt of the earth. They are the reason we keep moving forward and fighting. I could never have imagined that the two sons Kevin gave me would grow up to be so exquisitely exquisite. They have taken on the human form of comfort, joy, love, laughter, companion, cruise director. Exactly what the doctor ordered.

Kevin has loved having them home. Their companionship has helped to keep him focused on moving forward, and not dwelling on the past. Their friendship has allowed him to enjoy watching the Leafs hockey game, and not feel silly as he screams when they score, because he was not screaming alone! The house has felt more alive with them home, yes a little messier looking too, but who cares. The life that is in Kevin's eyes is irreplaceable. He has been up and moving more and more with the boys here. He has been smiling almost nonstop too.

If there was one thing that I want the boys to take away as they pack up and prepare to head back to school, it's this. You each have a man who loves you so much, and is so proud to be your Dad. I hope in a moment of silence, that you can recall and remember how amazing it feels to be loved so much. There will never be another man on the face of the earth who will love you unconditionally, purely, and without pause.

Your Dad.

You give him a reason to face down the yucky days, and to strive to get better. You are his motivation to rebound and get back into life. You quite simply are his everything.

There is something special between sons and fathers, and yes, I'm a bit envious. But having the three most important men in my life be in a love-fest with each other is something I will treasure forever. Troy and Liam, thank you for loving Dad so deeply and so effortlessly. One day you will truly realize how much it has meant to Dad, and to yourselves.

Can't wait to have you home for Christmas! We love you.

January 4, 2015 12:06 pm

Nothing is more precious than being in the present moment. Fully alive, fully aware.

~ Thích Nhất Hạnh

It has certainly been a whirlwind these past few weeks as one and all have been celebrating Christmas, Hannukah and the New Year. We have enjoyed so much having Troy and Liam home from school. They just add a greater feel of love and family. Since the last post, we have been very busy. Our friend Sally rallied a group of people to come to our home and help us de-clutter as we get ready to most likely move. Our garage and basement were loaded down with garbage, items waiting to be donated and treasures. Even though I am not what I would consider a pack rat, it was amazing how much "stuff" you can collect after 15 years in one spot. Under Sally's guidance, they made quick work of it and left us with such a feeling of relief.

We had a dear friend and incredible photographer, Kelly Billington, give our family the absolute best gift of a family portrait. It was something I wanted forever and there is no time better than the present, so we got it done. I have added some to this page for you to see. It made me feel like our family truly existed.

My staff at Patterson Elementary showered us with gifts for Christmas, making it a truly special time. It was even more so with my sister Karen and her kiddos James and Laura coming down to spend Christmas with us. For Karen and I, it has been decades since we woke up under the same roof on Christmas morning. Games, laughing, movies, dinners, salt caves, conversations hours long were the epitome of a wonderful holiday. It was also a blessing as Karen helped me pack boxes in the kitchen and worked with me in cleaning closets and under sinks. Looks great though!

The sheets on Troy's bed didn't even have time to rest before we were visited by our very dearest friends Steve and Julie Malecki. They drove down from Canada to spend New Years with us and to tackle Kevin's Honey Do list. Julie continued to help me with my laundry room and finally being able to see the floor, while Steve fixed the door bell, shower doors, railings, lights... the list goes on forever. Thank you friends for getting us even closer to the ultimate goal of moving.

While life was going on, Kevin had blood work and a CT scan done as well on Dec. 31. We meet with Dr. Hantel on Tuesday to discuss the results, but because of a surprise visit to the ER for Kevin, we were able to find out the results of those tests. Firstly, Kevin was sent to the ER after his scan and blood work because his blood pressure was really high. Thanks to not picking up his meds, and missing them for a few days, it set him up to spend about 8 hrs there. He was given a dose of his missed meds, and had an EKG, blood work looking for cardiac enzymes, chest x-ray etc. and passed with flying colors. Now for the rest of the story.

The CEA went from 23 to 108 which we all expected. He hasn't been on any chemo since October 19. The scan shows that any previous sights below his diaphragm are stable or decreasing in size, which is fantastic. The problem is above the diaphragm. While it has been mentioned before, there are lesions in his lungs that have grown since the last scan, and there are new ones too. The lesions are in both lungs. Kevin has been having a little shortness of breath, and the scan shows some scar tissue from the Cyberknife treatments last year. So, we know that surgery and radiation are not options available to us, which means we are waiting to hear from Hantel what kind of cocktail he wants Kevin to take. Dr. Hantel did talk about possibly taking two drugs, one that causes the marks on his face, and the other that causes diarrhea, nausea, fatigue etc. We are hoping that he lets Kevin take just the one drug that affects his skin, which will allow him to continue living a relatively normal life. If we have to implement both, lots of variables are thrown in again, some which will add incredible angst and stress on Kevin. But we have to wait and see what is suggested on Tuesday. We will be going with the boys so they are completely in the loop of what is going on.

In a sense, Kevin has developed a bucket list, and he asked me to do the same. My first thing on the list was to have a family portrait taken. Done. Kevin's list consists of selling the house so we can go on a family vacation. We have to check with our medical insurance company if Kevin can have any coverage if he travels outside of the US, in case of issues with his colostomy, or overall health. Here is hoping they say yes because Kevin wants to see the world (or parts of it at least)!

I received a book for Christmas from my friend Martha called "The Precious Present". It is a short book, but what a punch it holds. Essentially, it reminds us all that being in the moment is all we really have. If we think of the past, it's easy to become sad or despondent thinking about what has happened to Kevin and our family. If we think of the future, it can become overwhelming thinking of how it may look. BUT if we remain in the moment, we can continue to be happy and excited. The idea is divine, and attainable, although I do have to bring myself back sometimes from the future. It doesn't mean that you are in denial or unwilling to face what is happening. Rather it gives you a reason to keep smiling and enjoying life and wanting to keep moving forward. It gives you a reason to hug and kiss more, laugh and just be. Martha, thank you so very much for giving me "the Present". It's a great place to be.

We will inform you of our visit on Tuesday. Until then, prayers are appreciated, and try being in the moment or present yourself today. You may find it quite exhilarating.

Love Kim

January 7, 2015 9:48 pm

August 2010 diagnosed with colon cancer.

January 2015 beating all the odds and preparing to fight once again.

We met with Dr. Hantel on Tuesday to discuss the blood work and scan from December 31. Hantel's take on the scan was fairly optimistic—which is quite a word when used on a CaringBridge sight talking about cancer. He thinks the CEA number is not a reflection of the spots in the lungs. To him they are insignificant at this point. So he is assuming that the number is reflecting microscopic cancer somewhere in Kevin's abdomen. OK so now what.

Firstly, as a means of ruling out any possibility that the cancer has moved to the brain, or as Dr. Hantel said "to check to make sure there is something between the ears", Kevin will be having an MRI of his head. This is strictly to eliminate any unknowns as Kevin has never had a scan of his cranium. I am quite interested in how many jokes we can make out of this test once the results are back. Well, I might give him a pass... cuz he's cute!

In our discussions, Dr. Hantel left the decision of when we move ahead with chemo up to Kevin. Doc says there is no necessity to move into chemo immediately. He is encouraged that Kevin has gained weight, and is gaining strength too. In making the decision, we took a lot of factors into mind. Ultimately we have decided to delay starting Erbitux (yucky skin chemo) for a month. This is going to give Kevin more time to strengthen himself, continue working full time and enjoying life, even the smelly dog breath of Mya - our Newfoundland dog who loves to give kisses and loves to get hugs from us.

So for the immediate future, we will continue to live like "normal" and make the most of each day. Kevin is relieved in Dr. Hantel's response to the test results and I am relieved that Kevin is relieved.

I think once we start the first chemo, depending on the response of Kevin's body, they will add another one that is the nausea and diarrhea inducing one. But we are getting ahead of ourselves.

January 7, 2015 - Taking a deep breath and enjoying life.

February—March-ish, 2015 - Back to kicking ass.

Prayers of thanks from Kevin and I continue to travel upwards for all of you and all of your needs. May you all continue with good health and incredible happiness. We are wrapped in some warped form of happiness ourselves.

Love Kim

February 14, 2015 12:48 pm

There are exactly as many special occasions in life as we choose to celebrate.

~ Robert Brault

Much time has passed since I last posted, and not much new to report from the medical perspective. Kevin has not started chemo yet, although we anticipate that happening the first week of March. Our last appointment with Dr. Hantel was a good one in that he was agreeable that the chemo vacation could continue and be a good thing. It would allow Kevin to gain some much needed strength and weight, and would continue to allow his body and mind to heal and prepare for the treatment. Kevin's CEA numbers did go up to 308, but as Dr. Hantel said, he isn't breaking any records. We know there are spots in the lungs, and based on the number there is microscopic cells throughout his abdomen.

All this, and yet Kevin has never felt better, or in my opinion looked better. He is working full time, and has done some traveling for work to North Carolina, and Minnesota. And thanks to Steve and Julie for going with us, we also travelled to Las Vegas for a quick trip filled with card playing, gambling, laughing, site seeing and pure joy of being away from home.

Four and a half years is a long time to be on a ride that has so many ups, downs, turns and tumbles. It has brought anguish, hell, fear, overwhelmingness, happiness, joy, laughter, mindfulness, and anticipation. It has contained days of utter heartache, followed by weeks and weeks of pain. It has also had months and months of love, happiness, enjoyment and appreciation.

As Kevin's partner for life, and most recently as a caregiver, I have been on the ride with Kevin, albeit in a different seat. For those of you who know me, I do not do roller coasters or rides that contain that anticipation of not knowing what is coming next. Never has that been more clearly shown than this past week when I reached out, finally, to receive outpatient treatment for depression and anxiety. I am in a full day program M-F attending group therapy sessions, learning coping skills and life skills to help me as I continue on this ride.

Did I see this coming? Yes. And No. You see, part of the pitfalls of a caregiver is that your focus is clearly on the one for which you are caring. And in my case, that includes Troy and Liam.

I have completed four days, and have this upcoming week where I will be in treatment full time. I anticipate that I will continue on some sort of part time plan. And what's funny is, it's a totally different roller coaster ride. BUT - this ride offers you a heads up of when a big dip is coming, or when the turn is going to be sharp. AND it teaches you how to know when to hold on for dear life, or to let go and scream with delight.

I have always been considered the emotional one in my growing up family, and what that meant was that it only took a few words of correction to have me in tears. I cried at sad movies, when I was hurt, when something bad happened to someone I loved. I have struggled with that label all my life, and have slowly come to realize that in fact, I have been allowing myself to be who I am. And as an adult, I decide everyday that there is no shame in that.

Four and a half years of not having myself as my focus has caused me to reach levels of depression and anxiety that I hadn't before. So during this time of chemo vacation, you would think that I would be sailing through life without all those horrible feelings we have when we are knee deep in cancer. However, what happened instead was that I did not have an excuse to look past myself. The external noise settled down, and the internal noise erupted and could not be stopped.

The littlest things in life became completely overwhelming. I could not do laundry because I didn't know where to start. I DIDN'T KNOW WHERE TO START. That applied to everything. Finally I reached out, and took hold of the help that was presented. I'm learning so much, and I think the most important one for me, so far, is mindfulness.

If you have not read the book "The Precious Present" please look it up and take the 10 minutes it takes to read. It left an indelible mark on me, and started me to listen to the internal noises just before they erupted. Basically, the "present" time is all we have and if we stay in the "present" we can be utterly happy, no matter what is going on. If we look to the past, we start saying the shoulds, woulds, coulds. We cannot undo what has happened. If we look to the future, it is cloaked in fear, anticipation, sadness, worry, unknown. Both instances take us away from being truly happy right now. All we have is right now.

So everyday holds moments that we can turn to celebration. Right now I am happy that Kevin and Liam are watching a lacrosse game together and spending time together over something they both love. I am happy that I am writing this journal even though it is difficult, because my hope is that someone else may find something written here today and run with it. I'm proud of myself for stepping out of life for a short time and getting the help I need to be more often in the moment. I'm afraid of the future, and what it looks like. I miss the past when we were a family before cancer. But trying to be mindful and in the moment, I realize I am lucky to have this outlet which also serves as an inlet for your feedback.

So let's celebrate shall we?

Love Kim

March 4, 2015 8:19 pm

Relief. Renewal. Revitalized.

Words that on a page are just a line of letters, but, when said out loud and with respect to our lives they are exclamations of life and all, it's hope and joy.

Quickly, I completed my therapy and absolutely feel empowered. I feel relief that I am armed with resources and tools to help me be a healthier person, and to help my family through this journey. I have a sense of renewal and revitalization that makes me look at everyday as phenomenal and a host of potential. I am not "over" my anxiety and depression, but I am in control, at least for today, of what I do and think. Fantastic. Thank you to all for your supportive words and prayers.

Kevin had a scan on Monday and we met with Dr. Hantel today to discuss where we go from here. Being mindful of where this term comes from i.e., an oncologist, Dr. Hantel said he was thrilled with the scan. The spots in Kevin's lungs have remained ultimately unchanged since his last scan, some 2 months ago. That took a lot off of Kevin's mind as he was feeling some pain and discomfort around his rib cage and was afraid it was a result of the cancerous spots growing. Come to find out that the discomfort is attributed to the colostomy and the fact that Kevin has gained a bit of weight.

News about the rest of his abdomen however, was more grounding. It showed that there are new tumors in his liver and one small lymph node near the stomach. While this is not great news, it of course explains the increase in the CEA. The thrilling part is the fact that Dr. Hantel described these new sights as slow growing. I don't know that we have ever been able to describe Kevin's cancer as slow growing. Based on the scan, and Kevin's continual improvement overall, it was determined that Kevin will NOT go back on chemo quite yet.

When Kevin was told this, he was shocked. He was prepared to start this Friday, and had psyched himself up to having six to eight treatments. When we were told that there would be no chemo for now, Kevin had to take it all in. We were also told that when he does go on chemo, it would be for four treatments to see how it is working for him. Therefore it was a great visit and we are very happy with the outcome. We know that Kevin will always be trying to catch the cancer, but for him to be able to sigh with relief, feel a sense of renewal and an opportunity to continue to revitalize himself, he gave me a high five. "Normal" life can continue for now.

It's a great time in our home, as lacrosse season has also started which keeps Kevin busy every weeknight. It's what makes him tick. It's his greatest love outside of his family. The boys also begin their spring break this weekend. Liam is a starter for the lacrosse team, and will be traveling to Georgia and Tennessee to play games, returning home a week from today. Troy will be heading home this weekend after being asked by two different professors to join them in Ireland and Italy to study this summer and during the winter break. He will assist in research and have his name included on the published findings. I am back at work and am attending support groups to help keep me emotionally healthy. I should have done this long ago, but perhaps I wasn't ready until now.

I am sure that those reading the journal are smiling at the great news we are sharing. Please also note that this Friday, March 6 is Dress in Blue Day to remind everyone that March is colon cancer awareness month. Please join us, wherever you are, by wearing blue that day. And remember if you are 50+ years old, have a family history of colon cancer, or are showing symptoms that include blood in your stool, changes in bowel movements, unplanned weight loss GET

CHECKED AND FIND OUT WHAT'S UP YOUR BUM! Colon cancer is curable if found early enough. DON'T WAIT. Book a test during March and tell them that Kevin sent you!

Love to all and go blue!!

March 31, 2015 9:47 pm

The best thing about the future is that it comes one day at a time.
~ Abraham Lincoln

I didn't realize how much time has passed since the last post. I suppose that is a good thing because that means that we have been doing a lot of living... in the moment. And now is the moment to share an update.

Kevin visited with Dr. Hantel today and did blood work. Hantel was very happy with how Kevin looked, and that his vitals were good. As of this posting, we don't have the CEA back, but we know it will be going back up as Kevin has not been on chemo since October. That will change effective April 10, 2015.

You may recall that Kevin was finishing up chemo in October when he had a rupture of his colon. October 21 was the date, and I will never forget. Thankfully Kevin came through that very difficult time. It was a very serious situation, and I would not wish it for anyone. Kevin has been recovering from the emergency surgery and at some point he began, or should I say we began to feel what "normal" life was like again. It has been such a long time. As Kevin became stronger, and further removed from chemo, we began to enjoy everything at such a deeper level. We have been spending quality time with Troy and Liam and we have been visiting with friends. Kevin and I have been having a lot of date nights which have consisted of having dinner in front of the TV, watching Better Call

Saul. Kevin has been working hard, and of course it's lacrosse season, bringing with it a full calendar of practices and games.

We knew that the honeymoon from chemo would be coming to an end, but it kept being pushed back, making us all the more happy. But Dr. Hantel has decided that we should move forward with the treatment and he has booked Kevin in for April 10.

Kevin has had so much energy and enthusiasm for everything. He has been nonstop with all aspects of his life. However, more recently he has found himself quite tired (no surprise what with his schedule) and experiencing some pain in his groin and left leg. Dr. Hantel has said that it most likely is the lack of lymph nodes in that area that are causing an issue with drainage for the lymph system, and therefore putting pressure on some of the nerves in his leg. We just have to wait it out to see if it gets better once the treatments start. If it gets worse, we would have to go back.

So this is where my recent therapy comes in real handy. It's about staying in the moment, and not looking too far into the future. We have to continue to enjoy the moments that present themselves, and we have to continue to live life to the fullest. Don't tell anyone, but we are going away for Easter - just me and Kev for a long weekend in San Francisco. It will be an opportunity for us to gather our stamina and energy and clear our minds for the fight ahead. I know I say we, when it is Kevin who will physically be taking the biggest hit, but as I've learned, and stated numerous times, cancer affects everyone.

Kevin is not looking forward to the nausea and skin irritations. He is not looking forward to the fatigue. He is concerned as to how the chemo will affect his body, after the colostomy and surgery. I don't want to see the physical change in him, but we have to keep moving forward.

Abraham Lincoln's quote is simple yet profound. The future comes one day at a time. So for today, or what is left of it, I'm going to snuggle up with Kev, he is going to fill me in on the rest of his day, and we will fall asleep looking forward to tomorrow.

Thanks for your continued support and thoughtful words of love and encouragement. They do not fall on deaf ears. We wear them all on our hearts - it's what gives us the energy to face the yucky stuff, and keep moving.

Good night and love to all,

Kim

April 11, 2015 7.43 pm

Yesterday.

The first step in our newest journey.

Kevin's CEA is 1203 and according to Dr. Hantel our starting point.

Kevin began the first in at least four chemos Friday which beat him up pretty good, but not enough for him to miss seeing Liam play lacrosse downtown Chicago. The treatment is consisting of 2 drugs, erbitux and irinotecan (spelling?) and dragging over many hours. Kevin didn't make it home last night until almost 7:00 pm. He was slightly pale, nauseous and tired. Sleeping last night was constantly interrupted for him because of varying aches and pains. When he did get to sleep, it was peaceful. This morning he had to go in and get his neulasta shot to help keep his white cell count up.

I'm so very proud of Kevin and the way he is approaching this latest round of treatments. Not unlike the many times before, he is facing it head on and with his shoulders rolled back as well as his sleeves. It will get harder, but continuing to apply my newfound Mindfulness and "In the moment" schtick we are enjoying this beautiful day that was full of sunshine and warmth, the vision of our son playing college lacrosse, and the stinging bite of a loss on the field. When we came home Kevin slept for about 1 1/2 hours and he is now refreshed. Yeah for naps.

I also have to share a t-shirt that I bought and wore today that made Kevin and others laugh: It reads - My husband's wife is freaking awesome... true story!

Sorry for the short and succinct update but I want to get back to spending time with Kev. Enjoy the rest of your weekend everyone and try a random act of kindness.

Love, Kim

April 24, 2015 11:00 pm

The power of love to change bodies is legendary, built into folklore, common sense, and everyday experience. Love moves the flesh, it pushes matter around... Throughout history, "tender loving care" has uniformly been recognized as a valuable element in healing.

~ Larry Dossey

Power of Love... makes us realize how much "power" Kevin has in fighting against this disease. We are constantly inundated with kind words, prayers, hugs, acts of kindness, gifts, love, smiles, tears, friendship. And boy do we need it.

Kevin had number 2 chemo today and we found out that his CEA went from 1203 to 758 which is fantastic. It was almost a 50% drop and according to Dr. Hantel, Good News. It also took a lot out of Kev today.

As Kevin has been battling this for almost 5 years, (I can't believe that) and has a body that carries with it all the scars of surgeries and the sores of chemotherapy and radiation, the treatments are quicker to try and bring him down. He is taking two drugs and one of them, Erbitux, causes an incredible rash. It also makes him susceptible to sunburn. Of course you know Kevin as a white Irishman who turns to Larry the Lobster with short exposure to sunshine. Well after the first treatment, Kev was coaching the Marmion lacrosse team in a weekend tournament where he was doused with sunshine. Suffice it to say that his face is incredibly sore and raw. Each week this one drug will bring more and more rashes and acne to his face and chest that he was asked today if he wanted to dial back on Erbitux. Yep, he said NO. He received the whole kit and caboodle today.

The other drug, irinotecan, causes numbness in his fingers and toes. He is beginning to feel like he is wearing mittens again. He is experiencing a prickly feeling that makes it very difficult for him to get comfortable. He is fatigued and nauseous too and wants nothing more than to sleep until next week.

But the one thing that has not been touched by the cancer is Kevin's incredible positive energy and attitude. He wants to beat this thing (and by the way we are trying to come up with a name for the cancer - suggested by my therapist - so we can express our anger and hatred toward "it"). And the power of love that you bestow on him and our family gives him the strength to fight through these difficulties and to keep moving forward.

I am so proud to be his wife. He is an incredible man whose tenacity and persistence are second to none. He is working full time, coaching every night and on weekends, a husband willing to take on his share of household chores when he can and a Dad who misses his boys and can't wait to see them both. He is counting down the days that he can go fishing with Troy and is hoping he has the strength to make a trip to Iowa tomorrow to watch Liam play lacrosse.

Power of Love. Anytime that Kevin feels like he can't go on, we turn to this journal and see all the visits from all of you and the comments or likes left behind. It is the jolt that keeps Kevin charged and ready to keep going.

Thank you.

Love, Kim

May 7, 2015 9:14 pm

Chantal

What a beautiful name. What makes it even more so is that Chantal is an incredibly caring, trustworthy, genuine and professional woman. She is also our pharmacist.

People come and go in our lives but Chantal has been a staple in our medication dispensing life. Even before chemo came into our lives (and by the way, we named it Dick) we had the typical family prescriptions to be filled.

I have to admit that when your senses are not heightened because of a life changing event, you don't very often notice the people around you that are quietly doing their job and helping you while adding a smile to your order.

Fast forward to that life changing health crisis. Chantal, while not the only person who has helped us obtain antibiotics, pain meds, sleeping aids etc., she stands out among all. She is an incredible person who has truly found her calling. You can tell that she loves to help people. She is genuine in her concern for your health and always makes time to answer any and all questions. I have never appreciated someone in her role before, and tonight I let her know.

As we anticipate Kevin's third chemo treatment tomorrow, I tend to get a little melancholy. I began thinking about people in our lives who have made a difference, and Chantal came to mind. We had some prescriptions that needed to be picked up and when I called over to make sure they were in, Chantal answered the phone and I knew right away that I had to go over and let her know what a difference she has made.

She of course was deflecting of my accolades and said she was happy to help. I don't think she truly understands how much of a difference her smile, demeanor, and professionalism make as I drive up to collect the meds that help Kevin through his pains and anxieties. She always makes me smile and feel good. Hard to believe that you could say that about your pharmacist. But I can. And I did. Tonight.

Chantal, thank you from the bottom of my heart for the role you play in helping our family. You are a great gift and you will not soon be forgotten.

Chantal. Beautiful.

May 8, 2015 10:47 pm

Chemo 3 is in the books and the CEA went from 758 to 336!

The poison being pumped through Kevin's veins is kicking ass... and unfortunately Kevin too. He is sleeping now, after telling me how he felt as if he had been run over by a truck. No surprise as chemo's effect is cumulative, and Lord knows that Kevin is using every last ounce of the drugs to fight, fight, fight.

If you have ever questioned what a true superman looks like, look no further than tomorrow at Marmion Academy where you will find Kevy on the sidelines coaching and hosting the Marmion Cadet Challenge lacrosse tournament. Fourteen different teams from the surrounding area will compete on five fields in the hopes of taking home the dog tags and bragging rights.

So less than 24 hrs after completing his chemotherapy, rain or shine, nauseous or fatigued, Kevin will be there for his team, his guests and for himself. He is a walking example of indomitable spirit, strength, commitment and dogged determination. He will show us all how you can never quit, never give up on others or yourself. He will need to rest and be watered and rest some more somehow, somewhere. The only reason he will leave briefly tomorrow is to return to the cancer center for his neulasta injection to help build up his white cells and prevent infection.

He is amazing. You know earlier this week we both found ourselves wide awake at 3:30 am unable to settle down into even a fitful sleep. I quietly asked him after we held hands and spoke quietly, if he would dance with me. Without missing a beat he was up and had me in his arms. We danced in darkness to Thinking Out Loud by Ed Sheeran.

My Superman with the softest touch and gentle moves will be coaching his team to do their very best and then push for even more, all the while doing the same for himself.

Kevin Troy Griffin is truly a Superman. So if you can come out to watch a game or five, look for the guy without a cape. You may see that the kryptonite has weakened him in between the big plays but if you look close enough, you just might see the S on his chest. Superman. Survivor. Strength.

Love Kim

May 22, 2015 10:03 pm

Chemo 4 is bringing with it good news. The CEA went from 336 to 165!

Dr. Hantel was ecstatic. The cocktail is bang on. So much so that they have scheduled Kev for 4 more treatments and holding off on a scan until number 6 is done.

Kev is home resting and happy.

Yesterday I went for my colonoscopy to celebrate being 50, and to practice what I preach. It was so easy, and after they found and removed one polyp, certainly grateful that I kept my promise. Please go for a colonoscopy if you are experiencing symptoms or have reached the golden age. I will find out later next week if I have to go back in three or five years for another colonoscopy.

Thank you for your continued support and love. Kevin is doing it with a little help from his friends.

We plan on a lot of rest this long weekend, and hopefully a barbeque and some quality time with the boys!

Enjoy the weekend, short or long, depending on your geography!

Love Kim

June 9, 2015 12.08 am

So, often in the course
Of life's few fleeting years,
A single pleasure costs
The soul a thousand tears

Francis William Bourdillon

So much life has happened since I last posted.

The good news is that Kevin's fifth treatment has brought his CEA marker down from 165 to 96, another incredible reduction. It continues to feed us with hope and strength to see another day through its side effects. Kevin is without question the strongest man ever. His chest is bigger than Superman's and the S would shrink away on him looking more like a LaCoste label. Screw you nausea and fatigue. Take off headaches and tingling limbs. I'm here and fighting. Every day.

I'm sure most of you heard that Kevin was in a car accident recently, and thankfully escaped with only bruised ribs, and a broken hand. Oh yeah, and a few nightmares. When we were speaking with our friends in Canada, Steve and Julie, Steve joked about the "proverbial stepping off the curb and being hit by a bus". Realistically, it could have happened. BUT IT DIDN'T! We are so grateful that both Kev and his friend and coworker Steven were spared from serious harm. It will now be another story for Kevin to retell and store in his treasure trove of tales to entertain and enchant us all.

Simple things have occurred too. Liam cut his long hair short and is even more good looking than before. Troy has made a few batches of chili, and each one is better than the last. Work has called all of us in, and in our family a few evenings of hockey, "American Dad", and Deadliest Catch. Then everything stopped.

While working as a TA, I had the privilege of meeting and getting to know a fellow TA, Kelly. I worked with her for a few years before I moved to Patterson Elementary. Kelly's work with some of our friends in elementary school is beyond compare. Kelly as a person is caring, loving, funny, involved, a wife, mother. And as of Saturday evening, a mother who has witnessed the surprising death of her 16 year old son. His name was Matt and he died as a result of heart issues. They were known to the family, but Matt had been watched, under doctor's care and on medication and living a very full and active life. He played volleyball and basketball, and by all that I have gathered the past day or so, had many friends who loved him and are aching because of his passing. A sixteen year old son. Here one minute. Gone the next. Kelly's arms must be aching as they can no longer hug her son. Can no longer care for her son. No longer tousle his hair, or kiss his cheek. No longer.

Loving anyone in this world is going to bring with it some measure of pain. By investing our time, efforts, energy and love into someone else, we leave ourselves open to be crushed and shattered by their untimely death. Nothing can prepare us for the pain. I hurt for her, but understand that I can never know the thousand tears that she has released just in the short two days since Matt's death. It has for the moment, put things into perspective. Something that needs to happen for all, but too often not reviewed.

I wanted to share this with you as a means of making us all stop and take inventory of what is truly valuable in our lives, and what are things we can do without. Cutting someone off in traffic because you HAVE to get to where you are going faster than others. Getting mad because your drive through meal didn't come with the sauce you requested. Fighting with a fellow shopper over the last one of whatever.

Kelly can no longer hold her son.

Never close yourself off from loving others, and investing in their lives. Just remember to be kind to others, because you never know what is going on in their life. You may have missed a deadline, but Matt is gone. Forever.

Hug your loved ones a little longer. Remind yourself of your blessings. Show compassion to one another. Give the benefit of the doubt to someone. Smile at your neighbor. Wave to someone you see regularly. Stop and say a prayer for Kelly. And Matt.

Compassionately,

Kim

June 19, 2015 7:34 pm

Chemo is a poison that kills the cancer cells, and the good cells of a person's body. Chemo is painful, nauseating, day stopping pain. It is all encompassing. It holds our collective breath, and brings us to our knees.

And it also kicks ass!

Kevin's CEA dropped again from 96 to 51.7!

We are ecstatic.

Kevin is beaten down, but his spirits are high.

Dr. Hantel continues to be happy with everything. He is happy that we haven't had to add Avastin back into the mix because that is what caused Kevin's perforation back in October. He has also decided that Kevin's next treatment will be in three weeks, not two. I'm truly happy for that because Kevin has only been able to squeak out one or possibly two good days between treatments. This should give him a great boost.

So enjoy your weekend. We thank God for you as you continue on this journey with Kevin and our family. Your support and prayers are appreciated.

God is good. God is great. Chemo still sucks, but it kills cancer!

Love, Kim

August 20, 2015 4:12 pm

He who has a why to live can bear almost any how.

~ Friedrich Nietzsche

Today marks the fifth anniversary of when Kevin was diagnosed with colon cancer, some 1,826 days ago.

Every day that has gone by during this time is a blessing because Kevin is beating the odds. Every day he is winning, as are we. All of us who have Kevin in our life.

My hero has survived and thrived through so many surgeries, chemotherapy and radiation treatments. He has endured nausea, headaches, depression, fatigue, neuropathy, acne, dry skin, sleeplessness and chemo brain. He has a WHY to live and he can and does bear almost anyhow.

WHY

A few weeks ago Kevin was quite down, and feeling defeated. He said to me as he lay there with tears streaming down his cheeks that he wanted to give up and give in. With only a moment to take a breath, he then answered himself by saying that "only because of the love of my family and friends will I keep pushing forward through this dark time". That is why I chose the quote from Nietzsche. Kevin's why includes all who visit this site to read up on how Kevin is doing. Your love and friendships allow him to bear all the anguish and pain.

Tomorrow, Kevin will be returning to Dr. Hantel to see if his "maintenance" chemo treatment that he received two weeks ago is working and keeping the CEA number either the same, or at least not spiking. Depending on the result, Kevin will be facing the possibility of returning to a chemotherapy cocktail that has so many side effects. Right now he is receiving Erbitux alone which has minimal side effects.

But, after five years of treatments, his body is beaten up. Every chemical that goes in has the potential of doing more harm to the tissues and cells that are trying so hard to build upon one another working to hold off the bad cells.
Tomorrow is a pivotal day.

We want the CEA number to have stayed the same, or even fallen. We do not want a bigger number...please God.

Prayers are greatly appreciated.

I will post tomorrow after we get results. Love to all. And thank you for being the WHY.

August 21, 2015 5:28 pm

Number went from 40 to 52.6. Hantel wasn't there today so no real feedback at this time. Kev is resting and I am crying.

More updates when available.

September 20, 2015 8:05 pm

Stable - Used to describe either a place to house animals, or to describe a situation as not likely to change or fail.

Kevin is no horseman nor a fan of horses.

As a child, he attended company picnics with his family sponsored by his father's employer, SC Johnson Wax . One of the attractions at the picnic was a chance to ride horseback. Now the horses had been doing their thing all day, and were recognized with only brief respites from the sticky, screaming kiddos. When Kevin decided he wanted to partake in the attraction that children lined up for, and waited for, long into the afternoon, he couldn't have imagined the outcome.

When it came time for Kevin to ride the horse, he was assisted on, and in a matter of seconds, the horse that was Kevin's mount, decided that a rest was in order. It stopped, and lay down on the dirt with Kevin's leg pinned between itself and the ground. Kevin was ordered to not move as he would possibly break his leg because of the weight of the horse. I don't think Kevy had any inkling of moving, mainly because he couldn't. After what seemed a very long time, the horse was coaxed to get up and leave his rider clawing at the ground to get his leg out of the way. The "kicker" of this was that this happened to Kevin a second time, at a Johnson family picnic some years later.

Stable then, in this case, is being used to describe Kevin's CEA numbers and status. His treatment was Friday, and he also met with Dr. Hantel. His number went from 60 to 76. An increase, but in the world of colon cancer, nary a bump. Hantel reiterated that if it gets to 150, we would likely have to revisit Kevy's treatment plan and reintroduce another drug.

But for now, he is stable. No horses to be seen. Although he does appear to be staying in the race, close to the fence, with many fans in the stands cheering him on.

Love from Analogy Girl!

October 4, 2015 10:10 pm

Three little words that can change how you get through something difficult.

I AM HERE.

Three words that have never meant so much as they do during a moment of sheer angst and fear.

For the last week, Kevin was finding it incredibly difficult to stay awake and when he was up, the nausea was taking any and all joy out of everything. He struggled through each day, and made every attempt to be where he needed to be, see those he needed to see, and enjoy his down time with family. Needless to say, there wasn't a lot of down time. It almost always became sleep time.

Kevin was scheduled for his chemo treatment on Friday. As is typical, he had his blood drawn so they could check all his levels to make sure he was well enough to have the chemo. Dr. Hantel was the bearer of bad news when he came in and told Kevin that he would not be getting his chemo treatment because his blood work showed that his liver enzymes were way out of whack. He said that there was something going on, and that Kevin did not look good in yellow! Kevy finally admitted to having some discomfort and nausea for the last week, not to mention the lack of sleep and incredible itchiness. Dr. Hantel ordered a CT scan immediately, thinking that Kevin's bile duct was blocked.

Kevin had the CT scan on Friday and based on the results was told he would be having further testing. It was scheduled for yesterday *morning in Plainfield. Kevin went with Troy and the procedure was done so the doctors could have a closer look at the bile ducts. When Kevin returned home, he found himself in the bathroom urinating what looked like blood. He phoned the answering service for Dr. Hantel and it was suggested that he go to the hospital to find out what was going on.*

We got to Edward's Emergency room yesterday around 4-5 and Kevin had further labs done as well as another CT scan. It was determined from these tests that he had a kidney stone that was moving through his body, and his bile duct showed signs of being blocked by something. We aren't sure what that something is just yet... theories being considered include the liver itself, lymph nodes etc. Because Kevin has had so much done to his liver i.e.) three liver ablations, and two chemo embolizations, not to mention the rounds and rounds of chemo and radiation, his liver is misshapen and interferes with the bile duct system.

So as I write this Kevin is in Edward Hospital, and thinks that he has passed the kidney stone. Yeah. He is now waiting to hear when the temporary stent will be put into his bile duct. It will happen tomorrow, although time is not known just yet. Kevin is still itchy, a little less tired, and his labs show that the liver enzymes are less wonky. He has been given some intravenous antibiotics and was resting fairly comfortably.

It was wonderful to have the boys home this weekend, and, while it's not the kind of time we wanted to spend with them, they each got some good quality time with Kev at the hospital. I spent the evening with him, and have returned home to let the dogs out. (I know there is a song there... just not sure what to call it!)

Thank you for being here for Kevin, Troy, Liam and me. The strength and support may be invisible to the human eye, but our hearts can see, hear and feel it.

I'll let you know how Kevy makes out after the procedure.

Love Kim

October 15, 2015 9:57 pm

I have to be honest when I say that you have to stick around here because things can change on a dime.

So, after Kevin's stay in the hospital, he was released with two stents (one for liver bile duct and one for pancreas), a little less blood, and two prescriptions - one antibiotic for a possible infection after the surgery, and one to address Kevin's extremely low potassium levels. Released from Edwards on Tuesday night, Kevin had to go back for blood work on Thursday, was given the OK by Dr. Hantel and made a mad dash for the airport on Saturday.

You see, Kevin has always wanted to golf St. Andrews golf course in Scotland. He had always hoped that he would do so with his two brothers Jack and Brian and his Dad, Jack Sr. So, knowing the importance of this trip, Jack and Brian made it happen for the four of them. The four of them met up in Glasgow, Scotland and made their way to the Rusack Hotel right on St. Andrew's Golf Course. As of this writing, they have golfed three different courses; Carnoustie, St. Andrews Old Course and Kingsbarns. You will be forgiven if you have no idea what you just read! Suffice it to say, if you are a golfer you are probably drooling right now.

Kevin has figured out what has been wrong with his golf game. He needs to be in Scotland, and have a caddie. He shot 90, 86, and 88 respectively. I'm so happy for him! While golfing was the top priority, Kevy says the tea is incredible and he has had the best fish and chips ever. So many incredibly great moments.

I am sure to hear of the laughter that was shared and the teasing. I can't wait. While I haven't spoken to Kevin too much with him being gone, we did speak this morning. He told me that today during their last round of golf, he was very down, kinda blue. He explained to me that he was so looking forward to coming home, and at the same time was sad to know the trip was coming to an end. As Kevy explained, this experience was always one of those things he dreamed of, hoped to one day do, wished for so often, the making of a wish come true. And the wish has come true. That meant that this once in a lifetime experience will be behind him. It is profoundly final for Kevin.

It was something to look forward to and be able to take his focus off of cancer for a few days. It seemed to take forever to finally get here, and now it's almost over. The one great thing that Kevin said was that he talked to himself and essentially said in his mind that he was there and to enjoy what he was doing. He was being mindful. He was in the moment. He was able to turn his thoughts around and enjoy the final precious time he was having with his family.

Once that plane lands in Chicago reality will hit hard. Kevin will be returning to the hospital to have a permanent stent placed into his bile duct and the temporary pancreas one removed. Blood tests will begin again at a fever pitch and the two chemo combination will be slated to happen. Kevin's CEA went up to 136 before he left, and while the doctor thought some of the increase could be contributed to the inflammation and infection that Kevin was dealing with, he also said what we knew to be true. The cancer is still there and still needs to be tackled. Nausea, headaches, pains, fatigue will be the sand traps for this round. And the next and the next. Keep holding on Kevy. There has to be a cure somewhere. I want to see you eagle this, or at least get a birdie.

So, my sweet hubby, enjoy these moments with your Dad and brothers. Relish in their memories, and the making of new ones. Reminisce about each course you conquered so when you come home you will be bringing your best game to once again tee off on cancer.

~~~~~

Looking over the hundreds of journal entries that have been written since that horrific day in August of 2010 has proven to be agonizing, draining, cry inducing, heartwarming, uplifting, encouraging and hopeful. If nothing else, this is a love story in its truest sense. Everyone looks to be loved and to find others in which to harvest their affections. We were created as individuals and become intimate with few. We are raised in community from the earliest of days and given a name that is family. Love from one another is the prescribed golden rule and produces a strong foundation that supports our journey through life.

Love is ever evolving and embraces many who leave footprints on our heart. It is this particular journey that has assisted in making me a more grateful, humble, mindful and loving person. Like the "woods" that appeared so very far in distance from me and measured my harvested love, they offer an incredible analogy.

Walking through life you begin to plant saplings and bushes that will lay the way for our path. Through nurturing and loving relationships, the trees begin to grow strong and tall and the roots dig deep always searching for sustenance. Soon you may intersect paths with others and sometimes if you are lucky, begin meandering alongside someone who shares the same song.

It is at this moment when you begin to notice the green of the leaves and the abundance of branches. The path lays ahead, covered in dirt and the occasional leaf that has floated to the earth. When life events occur, depending on their intensity, present as a cleared walkway or raised knuckle like tree roots making for a treacherous go.

For Kevin, at 44, the path quickly turned rolling and jutting to and fro. Cancer had appeared and was not willing to meld into the background. It aggressively uprooted trees and strew them far and wide. It has done its very best to overtake the path and prevent us from moving forward. While the environment has called for a more determined stride, one that becomes too strenuous at times, it has also opened the passage to present the many many trees that have grown along with us. They are tall and strong and full of high reaching and low hanging wispy limbs. They are open enough to have the sun encapsulate us during the storms.

And it is at this point on our walk that we have come across an enormous low lying branch. It beckons us to rest for a while so that Kevin can gather his strength and go on to fight another day, another round, another tumultuous stretch along the path. So many tragedies have been passed and so many triumphant steps have been blazed. Kevin has been through so much, and has been helped along the way by the love, prayers, encouragement and faith of all who have read about his journey. But, I suppose, it's been our journey - all of us. And my love for Kevin is measured to the woods and back. How great that he finds himself smack dab in its middle.

Kim Griffin

Acknowledgements

Imagine all the people... ~ John Lennon

This book would not be possible without the help, support, dedication and love of so many people. Please forgive the writer for any missing names or characters - you all have a special place in my heart. To my mentor, Pat Casiello, an extraordinary author, woman, supporter - thank you firstly for your belief in me and this book and for your unending faith; to Emilie Procsal my book cover guru who never gave up on me when I was changing my mind and constantly challenging her; my editor Judi Fennell for reading and fine tuning all my words and thoughts; to Dr. Alexander Hantel and all the nursing staff at Edward Cancer Center in Naperville, IL - you have given us all more quality and quantity time with our Kevy; the visitors to the Caringbridge.org website (42,000 strong) who took the time to read, write notes of encouragement and storm the heavens with prayers for Kevin's recovery; my friends for rallying behind me and mine; for the Licata family, especially Rich and Maria and your ability to effortlessly fold our family into yours; to Reebie Storage and Moving, Kevin's employer of the last sixteen years, for encouraging Kevin throughout his career with them, and for their fundamental union with us from day one; for all the lacrosse players past and present at Marmion Academy who shaved their heads in support of "Coach", who visited Kevin during his numerous hospital stays and for never, ever, giving up on him, just as he has never given up on you; the Marmion community at large led by Fr. Nathanael for the endless meals, gifts, masses and special blessings bestowed; my home away from home Patterson Elementary and all the kiddos, parents and staff members who joined the meal wagon, offered gift cards, notes of support, shoulders to cry on, and for the fundraisers - not to mention the Friday Night Dance Parties; Brookdale peeps for never letting me feel alone and spearheading the meal calendar; our Game Night Buddies for the bellyaches from laughing at "Lightning Rod", and for wanting to make "trades" after Catchphrase; Kevin's brother from another mother—Randy Clark—and his entire family including wife Renee and kids Michael and Samantha. Your family has included us always. To Kevin's family far and wide with a special shout out to his Aunt Sue, an oncologist for over 30 years in Canada who walked us through the incredible mountain of test results and medical jargon; my own family led by the woman whom I first loved to the woods and back, my Mum "Trix"; my best friend and sister, Karen who has put numerous hours into collecting my tears and fears and being a soft place to fall; my son Troy who is firstly responsible for handing me the title Mom or "Mum" to my Canadian crew, and for his incredible intuitiveness and appetite for reading, listening and hugging me through tough times; my baby boy Liam, Yi Yum, former keeper of the blankie who shares his passion of music with me, who effortlessly makes me laugh aloud and is my tattoo buddy.

Finally, to the man who has been to the woods and back too many times to count, my husband Kevy. You make me laugh when I want to cry, feel warm when the frost is nipping at my ears, feel safe when I'm stepping outside of my comfort zone. You are the best part of me, my sailor and soldier and the only one to always be ready with my "shoes".

Lovingly and forever, Kim